International
Housing Policies

International Housing Policies

A Comparative Analysis

Chester C. McGuire
Capitol Economics Incorporated
Howard University

LexingtonBooks
D.C. Heath and Company
Lexington, Massachusetts
Toronto

363.58
M14i

Library of Congress Cataloging in Publication Data

McGuire, Chester C
    International housing policies.

    Includes bibliographical references.
    1. Housing policy. I. Title.
HD7287.M27   363.5'8   80-8815
ISBN 0-669-04385-0

m.R.

Copyright © 1981 by D.C. Heath and Company

Published simultaneously in Canada

Printed in the United States of America

International Standard Book Number: 0-669-04385-0

Library of Congress Catalog Card Number: 80-8815

Contents

v

JUN 6 '82

List of Figures

List of Tables

Acknowledgments

I would like to thank the Federal National Mortgage Association (FNMA), and especially Oakley Hunter, Chairman of the Board, Lester Condon, Executive Vice President, and Peter Treadway, Vice President, for their assistance and support for this project. I must also add, that although the research was sponsored by a grant from FNMA, that the views expressed herein are my own and not necessarily the views of FNMA.

Many of the materials used in preparation of this book were made available through the Office of International Affairs of the U.S. Department of Housing and Urban Development, and the assistance of Tom Callaway and Susan Judd.

This study involved considerable correspondence with housing officials in various countries. My special thanks go to: Mark Boleat of the Building Societies Association (London), Kazou Ohno of the Japan Housing Loan Corporation (Tokyo), J.M. Billaut of Companie Bancaire and R. Mathély of Companie Français d'Epargne et de Crédit (Paris), Camilla Lindberg of the Ministry of Housing (Stockholm), and officials of the office of the Federal Minister for Area Planning, Construction, and City Planning (Bonn).

Part I
International Comparisons

1 Housing Policy—An Overview

Government and the Private Sector

Housing policy refers to the range of activities that governments and private institutions jointly undertake to provide housing services for a population. In every society, the manner in which housing is produced, financed, and even consumed is determined by a combination of government activities, customs, and market forces. Because of this interdependence, consideration of housing policy cannot be divorced from the culture in which it operates.

The entire housing system is circumscribed by such factors as the level of national wealth, the political consensus concerning the amount of that wealth to be invested in housing, and individual tastes and preferences. Because of the intimate relationship of housing to family life, it is a pillar of social stability, positively related to social well-being and group satisfaction. Therefore, the very nature of housing makes it political and hence subject to political pressures in all of its facets—production, financing, and consumption. Housing manifests the political and economic climate found in a society as well as does any other facet of national experience.

The role that government assumes in the housing sector is the dominant aspect of a national housing policy. Government may take an active role, intervening directly, or a passive one, deferring to private market forces and individual consumer demand, to establish the level of production and prices. A multiplicity of national housing policies exist around the globe, as revealed by the ways in which governments have either intervened or refrained from intervention in the housing sector. Yet despite the enormous range of cultural and economic differences among nations, in actual practice the ways that governments intervene in housing are not as diverse as might be implied at first glance. Review of what is being done reveals that the methods of intervention in the housing sector are fairly limited in number, although the likely methods of implementation can vary enormously.

At one extreme are the centrally planned economies of the socialist countries, who view housing as a social right and hence assume responsibility for the provision of housing. At the other are the market economies, in which the individual bears the responsibility for housing himself. Where housing is seen as a social right, society tends to pick up most of its cost. Where it is regarded as a consumer good, it is entirely the responsibility of

3

households to provide for the entire cost of their housing accommodation. Representing the latter extreme is the United States, where housing is viewed as an individual responsibility requiring a high percentage of the individual's income. The former is represented by the Soviet Union, where as a social right housing expense takes only a small portion of an individual's income. The view of housing as a private consumption good tends to be reflected in market economies, and the opposing view is common in the socialist states of Eastern Europe and elsewhere. However, a variety of positions between these two extremes exist. Even in some market economies a considerable portion of the individual's housing cost is borne by the state, as is true, for example, in Sweden, Norway, and the United Kingdom. Of the Eastern European socialist countries, Yugoslavia and Rumania, for example, still leave the provision of housing largely to the individual.

The various systems are not as far apart in actual operations as they appear on theoretical grounds. For example, in the Eastern European countries considerable private ownership of property exists; and subtantial individual initiative goes into the provision of a family's housing. In the United States and in Western Europe there is considerable government intervention into the private housing market, by direct and indirect subsidies and tax preferences. What is common among both market and socialist societies is an acceptance by government that society as a whole is responsible for some measure of housing satisfaction.

Reason for Government Intervention

The reasons for state involvement in housing are many and complex, but the following are prominent:

1. To cure a housing shortage.
2. To aid the poor.
3. To improve general housing conditions.
4. To ease the affordability burden.
5. To stabilize production.

The Housing-Shortage Problem

Most nations at one time or another have had some type of housing problem. Usually it has been expressed in terms of a deficiency in the number of habitable units relative to the number of households. Urbanization has put heavy strains on all industrial societies to provide enough satisfactory housing. The persistence and extent of housing problems have been aggravated by wars and natural disasters.

After World War II Europe had a severe housing shortage. As much as 22 percent of the entire prewar housing stock had been devastated or rendered uninhabitable. But such devastation was spread unequally among the countries. Switzerland, which had not been a combatant, had only 4.5 percent of its housing units destroyed. Greece, which had been the scene of heavy fighting during the war, had some 50 percent of its housing demolished. In the Soviet Union, Germany, France, and Japan, the damage to the housing stock was extensive.[1]

After the war the highest priority the combatant nations faced was the restoration of their industrial capacity and the repair of losses to their infrastructure. Each nation first wanted to rebuild factories that had been destroyed, as well as highways, utilities, and other units essential to the economy. After 1950 most of the European countries and Japan had achieved their first objective in reestablishing their industrial sector. Housing was a lower priority, although each nation did immediately engage in replacing the housing that had been lost.

The housing situation in Europe was chaotic not only because of the war damages but also because during the prewar years little housing was built, despite increased urbanization. During the war people came into the cities to support the war effort, and after the war an enormous number of soldiers returned. These factors combined with the war's devastation created enormous housing shortages throughout the continent. A similar situation faced Japan, which after World War II had a housing shortage estimated at more than 4 million units.

Even in countries for which the war damage was negligible there were still tremendous postwar housing shortages. Britain, for example, which was not invaded, had comparatively little war damage. But the lack of new construction during the war years, despite increased population and urbanization, all contributed to an enormous postwar housing shortage. To a somewhat lesser degree the same was true for the United States, Canada, and Switzerland.

After 1950 the combatant countries were extremely active in building new housing. In Europe and in Japan, governments intervened to ensure high levels of housing production to eliminate the acute housing shortages. Using various measures—the direct building of war-torn areas by the French government, reliance on the private sector in Germany—all the countries succeeded in alleviating the war shortages. In fact, by 1970 it could safely be said that the housing shortage in Europe and Japan had ended. In Japan, which had extreme war damage, by 1968 the number of houses exceeded the number of households. Thus in a quantitative sense, Japan's housing shortage had also come to an end.

Not only was the housing shortage over by 1970, but in many Western European countries large numbers of vacancies then became a problem for the first time. This was quite noticeable in Sweden, Denmark, the Netherlands, and Germany, where large blocks of flats for rent stood vacant for long periods of time. The primary reason for the vacancies was that the housing shortage for which they had been created was over. Another factor was that people had acquired a taste for better housing than what had been produced to meet the postwar housing shortage. People now wanted more amenities than were offered in apartments that had been built with shortages in mind.

In the United States there was also a housing shortage after World War II, although no fighting was done on U.S. soil. Because of the Depression, virtually no housing was built in the United States during the 1930s. Whereas in the 1920s the rate of home building averaged 1 million units per year, in the 1930s the rate was half that. During the war that followed, very little housing was built, so that by 1945 there was a housing shortage.

During the postwar period there was a great deal of housing construction in the United States, which served to alleviate the shortage. In addition there was a tremendous upgrading of the housing stock through the repair and renovation of existing houses. Thus by 1960 there was no longer what could be considered a quantitative housing shortage, although a sizable portion of the housing stock (approximately 7 percent) was in need of replacement.

The housing shortages that existed across Europe, Japan, and North America after World War II have now been eliminated. Yet today, although there are fewer households than available habitable housing units, housing problems still exist and have become thorny political issues in most countries.

Assisting the Poor

Assisting those families that are too poor to obtain decent housing on their own is done in a variety of ways, such as direct provision of housing, the granting of housing subsidies, or the giving of welfare assistance, part of which can be used for housing expenditures. Many special groups, such as the poor, the elderly, and the handicapped, are recipients of such special treatment. Every advanced society has public programs to take care of the portion of this need that is not met privately.

The nature of the housing problem has tended to shift from shortages to problems of quality, affordability, and the ability of certain groups in the population to obtain decent housing. According to Hallett: "The housing problem usually refers not to whether the housing conditions of most people are somewhat better or somewhat worse, but whether the conditions of a sizable minority are catastrophic."[2] Even in advanced industrial societies with high per capita income, there frequently exists a sizable pocket of poor people for whom the housing situation is indeed catastrophic unless they receive substantial amounts of public assistance. In the United States, low-income, female-headed minority families have the greatest need of housing assistance. In other countries it is the elderly population in general and young households who have insufficient money to purchase housing.

Governments in the market-economy countries have tended to get into the provision of housing in some manner because of a distrust of the ability of the market system to take care of the poor. This leads to more active involvement to fill the void left by the private sector. With precisely this rationale Canada enacted a series of programs for low-income households with the pronouncement that:

> The presumption has always been that the needs of the poor would be met by a filtering process: as persons with higher incomes move out of existing houses or apartments and into new housing, the price of the older housing would fall and become accessible to lower income households. The filtering process has, in fact, never been able to provide sufficient accessibility, partly because of the tendency for substantial amounts of the older housing stock to be demolished in the process of urban commercial and industrial growth.[3]

Improvement of General Housing Conditions

Housing conditions affect public health and safety, especially in a dense urban setting. Accordingly, societies have established building-construction standards, housing-occupancy codes, and land-use regulations. The existence of negative externalities caused by the interdependencies of urban living has necessitated a substantial government role. Fire-prevention standards are among the earliest. Water and sewer standards have also become commonplace as the knowledge of disease transmission has become understood.

Aside from these basic health and safety issues, governments have become concerned about other kinds of housing conditions. Besides the provision of basic shelter, there are concerns of increasing the amount of space per family, the functioning of the unit, its attractiveness, and the quality of neighborhoods. It is now an article of faith in all the market economies that state planning enhances the ability of the private market to improve general housing conditions.

The Affordability Burden

Issues of housing affordability provide one of the traditional ways in which governments get into housing. Societies have different concepts of the proper percentage of income to be spent on housing. When the price of housing is likely to go above what the consensus in a society deems reasonable, government will be pressured to intervene in order to bring housing costs into line.

Europe and America have very different philosophies concerning the nature of the social responsibility for housing services. At the risk of over-simplification, it can be said that in Europe housing is considered a basic human right that should be distributed to everyone. Government's function is not only to provide housing for the poor but also to assist almost everyone. Therefore, the number of people receiving some type of housing assistance in Europe is typically higher than in the United States or Canada. In the United States social housing is considered to be housing for the very poor rather than for the middle class. People in the United States would consider many of those who receive housing subsidies in Europe to be too well off for such assistance.

In the centrally planned socialist countries a low level of housing expense, especially of rent, is considered a right. Typically, rents will range from 4 to 6 percent of a family's income, which is deemed an appropriate percentage to be spent on housing. This is extremely low by Western standards; the corresponding amount would be around 15 to 25 percent. However, within Western Europe differences exist. In Sweden around 10 percent of income is usually considered a decent figure for shelter cost, and government policies are aimed at lowering costs of rents and home ownership toward this relatively low percentage of income. In the United States about 20 percent is considered the most that a family can spend on housing, in order to leave enough in the budget to purchase other goods and services.

Another way to observe various kinds of national housing policies is to look at the relationship between need and effective demand. Housing need usually refers to some measure of what ought to be, in terms of housing costs, rents, or the level of production. Effective demand, on the other hand, is the concept of need tempered by the ability to pay. Since need is a normative concept, there is always a conflict between need and effective demand. However, demand is likely to be determinant since it is backed up by purchasing power. A market economy depends primarily on effective demand to allocate resources in the housing sector. One result of this is that housing policies in a free market are apt to err on the side of shortages, since effective demand is always considerably smaller than total housing needs. On the other hand, housing policies that are geared toward need rather than effective demand are apt to err on the side of producing housing surpluses. Although the two concepts are considerably apart in theory, in reality governments behave in such a way that need approaches effective demand by the use of subsidies and preferential treatments for housing that serve the purpose of increasing effective demand. For example, tax policies in the United States lower occupancy cost by 20 to 30 percent, thus greatly inflating actual demand. In the absence of such policies housing would be more expensive, and substantially less would be consumed.

Stabilize Production

Stabilization of the production of housing, and some insulation from the vicissitudes of the economy, have most often taken the form of regulations, assistance in the financial markets, and in some cases direct intervention of governments in housing production.

Stability of housing production is a significant reason for government intervention into the market. The history of housing production in most Western nations has shown cyclical variation. However, fluctuations in housing starts are most extreme in the United States, where the annual variations in production tend to be pronounced. But in any society extreme swings in production can be destabilizing and to have negative consequences. It has been pointed out that extreme fluctuations in the housing sector lead to inefficiencies in production and to unnecessary unemployment for construction workers who must leave the industry in slack times. Entrepreneurs in the construction sector are not able to take advantage of discounts and the economies that they might have with a stable, dependable level of production.

Housing and Social Policies

Housing policies also extend into social areas, as some governments have undertaken explicit housing policies that aim not at housing production or finance but at an equitable distribution of housing to all segments of the population. Most societies have opted, at least in their rhetoric, for the provision of housing in a manner that will not produce segregation by race, income, or social status. In countries that have racial problems, such as the United States and England, there are laws and regulations against housing discrimination based on race. These laws are aimed at making the widest spectrum of housing available to all without regard to race, religion, or national origin. Apart from the race factor, the presence in some European nations of a considerable number of guest workers of different nationalities has produced a corresponding problem resulting in the segregation of foreigners and their living under substandard housing conditions.

In racially homogeneous countries the avoidance of segregation by class and income is often a stated government policy that is implicit in all public-sector activities. Thus in Finland, for example, it is expected that housing should be made available to the middle class and the poor alike, with no social stigma attached to it. England has attempted to avoid stigmatizing public housing as lower-class housing by opening such housing to persons of a wider variety of income levels and occupations than is the case in the United States.

Swedish housing policy contains a definite commitment to the overall integration of people within the housing sector:

> It is an urgent task of housing policy to avoid segregation of any kind in housing, whether by age or socioeconomic or ethnic grouping. Segregation of the population isolates from each other people of different social groups, and contributes to an uneven use of service facilities . . . a good physical environment is one of the prerequisites for avoiding segregation. But it is also important to insure the different kinds of housing, with regard to size and form of tenure, are provided in one and the same area. These measures should be combined with measures intended to equalize differences in the ability of households to pay their housing costs.[4]

Although the urge for equality extends into the housing sector, housing remains the last significant refuge of inequality in almost every society. In the United States and in many other countries, housing quality depends on income, status, and race. The affluent are not scattered randomly across the landscape, and neither are the poor. The most extreme examples in the United States are the public-housing projects, which increasingly have become reservations for the very poor and for racial minorities. This kind of stratification is not found in British public housing, where there is a much greater social mix. But most countries recognize social and economic segregation in housing as a problem and have consciously set up policies to deal with it in various ways. However, housing segregation tends to be an accurate reflection of the basic values of a society. Segregation is less pronounced in homogeneous places such as Scandinavia.

Local Government and Housing Policy

Because of the inherent immobility and fixed character of housing, the administration of housing policy tends to be a function shared between national and local governments. In most countries, local governments are the principal implementing agencies of housing programs and policies.

In the United Kingdom the government's housing policy is carried out by a network of local authorities that have enormous powers. Sweden and Switzerland have had long histories of strong local governments. The communes have enormous power in the regulation of land for development. In Germany the *landers* (states) have been responsible for public housing. There, as in the United States, the provision of public housing is a joint endeavor shared by the states and the central government. Such examples of strong local participation in housing are common around the world.

In the Western European countries, and even in the Eastern European socialist countries, the relationship between the central and local governments is one in which the central government provides the financing and the units of local government implement the specific programs. In the USSR, for example, although macroeconomic decisions are made at the central level, the actual implementation of housing decisions occurs in the local soviets; the local people's councils play this role in the other socialist nations. Thus in the centrally planned states housing tends to be one of the most decentralized sectors of the economy. Local units of government in Eastern Europe have enormous latitude and power in housing production.

Basic Types of Government Policies

There are two basic types of government policies in housing: selective and comprehensive. Selective government assistance is the kind that is targeted toward special groups rather than applied to the housing sector as a whole. The United States, France, and Switzerland can be characterized as having selective government policies. In the United States direct housing assistance is given only to the poor, and there is almost always a means test for potential recipients of such assistance.

Comprehensive assistance refers to government plans that consider the entire housing spectrum rather than specific targeted groups. A comprehensive program aims at creating a large amount of housing without special regard for individual population subgroups. Comprehensive housing plans were in effect after World War II in Germany, France, Japan, and Scandinavia.

The categorization of policies as either selective or comprehensive is a generalization, and individual countries naturally tailor their housing policies to their specific needs. However, the tendency today is away from comprehensive kinds of treatment and toward selective targeting. The reason is that for all practical purposes the housing shortages of most industrial nations are now over. Thus there is no need for indiscriminate, across the board housing assistance merely for the sake of production.

Cycles in Housing Policy

Like most phenomena, housing policy tends to go through distinct phases. Lessons can be learned from the evolution of housing policies in the advanced industrial societies. During the nineteenth century extreme dislocations in all these countries were first caused by urbanization and then stimulated by an industrial society and later by the ravages of war. Such social disruptions have been partially resolved with political solutions, often expressed as national housing policies. Such policies seem to evolve through four distinct phases.

The first phase occurs in the face of an acute housing shortage in which the number of housing units falls far short of the number of households. This is now the case in less-developed countries and was the case in the advanced countries at the turn of the twentieth century and again following World War II. These situations require some state intervention to stimulate the level of housing production in order to ameliorate the housing shortage in a numerical sense. In order to solve the quantitative problem of too few housing units, new buildings are usually constructed to minimal standards, often with a stated goal of one housing unit per family.

The second stage occurs after the numerical shortage had been met, when the size of the housing units must be increased to meet the demands of the population for more space. Thus in the next evolutionary stage the goal is one room per person, and in this second stage the emphasis will be on building larger units.

The third phase involves increasing the quality of housing units. Once the basic numerical equivalency is reached, individuals will want a higher level of amenity. This may often involve the demolition of some of the earlier units that were built to minimal standards.

The fourth phase sets in once this upgrading of the housing stock has occurred. It manifests itself as a conscious attempt by the state to reduce the enormous financial burden it has had to assume for housing. This is currently being done through two devices. The first is to eliminate the indiscriminate subsidies to the housing sector and to concentrate subsidies only on those who specifically need such aid. The second and more subtle device is to encourage home ownership. Owner occupation significantly reduces the burden of housing on the state, first by eliminating the need for the state to build housing and then by reducing the burden of state maintenance over the life of the housing unit. If individuals purchase their own houses, the burden that might fall on the state is shifted to these individuals. This is not just a phenomenon in the Western market economies; it is also common in the Eastern European socialist countries, where owner occupation through cooperatives and the use of personal funds for housing are both encouraged as policies that will reduce the burden on the state. No country seems to be immune to these pressures, which are remarkably similar worldwide.

Despite the reluctance of some governments to expand their direct involvement in the housing sector, the public contribution to housing has tended to increase. Such contributions have taken various forms, such as

(1) state loans to individuals and producers; (2) direct subsidies to the housing consumer; (3) a variety of guarantees to producers, lenders, and consumers; and (4) preferential tax policies.

Review of the various kinds of government activities in the housing sector provides a recurrent theme: that governments, regardless of their political persuasion or economic system, eventually and invariably get involved in housing. Quite often government intervention in housing comes about as a result of an emergency situation. This has been most noticeable in the Western market economies. Government intervention became prominent in North America after the Depression of the 1930s, and in Europe after the devastation of World War II. Also evident is the reality that once governments are involved in housing, after a period of time they inevitably tend to retrench their efforts in the housing sector. However, political reality will not let a government withdraw from housing.

The reason for the eventual reluctance of government in the housing sector is that housing quickly becomes an extremely expensive activity to support. Housing is the largest item in the family budget; when a government picks up a large percentage of this cost, either directly or indirectly, its financial responsibility becomes enormous. Therefore, with competing government objectives and limited resources, at some point governments invariably decide to minimize their exposure in the housing area and to concentrate on health and education as alternatives.

> Western European governments tended to go into it (housing) hoping that one day they would be able to get out of it; they were wrong. Political and economic changes have made housing a focal point of every European country, have given it a place in the context of national economic and social development as a whole. Housing decisions have come to depend on non-housing policies and housing itself to be increasingly planned and programmed.[5]

Government housing policy is in time tempered by the reality that housing requires long-term involvement and hence a long-term perspective. Housing is expensive, calling for a commitment of enormous real resources. Additional expenditures are required to maintain it for as long as it is in service—a period of decades.

Even nations such as Switzerland that have little proclivity toward government intervention have found it difficult to get out of housing once they have ventured in. The temporary housing programs adopted by the Swiss after World War II to stimulate housing production were impossible to discard completely once the shortage was over and the programs had attained their original objectives. Political support for the housing programs tended to institutionalize them twenty years after they had been initiated as temporary measures.

Housing and Politics

In every nation the working class has rising expectations for housing. All governments have been at their wits ends to devise policies that will meet this increased desire of the working class not only for affordable housing but usually also for home ownership. This is a problem faced not only in the market economies but also in Eastern Europe and elsewhere. Many of the housing units built at minimal standards immediately after World War II are no longer considered satisfactory by the bulk of today's working population, who desire greater amenities, more space, and more architecturally and aesthetically pleasing surroundings. The task of devoting the required resources to providing such housing units are grave concerns across the spectrum of governments. The desire to continue to upgrade housing is one that crosses all national borders.

Many of the Western democracies have opted for special schemes that assist moderate-income families to obtain enough money for a housing unit. There are special savings schemes, bonuses, and interest-rate subsidies, which have been made available in most countries in one form or another. All these devices lower either the cost of acquiring a house or the monthly mortgage payments involved. In the Eastern European centrally planned countries the same things are taking place, with the governments allowing more individuals the flexibility to use their own funds to provide their housing. In Czechoslovakia, Poland, Rumania, Bulgaria, and Yugoslavia more and more individual families are choosing to participate as owners in cooperatives. The housing they tend to build for themselves is of higher quality and with more amenities than the housing that would be provided by the state alone.

Housing can become a fierce ideological battleground. Because of the intimate relationship of housing to the family and to the social structure as a whole, the provision of housing tends to reflect a nation's basic social system. For example, the political spectrum in Britain is almost evenly balanced between the Labor party, which leans toward socialism, and the Conservatives, who reject socialism in favor of a free-market approach. A Labor government's policies tend to be repudiated by those of a Conservative government, and vice versa, with housing policies set in place by one government often modified or overturned by another. The struggle over rent control and public housing in the United Kingdom serve as excellent illustrations of political and ideological fighting that spill over into housing.

Housing policies cannot be divorced from politics, nor should they be. This caveat should be kept in mind as one explores a variety of housing alternatives in different countries.

Notes

1. An excellent discussion of the postwar situation in Europe is found in the United Nations report, *Human Settlements in Europe: Postwar Trends and Policies* (ECE/HBP/18).

2. Graham Hallett, *Housing and Land Policies in West Germany and Britain: A Record of Success and Failure* (London: Macmillan, and New York: Holmes and Meier, 1977).

3. Ministry of State for Urban Affairs, Canada, *Human Settlements in Canada* (1976).

4. Ministry of Housing and Physical Planning, "Housing, Building, and Planning in Sweden," Monograph to the United Nations (1978).

5. United Nations, *Human Settlements in Europe*.

2 Housing Investment

The Cycle of Housing Investment

A nation's investment in its own housing tends to be correlated with its overall stage of economic development. Mature economies will differ from developing nations in terms of the amount of resources devoted to housing, which reflect differences both in ability and in priorities. Even among the developed industrial nations, differences exist. One factor is that the pace of urbanization has not been uniform. England, one of the first nations to industrialize, had to face pressures for urban housing for the working class half a century before Sweden, which industrialized much later. Also, World War II took its toll unevenly among the combatant nations. Thus by 1945, based on the pace of urbanization and the extent of war damage, each of the industrialized countries of the world had charted a different course in its manner and amount of investment in housing.

Nevertheless, taking into consideration the difference in rates of urbanization and the special ravages of war, a general pattern with regard to national housing investment does emerge. As an economy matures, housing investment as a percentage of its total output (as measured by its gross domestic product) will tend to increase up to a point and then to decline steadily even though gross domestic product (GDP) continues to increase. Not until an economy is mature will significant resources again be devoted to the housing sector.

Rapid urbanization places great strains on a society's ability to house its population adequately. Problems of inadequate housing that could be ignored in the countryside are manifest in the cities. Perhaps the best example is provided by England, which not only advanced manufacturing technology but also gave the world the tenement. Tenements were built in response to the social pressures to upgrade workers' housing. In retrospect it is evident that improvement in the housing of workers was a necessary precondition to continued industrial development. In England, as elsewhere, industrial development continued hand in hand with an increasing investment in housing stock.

Investment in the housing sector tends to proceed grudgingly once the industrialization process is underway. Governments initially prefer to put scarce resources into the industrial sector and agriculture rather than into housing. Certainly during the early stages of national economic development

17

there is great stress on industrial goods and infrastructure. This is found today in most nations in the third world. Brazil is an excellent example of a nation that, while developing its industrial base, is at the same time determined to devote some resources to housing. Comparable situations prevailed a century ago in Europe, when choices had to be made between housing and other kinds of investment. The usual reaction has been to attempt to postpone housing investments for as long as possible. This results from a rather traditional view of housing as a consumer of scarce resources rather than as an investment in itself. This traditional view is now being challenged by those who see the housing sector as contributing positively to economic development by: (1) providing jobs in the construction sector; (2) fostering a building-materials industry; and (3) increasing the well-being and hence the productive capacity of society.[1] But this is a slowly evolving position that does not yet have universal acceptance.

In some countries there has been a gradual shifting of opinion as to whether housing is a consumption good that can be easily postponed or social capital in terms of personal and social investment. As a consumption item housing can be given low priority, just as can any other consumable item. This has been the view of centrally planned governments in Eastern Europe, for example, as well as a common view among the less-developed nations of the third world. From this perspective the housing problem is seen as one that will be solved primarily through economic development. The resulting premise is that as an economy produces more goods and services and expands, more surplus will be available to be spent on housing. This conventional wisdom has tended to limit the provision of housing in many societies. Where national priorities are heavily committed to capital formation and industrialization, housing is often slighted.

This traditional view is shifting even in the Eastern European countries and in many nations of the third world. For example, in the centrally planned socialist countries housing is being thought of more as an investment, since it is a durable good, and as one that provides many jobs in both its creation and its maintenance. Good housing also elevates the standard of living of a society, which goes hand in hand with technological advance and increased production efficiency. According to this reasoning, improvement is then not just an adjunct to economic growth but an integral part of it. The position of housing in the central-planning process thus tends to be elevated above that of mere consumption. Furthermore, there is a great deal of popular and political agitation among citizens for higher housing standards, no doubt a very influential factor in shifting the view of housing in centrally planned economies.

Among the so-called developing nations of the third world, the view of housing is also tending to shift in a more positive direction. What has heretofore been considered a housing problem is reflective of the social and economic problems of the population. The housing problem is linked directly to the entire process of urbanization and becomes evident as a surplus agricultural population attempts to start life in the cities. Increasingly evident in the developing countries is the understanding that a national development policy must contain a housing component. Of course, in the developing countries a housing component will depend on the resources that are available, in a context in which resources for investment are in short supply.

Housing investment tends to become significant at a later or second stage of industrial development. At some point wealth will have increased to the point at which a relatively large amount of resources can go to housing. This will occur some time after the nation is reasonably secure in its role as an urban industrialized state, and will tend to last until there is enough satisfactory housing for its population. For North America and Western Europe this second period began after 1900 and lasted until a decade or so after World War II. Except for the periods of two wars and a depression, there was continued investment in the housing sectors of the industrial nations as measured by the percentage of GDP devoted to housing.

A third stage emerges in the absence of widespread housing shortages when the housing sector enters a steady state. At this time emphasis is primarily on upgrading the housing stock and on providing housing with a greater amenity level. Much of the housing from the second stage—for example, the tenements—will be demolished to make way for modern sanitary dwellings.

In commenting on the housing construction that had taken place in the European countries after World War II, a United Nations report stated:

> It may be said in passing that in the early 1950's most countries were building houses which were too small in order to make the most of their resources. This spotlights a recurrent dilemma of government authorities responsible for housing. Does one build more smaller, simpler houses to get people off the long waiting lists, in which case one may be creating the slums of the future? Or does one build fewer but larger and better-equipped houses which are less likely to become obsolete, but leave an immediate political problem?[2]

It can be seen, for example, that in the Soviet Union much of the housing built in the 1950s was of such poor quality and so lacking in amenities that it was obsolete by the 1970s. A somewhat similar fate confronts much of the French housing built immediately after the war, which is now shunned by consumers.

Housing Production

One of the commonly used indicators of the level of housing production is the amount of new housing completed per year per 1,000 inhabitants. This measure places the effort of countries into perspective without regard to

their absolute size, and thus provides a good indication of the relative contribution made by each country in providing housing.

In the postwar period the United States has been building new housing
at a rate of between 7 and 8 dwelling units per 1,000 inhabitants. The
highest level of production occurred in 1950 when the rate per 1,000 exceeded 10. Since then the rate of production has tended to decline.

The extensive war damage suffered by many countries in Europe and
Asia obviously influenced the level of housing construction in many of the
countries. The Western European countries and Japan have exceeded the
rate of housing production of the United States, as can be seen in figure 2-1.
However, the rate of construction among the centrally planned economies
in Eastern Europe has been comparable to the rate of housing construction
in North America.

Sweden, which had not been a combatant in World War II, nevertheless
had for many years the world's highest level of housing production. Between 1965 and 1972 its rate of production was an astounding 12.8 units per
1,000 inhabitants. Since then its rate has subsided and currently approaches

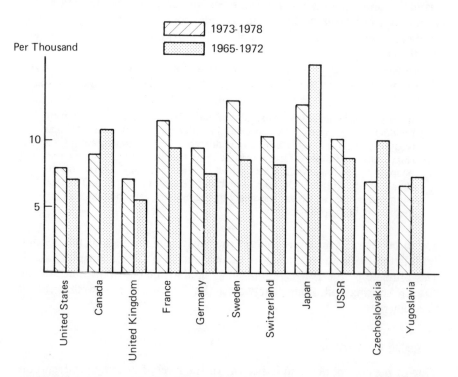

Figure 2-1. Completed Dwelling Units per 1,000 Inhabitants, 1965-1978

the rate found in the United States and in many of the other European countries. Sweden's remarkable rate of building was related to urbanization pressures; after the war much of the population moved from the countryside to the city, creating enormous housing shortages. The Swedes resolved to end their housing shortage by building a large number of units, especially apartments in large blocks of flats.

The world's current leader in housing production is Japan. Its performance, especially since 1972, has been astonishing in terms of the number of units provided. Although Japan has only half the population of the United States, the actual number of new housing units built has been comparable. In terms of its population Japan's rate has been sustained at over 15 units per 1,000 inhabitants, a rate unique in the world. In 1973 production exceeded 18 units per 1,000 inhabitants, a truly prodigious effort.

Another measure of relative housing production is the percentage of housing investment accounted for in a nation's gross national product (GNP). Since the war the level of effort devoted to housing by the United States has averaged between 3 and 4 percent of GNP. The highwater mark occurred in 1951 when more than 5 percent of GNP was devoted to housing. Since then, however, there has been a secular decline in the level of housing investment in the United States.

According to this measure of the level of effort, the current world leader is again Japan, followed closely by France. As can be seen in figure 2-2 France devoted an exceptionally large amount of its national income to the provision of new housing during the 1970s. Also impressive was the level of housing production in Germany.

In order to put all these housing-production figures into perspective, it must be stated again that there are definite national cycles in housing production that depend on the state of a country's economy, the condition of its housing stock, and the priority afforded housing in relation to all other goods and services. The reason that the United States and the United Kingdom devote such a low percentage of GNP to housing, as compared to other nations, is that their inhabitants are relatively better housed at the present time. There are more sound housing units per numbers of inhabitants and much higher levels of owner occupation than are generally found elsewhere. Also, the fact that the United States and the United Kingdom were not theaters of actual fighting during World War II spared a considerable amount of the housing stock.

Housing production can be categorized by the type of investor, as shown in table 2-1. Private investors, who are typically owner occupiers or profit-motivated owners of rental housing, are the most common investors in most countries of the world. In North America private investment is most pronounced, accounting for almost half the total. Private investment is also found in the centrally planned socialist countries of Eastern Europe.

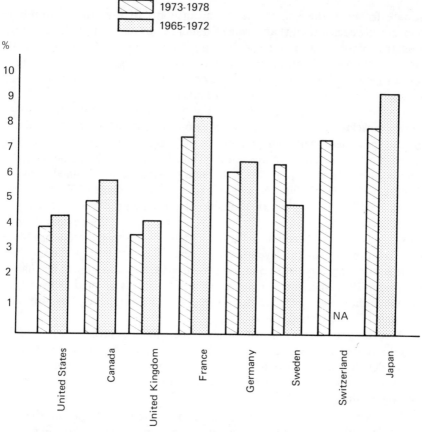

Figure 2-2. Percentage of Housing Investment in Gross National (Domestic)
Product, 1965-1978

Direct government investment in housing is not extensive in Western
Europe and North America. The notable exception is the United Kingdom,
where about half the new housing, known as council housing or public housing, is provided by local government.

Between the private and government sectors is a kind of investor that is
a little bit of both, investors that are difficult to classify as either private or
public. For example, in France private entities, Habitation à Loyer Modéré
(HLM organizations), borrow money directly from the government at
below market rates and build moderate-income housing. The preferential
treatment they receive and their close associations with the local and central
governments distinguish them from strictly private-sector investors. Yet
they are technically not "government." In other countries, such as Germany and Sweden, large independent cooperatives build housing. Although

Table 2-1
Housing Production by Type of Investor in 1977
(percentage of total)

Country	Private	Nonprofit Semipublic	Government
Canada	93	6	1
Germany	64	33	3
France	77	22	1
Sweden	72	26	2
Switzerland	88	8	4
United Kingdom	45	—	55
United States	99	—	1
USSR	19	10	71
Yugoslavia	59	—	41
Czechoslavakia	29	46	25

Source: United Nations, *Annual Bulletin of Housing and Building Statistics.*

they are private, they receive considerable government assistance and preferences that private, profit-motivated investors could not obtain.

Nonprofit entities are a very important component of the European housing sector. In Eastern Europe nonprofit corporations, especially cooperatives, are organized by the state and frequently are run by state enterprises at the local level. In Western Europe the most prevalent nonprofit housing entities are those that are offshoots of labor unions. The labor movement has been very active in housing, especially in supporting the development of cooperatives. France, Sweden, and Germany provide the best examples. The nonprofit sector is much less important in the United Kingdom, accounting for a relatively small amount of annual housing construction. In the United States nonprofits are a negligible factor in housing. Most are engaged in building cooperatives and in government-subsidized housing for low-income families. Cooperative housing in the United States tends to be concentrated in the Northeast, with New York City having the largest concentration.

In some countries, notably Germany and Scandinavia, the nonprofit enterprises have to compete against profit-motivated entities in the provision of housing.

This problem of the scarcity of resources in relation to potential demand does not depend on any type of economic system, nor do good intentions free a "non-profit" enterprise from the same economic constraints as those facing "profit-making" enterprises. A non-profit association, unless it is subsidized, has to cover the cost of housing construction, including a competitive rate return on borrowed capital. Apart from the freedom from taxation, which involves a small subsidy, it can only, in the long run, produce more cheaply than competitors if it can build more efficiently. There is no evidence that non-profit enterprises are more efficient than profit-making firms. On the other hand, there is no evidence that they are less efficient.[3]

The exact kinds of housing investors in any country and the styles in which they operate appear to be the product of three forces: (1) political ideology, (2) historical customs and practices, and (3) sheer practicability.

Political Ideology

The sharpest divisions between public and private investors are drawn along lines of political ideology. In socialist countries with centrally planned economies, the dominant investor is often the state itself. The USSR provides the best example of the triumph of ideology. In the USSR it is the state's duty, as spelled out in its constitution, to ensure and provide decent housing. Therefore, government entities provide more than 80 percent of the new housing built in the cities. Commitment runs very deep, as exemplified by attitudes toward rent: in the USSR the level of rents set by Lenin after the revolution has not risen. The level of rents is frozen for ideological reasons rather than for practical considerations, as wages have risen along with the prices of food and other necessities.

The United States represents the other ideological pole, wherein the dominant investor is the private sector. In the United States direct government production and/or ownership is almost insignificant, accounting for approximately 1 percent. Since colonial times real property has been the province of the private sector. Government has tended to own no more land and property than necessary to carry out its official functions. Of course, in the case of the United States a caveat is in order. Although government does not as a rule either build or own housing, it is involved indirectly, through such devices as subsidies, tax policies, and land-use regulation. However, when all is said and done, the primary reason that direct government investment in housing is slight in the United States is one of political ideology rather than anything else.

In the United Kingdom the ideological divisions over housing are deep and tend to follow party lines. In light of this it is not surprising that approximately half of all housing is provided by the state for rentals and the other half by individuals for ownership. When the Labor party is in power the public sector is favored; when the Conservatives are in power, private home ownership is encouraged. A Labor government appropriates funds for the buying up of private rentals and putting them under local authority ownership. A Conservative government will quickly move to sell off as much council housing as possible.

Historical Customs and Practices

Ingrained customs often take precedence over political and economic
ideologies, and the housing sector often produces anomalies—situations at
variance with professed ideology. For example, in most of the socialist
countries with centrally planned economies, where private property is
eschewed as doctrine, significant private home ownership exists. The urge
to provide one's own housing, to own it, and to bequeath it to one's
children is stronger than socialist dogma. All socialist states have had to
modify their doctrine in order to rationalize individual property ownership.
In socialist Yugoslavia 70 percent of all housing is privately owned. The majority of housing units built in Czechoslovakia, Romania, and Bulgaria are
also privately owned. Even in the Soviet Union private cooperatives account
for 10 percent of construction in the cities. In the rural areas fully one-third
of all housing is privately owned.

In those countries that had widespread property ownership prior to
their turn to socialism, property ownership persists. The custom is too
deeply ingrained to eradicate.

In the market economies the nonprofit sector is a reminder of the en-
durance of custom. Private philanthropy has since the Industrial Revolution seen as one of its missions the provision of decent housing for workers
and the poor. The present nonprofit housing groups are offshoots of this
movement. Although profit motivation may be the dominant force in most
market economies, the nonprofits have not only endured but have also
flourished.

Practicality

Sheer practicality sustains some housing investors. Some investors have
neither an ideological nor a historical claim to their existence, but since they
can produce housing they are tolerated and sometimes even encouraged.

Cooperatives fall into this category. Ideologically they belong neither to
the left nor to the right. The cooperative is a form of private ownership that
is a bit too communal for doctrinaire conservatives, whereas its ownership
aspects repel ideologues on the left. But cooperatives have proved their
ability to provide moderate-cost housing under a variety of economic
systems.

In market economies the state is called on to provide housing for the
very poor. Public housing in the United States, Canada, and Japan are examples. In the United States there are many instances where private provision of housing for the poor has been neither practical nor feasible. In

socialist countries it is more practical to let farmers build and own their own houses and small plots of land. This is only tolerated in the USSR but is encouraged in other socialist countries.

A Concluding Note

The point at which there is a reasonably satisfactory roof over each family's head is usually the high-water mark for housing investment. This occurred in the United States in 1950, when more than 5 percent of GNP was devoted to housing and when the wartime housing shortage was just about over. Since then there has been a secular decline in the investment in housing. The cycle has presented itself elsewhere. In Sweden during the 1960s an exceptionally large contribution, 8 percent of GDP, went to housing. This rate persisted until the numerical housing shortage was over, after which the rate dropped to 5 percent in 1978.

Another way of stating this principle is that once basic housing needs are satisfied, the demand for other goods and services tends to occupy a greater proportion of the national and household budget. As a result, as incomes tend to rise and after basic housing needs are satisfied, demand shifts elsewhere. This is a secular trend that is evident in all advanced societies.

Notes

1. United Nations, *World Housing Survey* (1974).

2. United Nations, Economic Commission for Europe, *Human Settlements in Europe: Postwar Trends and Policies* (ECE/HBP/18, 1976).

3. Graham Hallett, *Housing and Land Policies in West Germany and Britain: A Record of Success and Failure* (London: Macmillan, and New York: Holmes and Meier, 1977).

3 Housing Finance

Observation of housing production around the world reveals that the major obstacle to any country's sustaining a program of housing development is the lack of a constant and guaranteed source of money. To sustain housing production year in and year out and to provide the mortgages for investors and home owners requires the availability of funds from dependable sources at reasonable rates. This chapter examines the various methods societies used to fashion housing-finance systems.

Housing-Finance Systems: Characteristics and Constraints

Housing finance has been defined by the United Nations as money provided by any source other than the residents or builders of the dwelling for the construction or purchase of housing. It includes construction funds loaned to builders and mortage funds loaned to individual families by private or public banks and by a wide variety of other types of financial institutions.[1]

A housing-finance system brings together lenders, builders, consumers, and often the government. It consists of all the institutions that are essential to sustain the flow of money into and through the housing sector. It is necessarily a very broad network encompassing government regulation on the one hand and the private institutions that mobilize savings and investment capital on the other. It also includes various types of housing subsidies provided by government agencies, which are alternative sources of finance.

Some form of housing finance is required for the construction of almost all housing built in the world today. For owner occupation the housing-finance system permits the household to borrow enough money to cover most of the acquisition cost of the property. For rented housing the landlord in effect provides the tenants financing, while recouping this financing through rents. Therefore, a functioning housing-finance system benefits households regardless of tenure.

Sources of funds for housing tend to be the same for all countries, private lenders, government appropriations, insurance companies, pension funds, building societies, savings-and-loan associations, commercial banks, and other kinds of depository institutions. All over the world these are the kinds of institutions that are active in the financing of housing.

Institutions that can attract private savings are the most common vehicles for housing finance, especially in the market economies. Savings-and-loan associations in the United States and the building societies in Europe are the best examples. But thrift institutions also play a prominent role in the centrally planned socialist countries. Bulgaria, Czechoslovakia, Rumania, and Yugoslavia, for example, have savings banks that make loans for housing to individuals; and such financing accounts for a sizable amount of the total housing constructed. Nor are thrift institutions restricted to the advanced industrial nations; they are also found widely in Latin America, Africa, and Asia. And everywhere they are found, their functions are remarkably similar.

The long-term capital market is an alternative to aggregation of individual savings. In some countries mortgage bankers specialize in tapping long-term investment funds for housing. This is most common in Northern Europe, as practiced in Germany and Scandinavia. However, to lesser degrees the harnessing of long-term funds is found in other systems as well.

Private pension funds and government pension and social-security funds are often sources of housing capital either directly or indirectly by their purchase of housing-related securities. Both France and Brazil use such funds to make direct housing investments. However, in most other countries the public and private funds are encouraged to purchase housing securities issued by mortgage bankers.

Governments provide various degrees of direct investment capital, subsidies, or some combination of the two. Each nation tends to devise its own set of direct and indirect subsidies for the housing sector. Government involvement is so pervasive, even in the market economies, that government must be included among the financial institutions active in the housing sector.

The government can be instrumental in establishing private and semiprivate financial institutions. For example, savings-and-loan systems were established in Brazil and several other Latin American countries at the instigation of their governments. Increasingly, many countries are turning to the national housing-bank model. There are models to be emulated such as the Federal Home Loan Bank in the United States, Crédit Foncier in France, the Brazil National Housing Bank, and the Housing Loan Corporation in Japan. These are all government-sponsored entities with strong ties to the private sector.

Each society has a legal framework that regulates savings and lending functions. Such regulation has evolved over time; much of it, however, dates from the 1930s. Even market economies have extensive regulation of financial institutions—regulation unparalleled in the industrial sector. Banks, savings banks, savings-and-loan associations, building societies, insurance companies, and other lenders are heavily regulated. The extent of regulation will vary with each country, but government regulation is commonly far more extensive in finance than in other sectors of the economy.

The central banks assume a leadership role over the commercial banks and in some nations over other kinds of lenders as well. There may also be specialized central banks for housing lenders. There are laws that govern the system of property-title conveyance. Mortgages themselves are legal instruments.

There may be special arrangements for housing (or "special circuits," as they have been called), which nations can use to insulate the housing sector. The variety of preferential measures taken as incentives for investment in housing and for housing production include tax breaks, interest-rate supports, and bonuses for saving.

One important and necessary function that government can provide for the housing sector is economic stability. This is perhaps its most important function, although history attests that it can be very difficult to achieve.

There are constraints on any housing-finance system that determine the barriers beyond which the system cannot grow. The most obvious constraints are the level of national income and the distribution of income within a country. The national income will determine the limits on the funds that are potentially available for investment purposes, including those that can be invested in the housing sector. A poor nation will have difficulty in developing an extensive housing-finance system, no matter how willing it may be, if the funds simply are not there. Distribution of income is important because that will determine which segment of the population can be served by the housing-finance system. If income distribution is highly skewed, then only the wealthy minority will be able to take advantage of the housing-finance system.

The amount of public resources that can be devoted to housing is also a function of the level of national income. Given adequate national income, the government can subsidize some segment of the population that is marginally outside of the private housing sector by both direct and indirect subsidies. But the willingness and fiscal capacity to subsidize those marginal households determine the limits of such assistance.

It should be noted that not all nations have effective housing-finance systems: the capital may not be present, there may be no functioning institutions that can mobilize savings, or there may not have been sufficient trust built up over the years to inhibit hoarding and promote investing. Where there are no effective systems of housing finance, it is impossible to bring together builders, lenders, and the households that desire the housing. As a result, little housing will be built on an organized basis.

Mobilization of Savings

Most housing-finance systems, at least those in the market-economy countries, depend almost entirely on personal savings. Savings from individual households provide the bulk of the funds that make the financing of housing possible. Both specialized and general-purpose institutions exist to take these private savings and put them to productive use.

People will only invest their funds if they believe that the value can be protected from loss through mismanagement or calamity. In all cases there must be faith that the institutions are sufficiently solvent, reasonably honest, and well enough managed that persons who entrust savings to them will not be taking an undue risk. Such measures as deposit insurance, common in the United States and Canada, give investors confidence in the safety of savings institutions. Other systems, such as the building societies in the United Kingdom, stress their probity and prudence rather than insurance.

Propensities to Save

Societies have different propensities to save, as can be seen in figure 3-1. Some nations, such as Germany, France, and Japan, have high rates of savings. Others, such as the United States, the United Kingdom, and Sweden, have low savings rates. Nevertheless, regardless of national rates of savings, each of the advanced industrial nations has been able to establish and sustain savings institutions that depend on individual thrift. Savings banks are as much a feature among the low savers as among the high.

Individuals save for a variety of reasons—for a "rainy day," perhaps, or in order to purchase expensive items. For most people saving involves the postponement of immediate gratification to obtain comfort or security by that act or to purchase something in the future. But of all the reasons to save the strongest is to purchase a house of one's own. The establishment of building societies, mutual savings banks, and savings-and-loan associations was rooted in this desire. It is not only in the wealthy nations that one finds this phenomenon; thrift institutions in which people save for housing have been successfully established in poor countries as well. Even in the less-developed nations, poor as well as middle-class people will save for a house.

A successful housing-finance system must tap the savings of those who are not saving for a house, either because they already have one or because they are content to rent. It is not possible to provide the enormous amounts of money needed for housing finance from only those savers who are potential home purchasers. The ages at which people are most prone to buy houses are different from the time of life at which they are most likely to save. The bulk of savings comes from people who are at their peak in earnings but are past their prime home-buying years. This can be seen in table

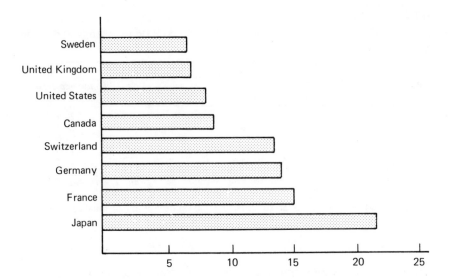

Note: Average rate from 1970 to 1975.
Source: United Nations, *Yearbook of National Accounts Statistics.*
Figure 3-1. Average Savings Ratios: Personal Savings as Percentage of Personal Disposable Income

3-1, which shows savings by age groups in the United States. The largest share of savings comes from those over 55 years old. These savings, resulting no doubt from a desire for security in old age, also represent peak earnings at a time when household expenditures, especiallly those related to to family rearing, are at a minimum. Thus the older households have a disproportionate share of all savings, at precisely the time when they are no longer in the market for new housing.

The system must have features that allow the two types of savers to be treated differently. For the saver who wants a house, the overriding consideration is to accumulate enough funds in a reasonable period of time, with some assurance that at the end of the savings period a mortgage will be available. The second saver is saving not for home ownership but for income, and the rate of return on the savings is of paramount importance.

Retail and Wholesale Savings

The process of obtaining money for housing can be seen in terms of retail and wholesale methods for raising funds in the capital market. The retail side consists of endeavors to raise money from households and small businesses. These funds are always raised in relatively small amounts. The wholesale side, on the other hand, refers to raising money by tapping large

Table 3-1
Savings and Income by Age Groups in Typical American Savings-and-Loan Association

Age of Head of Household	Share of Savings (%)	Share of Household Income (%)
Under 34	6.8	26.9
35-44	8.4	20.6
45-64	16.5	23.9
55-64	25.4	17.0
65 and over	42.9	11.6

Source: K.F. Thygerson, "How Old Are Your Savers?" *Savings and Loan News* (February 1976).
Note: In this table, "savings" refers to actual amounts on deposit in individual accounts, and is not to be confused with savings as measured in GNP accounts.

financial organizations and international investors. To tap the wholesale market, bonds are usually issued in large denominations.[2]

One advantage of the retail side is that the savings of households are a dependable source of money. Over-the-counter flows into thrift institutions can usually be counted on year after year. There is some volatility in this market, as occasionally small savers will withdraw their money.

Thrift institutions such as banks, building societies, and savings-and-loan associations are financial intermediaries that take individual savings and lend them to businesses or other households in need of funds. Surplus funds that are unused by households are put to productive use, providing a valuable intermediate service. However, it is possible for savers to put their money to work directly, bypassing the intermediaries. This occurs when households buy the bonds and notes of financial companies and governments, a process called disintermediation. When higher interest rates can be obtained by going directly into the capital market, the savings institutions will be bypassed.

All depository institutions run some risk that depositors will withdraw their money. The building societies in the United Kingdom and the savings-and-loan associations in the United States have nominal restricions against immediate withdrawal since the funds on account are technically shares rather than real deposits. Advance notice of thirty days is required for withdrawal of money. At least, this is stated in small print on the passbook. However, this requirement is seldom enforced since a share is virtually indistinguishable in practice from a deposit. It would be unusual for an institution actually to require the thirty days' notice. By the time word got out to other savers that their money was not available on demand, there would be panic. The risk that savers will withdraw their funds is real. Therefore, the yield paid to small depositors must be consistent with what they could otherwise obtain. Otherwise, they will take their funds elsewhere.

There is also a risk with depository institutions that their spread will be eroded. The spread is the difference between what an institution pays depositors as interest on their accounts and the rate that it charges its customers on mortgages. This margin is what the institution uses to pay all operating expenses and profits to shareholders. The anticipated spread can be eroded during a period of rising interest rates if the institution is required to raise the amount that it pays to its passbook savers in order to be competitive but cannot raise interest charges on its portfolio of mortgages to a commensurate level. Where mortgage rates are fixed for a long term, this can be devastating during periods of rapidly rising interest rates. If the rate on existing mortgages is allowed to rise, the spread will remain intact.

To prevent disintermediation in a savings-bank system, lenders must be attuned to market signals. The primary signal to raise interest rates is a drop in deposit receipts. Once institutions see that their rate of inflow is tapering off, as a defensive measure they will have to raise the interest rate offered to depositors.

The cost of raising funds from personal savings is relatively high because individual deposits are small and must be constantly serviced. Also, the operation of branches of savings institutions is costly. To obtain over-the-counter savings efficiently, branches must be established in close proximity to a residential population. Therefore, savings institutions have tended to develop extensive—and expensive—networks of branches in order to be close to the sources of individual deposits.

In the retail market the interest rate paid to individual depositors tends to be low, primarily because of the high cost of servicing a small account. For example, in 1978 the interest paid on passbook accounts at savings-and-loan associations in the United States was only 5.5 percent, lower than rates on other investments. However, the minimum requirements for alternative investments exceed those for savings accounts. Whereas any small amount can be deposited over the counter in a passbook savings account, corporate bonds are usually sold in denominations of $10,000. On the whole, gathering funds via the retail method is more costly per dollar obtained, compared with gathering funds wholesale in large denominations.

A savings-bank system relies almost exclusively on individual household savings and is therefore dependent on the stability of personal savings. Fortunately, personal household savings in most countries have tended to be stable over time, although there are occasional violent fluctuations.

Although the bulk of money in most savings institutions comes from the flow of small savings, institutions also seek to attract investors with large amounts of money who are seeking the highest interest rates. As a compromise measure to attract larger deposits, certificates of deposit or other contractual arrangements are used. The interest paid on term deposits exceeds that on passbooks, but the money is locked in for a specific time period.

Methods used to lock money into the housing sector for longer terms vary. In Britain the building societies offer 0.5 percent over the going rate on shares for five- to ten-year contracts. In the United States there are long-term certificates of deposit with interest-rate premiums ranging from 0.5 to as much as 2 pecent over the going passbook rate. In Canada most savings are in the form of one- to five-year certificates.

Contractual Savings Schemes

Several countries have developed saving schemes whereby individuals contract to save a specific amount of money and are rewarded for their efforts with bonuses and other advantages from the government. Some systems are strictly for housing, as in Germany and Austria; others are mixed, as in France, where individuals can save for housing or for other purposes. Contractual savings schemes create a community of interest between savers and borrowers, who tend to be the same people. The people saving are principally those who eventually want to purchase houses. The institution in which the savings are held will in time provide the mortgage.

Contractual savings schemes have an advantage over ordinary savings accounts in that they insulate a portion of the housing-finance sector from the vicissitudes of the market. Because savers are contracting for specific future benefits, the rate that they are paid on their savings can be divorced from market interest rates by the commitment to a low mortgage rate sometime in the future. With the guarantee of a mortgage at a low interest rate when the time arises, a person may be satisfied to receive a low rate of interest on his or her savings. Usually in these savings schemes, if the individual fulfills the contract, the government will supplement the interest earned with a bonus. The combination of a bonus on top of the low nominal interest produces a satisfactory effective yield. The true yield is even higher if the interest and bonuses are tax free, as they are in France and Germany.

Contractual savings schemes have another benefit, since they can be targeted specifically to those who are in need of housing when they are subject to eligibility criteria. Such schemes are usually intended for the benefit of first-time purchasers of moderate income who are saving to purchase their first home. Home ownership can be stimulated precisely among the group most in need of some type of subsidy to purchase a first house.

The money that is deposited in these contractual savings schemes tends to be locked in for a relatively long term. Savers must agree to deposit a certain sum over a period of time. At the end of that period the savings institution agrees to make a loan for a stipulated amount at a below-market interest rate. Interest rates in such schemes are not market rates. The saver is paid a very low interest rate, in the neighborhood of 2 or 3 percent per annum; but the eventual loan is written for a correspondingly low rate of 4 to 5 percent.

With contractual savings schemes it may take a long time to save any meaningful amount of money. Even with the assistance of government bonuses, it would likely take several years to accumulate enough money to make an appreciable impact on home financing. It often happens, as is the case in Germany, that when the amount saved plus the bonuses is not enough to cover the total amount needed, an additional loan can be obtained. Even if such contractual schemes cannot provide enough money for a complete house purchase they are extremely useful in encouraging thrift, especially for first-time buyers.

Contractual savings schemes must necessarily play a supplementary role in housing finance. The savings capacity of individuals is limited, especially at the stage in the life cycle at which they are trying to accumulate equity for the first house. Therefore, contractual savings schemes have limits because the participants cannot possibly supply all the money required.

An advantage of contractual savings schemes is that they tend to reduce the housing-cost burden by providing a high down payment, which lowers the monthly carrying cost. Another advantage is the low rate of interest on the mortgage, which has the practical result of making the repayment period much shorter. When mortgages are written at high interest rates, the term of repayment tends to be long in order to make the monthly payments reasonable.

Variations of contractual savings for housing plans are found in Austria, Belgium, Denmark, Finland, France, Germany, England, Ireland, Italy, and the Netherlands. They are not strictly creatures of the Western democracies, since comparable schemes are found in the Eastern socialist countries of Czechoslovakia, Rumania, and Bulgaria.

Mortgage Banks

An alternative method of raising housing money is the mortgage-bank method, wherein funds are raised not through individual savings but by issuing bonds in the capital market. Such systems are found in Denmark and Italy and to some extent in Germany, Norway, Sweden, and Finland.

A mortgage-banking system is not vulnerable to swings in short-term savings deposits, since the money is raised in the capital market. It does not tend to suffer the occasional famines experienced by a savings-bank system. In a mortgage-banking system money can always be raised in the capital market, although often at a high price. Money raised in the capital market has a higher cost than does money raised in over-the-counter savings. The price depends on how crowded the bond market is at the time the mortgage loan is made.

The funds raised in the capital market in large public offerings have lower unit costs than do savings deposits. Offsetting this is the tendency for bond rates to be higher than the rates paid on individual savings accounts. Also, in some systems the bonds themselves are issued on a retail basis. For example, in Denmark an individual bond is sold in the market for each mortgage, which tends to negate economies of scale. On the other hand, the German mortgage banks raise large quantities of money in wholesale fashion and use the proceeds to make mortgage loans.

A mortgage-banking system that raises its funds through issuing long-term loans and notes in the credit market runs the risk that borrowers will prematurely redeem their loans. Loans are constantly being paid off as houses with mortgages are resold. There is also the danger of premature redemptions should interest rates go down and mortgagors seek better terms.

When mortgages are prematurely redeemed, the mortgage bank has the problem of reinvestment. It will either have to reinvest the proceeds at a rate sufficiently high to pay the intrest on the outstanding bonds, or have to redeem a corresponding amount of bonds outstanding to match assets to liabilities. Thus in such a system there are often severe prohibitions or penalties against premature redemption. In Denmark, for example, bonds are selected at random periodically for redemption. Since mortgage bonds are usually sold at deep discounts, this possibility of early redemption by lottery presents an opportunity of a bonus yield to the lucky bond holders.

Business-Enterprise Participation

In some countries business enterprises make loans for housing. In Japan it is commonly accepted that some industrial enterprises will provide some of the housing for their workers. They are encouraged to do so by the government, which will make loans from employee pension funds to provide housing for workers. In addition, some companies will even lend employees money for a house purchase. In Eastern Europe it is common for some of the state-owned enterprises to build housing and, additionally, to make housing loans to their workers.

France has a system requiring a 1-percent contribution of total wages into a special housing fund that can be used in a variety of ways to provide moderate-income housing. Brazil taps the national payroll tax to make direct housing loans. There are really no counterparts to these devices in the English-speaking world.

An indirect form of this kind of assistance is to encourage various institutions, such as pension funds, to purchase mortgage bonds. In both Sweden and Italy, government-backed mortgage bonds can be used as legal reserves for banks and insurance companies; this is an inducement for their purchase. This tends to be a "semicompulsory" method of directing private investment into the housing sector.

Terms and Conditions on Mortgages

Sources of Funds

The terms offered to borrowers by mortgage lenders are influenced by the way in which the funds are raised. For example, whether or not interest rates are fixed or varied over the term depends on whether or not the lender raises short- or long-term money. Where the lender raises funds through short-term savings deposits, the interest rate is likely to vary. This is the system commonly used in the United Kingdom, Germany, France, and Switzerland. This is not universally true, however, since the United States depends on short-term savings from savings-and-loan associations and mutual savings banks, which issue fixed-rate mortgages. However, as inflation persists, the use of the variable-rate mortgage is becoming more popular among lenders in the United States.

The savings-bank method, which entails borrowing short and lending long, is assumed by most commercial bankers to be the sure road to disaster, a situation they have attempted to avoid for years. Commercial-bank lending is primarily for short-term business needs, which provide a good match with the short-term nature of their deposits.

All lending institutions seek some kind of immunity against the risks inherent in mortgage lending. One method is to match assets and liabilities. For example, a deposit in a savings institution is a liability on its books, whereas mortgage loans are carried as assets. For savings institutions it is impossible to match assets and liabilities exactly because mortgages are written for long terms of twenty to thirty years, whereas deposits are short-term funds with no guarantee of a minimum deposit period.

One important aspect of mortgage lending tends to mitigate the borrow-short-lend-long hypothesis. Most mortgages are amortized with a fixed schedule of periodic repayment. Repayments to the lending institutions generate a considerable cash flow, as much as one-third of their entire capital. At any given time, this steady reflow of capital is a stabilizing factor.

When funds are raised in the capital market, there is a tendency to fix a rate of interest on mortgages for the duration of the term. Funds raised in the capital market are long-term funds and usually carry a fixed interest rate. A mortgage bank, for example, can closely approximate a matching of assets and liabilities, since it can grant long-term mortgages as assets and issue long-term bond liabilities to raise the funds.

The renewable or rollover mortgage in which the rate is fixed for a term that is shorter than the period of amortization is used in Canada. The Canadian system is somewhat of a compromise between a savings and a mortgage-banking system. Savings accounts tend to be in the form of term deposits of one to five years and are therefore similar to bond instruments. Since the mortgage term of one to five years matches the term of the savings accounts, the two are compatible. This arrangement tends to mitigate the problem of disintermediation, since savings rates can rise to meet conditions and mortgages when due are renegotiated at the market rate.

Mortgage-Loan Repayment Methods

All mortgage systems tend to be based on the annuity principle of equal installments on a monthly or quarterly basis. The annuity principle, first devised by the British building societies, has now become commonplace in all systems of mortgage finance. The alternative is the balloon or nonamortized loan where at the end of the term, usually five or ten years, the mortgage is refinanced. However, in the German speaking cantons of Switzerland the interest-only mortgage without a fixed term is common. The principal never comes due and is paid off only at a sale.

The average term for a mortgage in Europe and North America is twenty to thirty years. This length is common when the mortgage interest rate is a market interest rate. When the interest rate is kept artificially low through special subsidies or special contractual savings programs, the low interest rate will produce a shorter repayment period. With low interest rates the repayment period can be as short as ten to fifteen years and still provide moderate monthly payments.

In the United States most mortgages are written with interest rates fixed for the term of the mortgage. This arrangement does not provide a satisfactory match of assets and liabilities. Loanable funds come from short-term deposits, and mortgages are contracted for twenty to thirty years. The situation in the United States was tolerable from the 1950s through the mid-1970s because interest rates were moderate and relatively stable. However, the inflation of the late 1970s has put an inordinate strain on the system of fixed-rate, long-term mortgages. Lending institutions began in the late 1970s to issue mortgages with provisions to change the interest rates as money-market conditions change.

The variable-rate mortgage (VRM) is flexible, giving the lender power to alter the contract rate of interest as conditions warrant. The VRM represents a sharing of risks between savers, borrowers, and lenders. Critics of the VRM contend that it shifts a burden that ought to be borne by the lending institutions, since they are primarily in the business of taking risks, and the risk of interest rise is one that they can reasonably be expected to bear. However, the lending institutions argue that sharing the risk increases the availability of money and tends to lower the interest rates charged. If lenders were not free to vary the rate of interest, they would have to charge enough in the fixed rate to compensate them for the possible losses that might occur in the future.

The variable-rate mortgage is popular among lenders primarily because it provides the institutions a match in their cash flow. It is not really a match between assets and liabilities since the liabilities are still short-term deposits, but it does allow interest income to rise or fall in step with market conditions. Allowing an increase in the rate that savers can be paid keeps money in the institutions; allowing an increase in the mortgage rate keeps the spread from being eroded.

The British method of adjusting for interest-rate changes includes a provision for lengthening the amortization period in order to keep the monthly payment constant. Rather than letting the monthly interest payment rise as the interest is revised upward, it is possible to maintain the same monthly rate by merely extending the terms. This system works fairly well until mortgage intrest rates become so high that the payment will no longer cover the interest on the loan. This is the point at which the advantage of lengthening the repayment period becomes null.

Accommodation of Marginal Home Purchasers

Most countries have instituted some type of flexibility in their mortgage systems in order to make mortgage lending more lenient, especially to members of lower-income groups and young households who may aspire to home ownership but who do not have the necessary savings or earnings. Aspiring home owners have two problems, accumulating the down payment and qualifying for a mortgage, that are caused by low income due to their stage of the life cycle. More lenient mortgage terms are necessary to overcome these two obstacles.

A housing-finance system can accommodate marginal home purchasers in several ways without resorting to direct government subsidies. Some of the alternatives are: (1) reduce the size of the loan needed, (2) reduce the interest rate, (3) lengthen the repayment period, and (4) provide for graduated repayments.

Reduction in the size of the loan required can be accomplished through various contractual savings schemes. Incentives to save permit the potential borrower to build up a larger equity than would be normally the case. Since there would be a smaller sum to be repaid, the monthly mortgage payments would be less of a burden. However, the social pressure throughout most of the world is in just the opposite direction, toward providing higher-valued loans rather than requiring greater down payments from savings.

The interest rate can be reduced, but this usually requires some form of government subsidy. The only way to reduce the interest rate without subsidy is by the use of contractual schemes in which both borrowers and lenders agree in their mutual interest to a below-market rate of interest. Under the German and French plans the lender has four or more years of deposits on which the interest paid is low, and in time the borrower obtains a low-interest mortgage as quid pro quo.

Lengthening the repayment period will reduce the monthly outlays for the individual household. However, there is a limit on the benefits that occur after a term of thirty years. There is very little advantage in lengthening a mortgage-repayment period more than that, since the successive reductions in monthly payments are slight.

Another idea that is receiving increased attention throughout the world is that of provision for a system of graduated repayment. In the GPM (graduated-repayment mortgage) the repayment in the early years is lower than that in later years. Most GPM schemes envision some start-up period of five to ten years during which the rate of repayment is kept low. In many schemes, such as those in existence in the United States and Canada, the annual repayments in the first few years are less than the interest required to amortize the loan. This has the result of actually increasing the loan principal as the interest deficit is added to the outstanding balance. Ater the period of graduation, the loan is amortized with a constant repayment over the existing life. The GPM therefore requires a greater total payment over the life of its contract as compared with the normal fixed-rate, level-payment mortgage.

The GPM is a method for overcoming the inflationary gap in mortgage lending. Such a gap occurs because of the way the market interprets the inflationary environment. Although it is quite probable that a borrower's income will grow over the years and that a family will be able to one day afford a house, in the present this may be impossible because of insufficient current income. Ironically, the market price of the house tends to reflect inflationary expectations. With a GPM a house can be purchased today on the assumption that tomorrow's income will rise to match inflation. For some this is a safe risk, but not for all.

A disadvantage of the GPM from the lender's point of view is that during the early years the repayment of principal is nonexistent—even negative in the first few years. Since as much as 40 percent of the funds that lending institutions have on hand come from repayments, this is a critical factor. The system as a whole can stand only a small fraction of its mortgages being GPMs. Revell offers another criticism of the GPM:

> Their adoption must therefore depend on a complete disbelief in the part of the authorities to bring inflation under control within the next 20 or 25 years or in the possibility of economic slump of such a magnitude that the price level and the rate of growth in real incomes fell sharply.[3]

Mortgage Interest Rates

In the market economies mortgage interest rates tend to be set in the market by the forces of supply and demand. Accordingly, mortgage rates bear a direct relationship to other rates of interest and tend to rise and fall with the general movements of interest rates in the economy as a whole, as can be seen in table 3-2. Although this is true in general, many caveats are in order. First of all, there are a variety of preferences afforded to housing that to some degree provide insulation from money-market movements. These measures will tend to vary with each country.

Where a large portion of the mortgage money comes from the government, the rates charged may reflect administrative decisions rather than market conditions. In order to provide perspective on mortgage rates among various nations, the following synopsis is presented. (Figure 3-2 compares mortgage interest rates for various countries.)

United States and Canada

Mortgage rates are market rates that are not shielded or insulated from general conditions in the capital market as compared with other relatively free market rates, leading to considerable fluctuation. However, monetary authorities impose interest ceilings on deposits, which have some effect on rate movements. The mortgage rate is typically 3 points above the short-term treasury-bill rate and 0.5 to 1 point above the rate on long-term high-grade corporate bonds.

United Kingdom

The mortgage rate at building societies is set by the Building Societies Association (the industry cartel), based on actual market conditions. Therefore, virtually none of the U.K. mortgage market is insulated from

Table 3-2
Selected Interest Rates for 1960-1978

	1960	1965	1970	1975	1978
Canada					
Treasury bills	3.25	4.54	4.44	7.78	9.17
Industrial bonds	5.61	6.05	8.83	10.94	9.93
Mortgage rate	6.50	6.25	9.79	10.90	10.19
France					
Treasury bills	3.68	3.39	7.33	10.17	10.35
Industrial bonds	6.55	7.22	8.65	10.73	10.71
Mortgage rate	—	—	9.90	10.56	10.89
Germany					
Treasury bills	3.79	3.91	5.83	3.93	2.67
Industrial bonds	6.10	7.60	8.40	9.20	6.20
Mortgage rate	6.2	7.7	8.20	9.10	6.60
Japan					
Treasury bills	6.08	5.71	5.80	6.06	3.39
Industrial bonds	8.69	8.54	8.83	9.39	6.38
Mortgage rate	—	—	9.0	9.36	7.56
Sweden					
Treasury bills	4.50	5.70	8.25	6.25	5.75
Industrial bonds	6.00	6.50	7.50	9.25	10.00
Mortgage rate	5.70	6.45	7.45	9.20	9.95
Switzerland					
Treasury bills	3.02	3.98	5.70	6.50	3.25
Mortgage rate	3.76	4.42	5.43	6.86	4.52
United Kingdom					
Treasury bills	4.35	5.52	6.82	10.48	9.17
Industrial bonds	6.54	7.14	10.82	19.36	12.87
Mortgage rate	6.30	7.10	8.98	11.71	10.33
United States					
Treasury bills	2.93	3.95	6.46	5.84	7.19
Industrial bonds	4.41	4.49	8.04	8.83	8.73
Mortgage rate	—	5.81	8.45	9.01	9.30

Source: OECD

market forces. However, political tradeoffs between the cartel and the government keep the actual mortgage rate below the market clearing rate. There is no real market for corporate bonds in the United Kingdom, so comparison of bond and mortgage yields is not relevant. The spread between short-term treasury bills and mortgages is only around 1 percent.

Germany and Switzerland

Mortgage rates are set competitively in the capital market. The only exception is the German contractual savings plan, which produces a mortgage rate

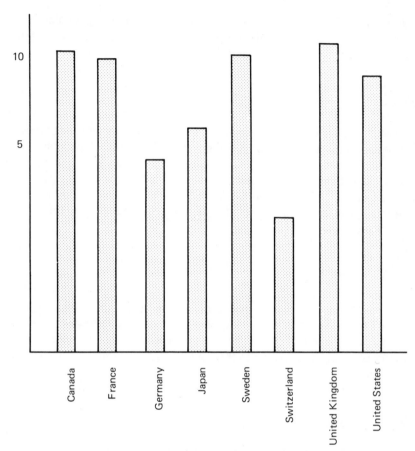

Figure 3-2. Mortgage Interest Rates, Year-End 1978

roughly 3 percentage points below market rates. Mortgage banks raise funds by issuing bonds at market rates. Neither Switzerland nor Germany has any special circuits that insulate housing finance from the market.

Interest rates in both Germany and Switzerland are low in comparison with those in other market economies around the world because of the relatively low rate of inflation in those countries.

Sweden

Virtually all housing is financed in part by the government through the device of the second mortgage granted by the state. The first mortgage obtained from a private bank is at the market rate. The second mortgage from the state, for 20 to 30 percent of value, is at a rate initially 3 points below market but graduated to market levels in twelve years. Thus the composite rate is slightly lower than the market rate.

France

Although France is a market economy, it has insulated a significant portion of the mortgage market with special government-supported programs. The accession-to-ownership and the rental-housing-assistance programs are at below-market rates (approximately 3 percent below the going rate). Contractual savings schemes produce mortgage rates a full 6 or 7 percent below market. Therefore, only a fraction of mortgage loans are actually on a market basis.

Japan

The Japan Housing Loan Corporation (JHLC) accounts for one-third or more of all mortgage lending. JHLC loans are issued at a low rate, which is approximately one-half the rate in the private market. It also varies the rate of interest charged according to the kind of housing produced—new, used, or urban redevelopment.

Mortgage Insurance

Mortage insurance is an innovation in housing finance that is used in some countries, but it is certainly not a ubiquitous feature. It is an interesting use of the principle of insurance since it is the lender and not the home purchaser who is insured. The value of mortgage insurance is that it provides protection to lenders, reducing their risk and thereby making mortgage terms more lenient.

Mortgage insurance was pioneered in the United States in 1934 by the Federal Housing Administration (FHA), which held a monopoly on the practice until the early 1960s. Since then, private mortgage-insurance companies have been introduced, which have tended to exceed the FHA in the volume of such insurance underwritten.

Canada has also developed a strong system of mortgage insurance. The Canada Housing and Mortgage Corporation is the government entity responsible for underwriting such policies. Like the United States, Canada also has private mortgage insurance, which exists side by side with the government program.

Aside from those in the United States and Canada, no really vigorous programs of mortgage insurance exist. Although many countries have set up the legal and administrative apparatus for national mortgage-insurance programs, such programs are not operating on an appreciable scale.

Crédit Foncier operates a French mortgage-insurance program that is patterned after the FHA in the United States. However, it receives very little use. Similarly, the mortgage-insurance program of the Japan Housing Loan Corporation is not heavily used. In Brazil all mortgages are insured by a consortium of private insurance companies, which are not specialized mortgage-insurance companies like those in the United States and Canada.

Many Latin American countries have established mortgage-insurance programs. The United States has provided much technical assistance to these countries to establish housing-finance systems. They have tended to copy the U.S. model, including FHA-type programs.

Mortgage insurance as such is not found in the United Kingdom, Germany, Switzerland, or the Scandinavian countries. In the United Kingdom the building societies feel that their own probity and prudent lending are sufficient. Housing values are so high in Germany and Switzerland, where real estate has high investment status, that mortgage insurance is not considered necessary to protect lenders. In Scandinavia the governments are already heavily involved not only in housing finance but also in determining building and land-planning standards. Furthermore, where waiting lists for individual houses exist, there is little perceived risk in mortgage lending.

Lender of Last Resort

A lender of last resort in the housing sector is that entity that has both regulatory powers and some capacity to grant credit to institutions that make housing loans. There are several models of such an entity.

In the United States the Federal Home Loan Bank Board comes closest to filling such a role, since it regulates and lends to the savings-and-loan associations. However, the savings-and-loans cover only half the mortgage market. Other contenders that have some claim to the title are the Federal National Mortgage Association, because of its extensive trading in the secondary market, and the Government National Mortgage Association, a part of the Department of Housing and Urban Development.

Canada has a much less ambiguous lender of last resort in the Canada Housing and Mortgage Corporation, which has considerable power. It issues mortgage insurance, operates subsidy programs, and makes direct loans when conditions warrant.

In Sweden the Ministry of Construction would be regarded as lender of last resort. The state not only sets housing standards but also makes loans.

The rate of building and the type of housing constructed are influenced by the lending policies of the state.

The National Housing Bank (BNH) of Brazil dominates the housing sector. It regulates the housing-finance system and provides money to developers and lending institutions. Its subsidiaries also build low-income housing.

Crédit Foncier is the dominant entity in the French housing sector having the power to determine lending standards, to make direct loans, and to serve as a discounter to private lenders.

The United Kingdom has no entity that one might consider as lender of last resort. Private housing finance is almost completely dominated by the building societies. Their cartel is self-regulated, obviating the need for extensive government regulation. But there is no entity, government or otherwise, to which the private lenders can turn in times of credit stress.

Secondary Mortgage Markets

Mortgage markets have two tiers: a primary market in which mortgage loans are issued and a secondary market in which mortgages are subsequently traded.

The primary market has three basic functions: (1) origination, (2) service, and (3) holding for investment.

1. Mortgages are originated by a variety of entities: savings-and-loan associations, building societies, savings banks, mortgage banks, commercial banks, insurance companies, government agencies, and pension funds.

2. The servicing function, usually performed by the originator, consists of receiving payments, accounting for the amortization, and instituting foreclosure proceedings in case of default.

3. Income received from the portfolio of mortgages is required to pay depositors (and for all other expenses of raising funds) and for the overhead. Therefore, mortgages originated tend to be kept by the lenders as their primary investment.

A secondary market may come into being when those that originate mortgages sell them to other investors. However, even when mortgages are sold, the originating institution is apt to retain the servicing at a fee. The investors who purchase the mortgage receive the loan payment net of servicing fees. There are investors who are attracted by the relatively high interest rate on mortgages, which in many countries exceeds the rates of both government and corporate bonds.

Originators may wish from time to time to sell from their mortgage portfolio to obtain cash in times of credit stress. When there is a decrease in deposit inflows or an abnormally large demand for loans, it may be advantageous for a lender to sell existing mortgages to raise cash, which can be done if such a market exists. If there is no such market, it will be difficult for a loan originator to find buyers.

There are several variations on secondary-mortgage-market operations. When secondary mortgage markets exist, one or some combination of these techniques is used.

1. Mortgages can be traded outright. This usually entails that title to mortgages be changed or assigned and recorded, much as common stocks or bonds are traded.
2. Participations rather than whole sales may be traded. In this case a purchaser does not buy the mortgages as such but only an interest in them.
3. Bonds that use mortgages as collateral can be traded. The actual possession of and title to the mortgages will reside with the originating institution.
4. Mortgages can be accumulated into pools, and participation in the pools can be sold.

United States

Approximately one-third of all mortgages originated will be traded in the secondary market. The largest purchaser of mortgages is the Federal National Mortgage Association. The Federal Home Loan Mortgage Corporation, a part of the Federal Home Loan Bank System, is also a major secondary-market participant. Private insurance companies and banks are also active packagers and traders on the secondary market.

Canada

Only 4 to 6 percent of all mortgages originated are traded in the secondary market. Because of the unique features of the Canadian mortgage market, a large secondary market has never materialized. The utilization of renewable mortgages providing for periodic interest-rate changes leads to lenders holding onto their portfolio. The national branching and large size of Canadian institutions produce a situation wherein they can raise and transfer money internally, without the need for an external market mechanism.

United Kingdom

There is no secondary market in the United Kingdom since building societies keep all of their mortgages. Like the Canadian institutions, building societies are large organizations that branch nationwide and can

vary interest rates on mortgages. There is no demand for second-tier transactions.

Germany

Secondary trading in mortgages is unknown in Germany. Savings banks
hold the mortgages they originate. The mortgage banks also hold their
mortgages as assets against their bond liabilities.

France

Crédit Foncier operates a secondary market in France. Eligible mortgage
lenders may be authorized by Crédit Foncier to issue bills of mobilization
(bonds) backed by mortgages. The bills are sold to insurance companies,
pension funds, and commercial banks.

Brazil

The National Housing Bank (BNH) serves as a discounter for mortgages.
Lenders in the housing-finance sector can present mortgages to the BNH for
sale. The rate of discount is related to the value of mortgages, with low-
value mortgages receiving the highest yield.

Both Denmark and Italy make extensive use of bond financing for
mortgages. This system has some similarity to a secondary-market operation. A lending institution will obtain funds for a mortgage by selling bonds
(or helping the borrower sell his bonds) in the capital market. But this is
really a form of primary transaction, rather than what would normally be
considered a secondary-market transaction.

In summary, France is the only European country with a vigorous
secondary mortgage market. In North America the United States has a large
and active secondary market, but Canada does not. Latin America has
secondary mortgage markets, with Brazil being the leader. In Asia (including Japan) and Africa, vigorous secondary markets have yet to emerge.

Inflation and Housing Finance

One of the most difficult problems that a housing finance system faces is inflation. Both sides of the system—savings and lending—are adversely affected in inflationary periods because of the impact of inflation on interest

rates. The nominal rate of interest has two components: the real rate and a premium equal to the perceived rate of inflation. The greater the rate of inflation, the higher are nominal interest rates on all financial assets, including savings accounts and mortgages.

Depositors demand higher rates of interest on their savings to compensate for the erosion of their capital. If the interest income on a mortgage portfolio is fixed, increasing the rate paid to savers will erode the institution's spread. If rates on existing mortgages can be raised, this situation can be avoided. Therefore, for savings-bank systems, variable-rate mortgages provide a first line of defense against cash-flow imbalances brought about by inflation.

In a fixed-rate mortgage system, as in the United States, savings institutions face unpleasant options under inflation. They can sell their existing mortgages at a loss, hoping to recover in the future by reinvesting the proceeds at the going rate; but this erodes their equity base. They can hold the existing mortgages and thereby watch their margin shrink. They can curtail making new loans. They can borrow funds from nondeposit sources and continue to make loans, but this is high-cost money.

The building societies in the United Kingdom and Germany have avoided these pitfalls by using variable-rate mortgages, which provide a more even match of cash flows during periods of inflation. The Canadians have fared well with term deposits and renewable mortgages with comparable terms, thus providing a match on both asset and liability sides.

Brazil has resorted to universal indexing of all financial assets and wages at rates equal to the inflation rate. Thus capital is not eroded. Indexation has kept the banking system coherent and has made mortgage lending possible despite triple-digit inflation rates.

Comparable indexing of financial assets is found in Brazil's neighbors Argentina and Chile, where the rate of inflation is even greater. But other than in these Latin American countries, indexing of mortgages has not been widely used. For a short period in the 1960s Finland indexed mortgages as well as other financial assets, but the system was abandoned in 1967. Finland's experience was unique in Europe.

The Perfect System

After reviewing the major housing-finance systems of the world, one might at this point attempt to describe the perfect system. First of all, such a system would have assets and liabilities that were evenly matched in terms of maturity. There would be neither premature redemption of bonds on the liabilities side, nor of mortgages on the assets side. Balances on deposit in savings accounts would not be withdrawn. There would be variable interest rates that would tend to match cash flows of both assets and liabilities. There would be stable operating expenses. There would also be an ample and assured supply of funds. There would be a secure regulatory environment that would positively encourage both savings and mortgage lending. This is the perfect system, but of course it does not exist.

Notes

1. United Nations, *World Housing Survey* (1974).

2. For a more complete discussion of retail and wholesale aspects of banking see Jack Revell, *Flexibility in Housing Finance*, Organization for Economic Co-operation and Development (Paris, 1975).

3. See ibid.

4 Housing Consumption

The Preference for Home Ownership

The right to own real property is recognized in some way in every society. This is especially true of home ownership, which despite ideology or economic system is ubiquitous. Even in Eastern Europe, where land has been nationalized, there is extensive home ownership at rates that exceed those in many of the market-economy countries. Home ownership is not restricted to the developed nations but is the majority form of tenure in most less-developed countries as well (see table 4-1).

In Europe and North America, owner occupation has been on the rise since the turn of the century and especially since the end of World War II. Governments have been nearly unanimous in encouraging this trend, using various methods but increasingly using the housing-finance system and taxation. Interest-rate subsidies for mortgage loans, special savings schemes, tax deductibility of interest, and preferential capital-gains taxes have been the primary means of encouraging owner occupation.

Governments have given official support for home ownership. For example, the British Green Paper states:

> The Government welcomes the trend towards home ownership because it gives people the kind of home they want. It reduces the demands made on the public sector. It helps with problems of mobility, particularly for people who need to move to a new area when changing jobs.[1]

In the United Kingdom the level of home ownership has doubled since the end of World War II. The strong demand for ownership was made evident in a survey that showed a large unsatisfied demand for owner occupancy, especially among members of younger rental households.[2] Most young marrieds stated that they were prepared to make sacrifices for home ownership. On the other hand, the survey found that few inducements, financial or otherwise, would cause owners to become renters. For most renters who did not aspire to home ownership, the primary reason was their age rather than any other consideration. The most common response to the question of what the government ought to do in housing was that it should "enable people to buy their own homes." The British responses to these questions would probably be typical throughout the world.

Table 4-1
**Per Capita Income and Percentage of Owner-Occupied Dwellings in
Selected Developed and Developing Countries**

Country	Per Capita Income ($)	Percentage of Owner-Occupied Dwellings
Belgium	2,633	55.9
Canada	3,636	60.0
France	2,901	44.7
Germany (West)	3,034	34.3
Italy	1,727	45.8
Japan	1,911	58.2
Sweden	4,055	35.2
Switzerland	2,910	27.9
United Kingdom	2,128	48.0
United States	4,734	62.9
Columbia	409	61.3
Guatemala	330	69.3
Honduras	266	72.5
Iraq	343	83.0
Republic of Korea	256	69.0
Nicaragua	407	66.1
Paraguay	249	69.2
Phillippines	303	78.7
Portugal	653	44.5
Sri Lanka	173	63.3

Source: United Nations, World Housing Survey, as appears in Caroll Melton, *Housing Finance and Homeownership*. (Chicago: International Union of Building Societies and Savings Associations, 1978).

Consumer preferences in housing can shift over time. For example, in the 1960s, 70 percent of the construction in Sweden was of apartments. However, the demand shifted so thoroughly toward owner occupation that by 1975, 75 percent of the construction was of single-family houses. Consumers had rejected the large blocks of flats that had been built in earlier years to satisfy the pent-up housing demand.

Condominiums, a form of ownership, are increasingy supplying homes for the mass market in both the East and the West. Condominiums (and cooperatives) originated under Roman law and have been in use for centuries in Latin countries. They are widely found in Spain, France, Yugoslavia, and many other European countries. However, acceptance of condominiums in English-speaking countries has been recent. Today the condominium form of ownership is widely used throughout Europe for both residential and commercial property. Condominium ownership is also common in Japan, where it provides most of the housing for ownership by workers.

Cooperative housing has been common in both Northern and Eastern Europe; the Germans and Scandinavians have been particularly strong builders of cooperatives with the work of large labor-union-sponsored cooperatives. However, more cooperative housing is found in the centrally planned socialist countries than in Scandinavia and Germany. Coops are flourishing in Rumania, Czechoslovakia, Yugoslavia, and even the USSR. Cooperative housing has never developed a wide appeal in the English-speaking countries. In the United States, Canada, and the United Kingdom, cooperative housing represents only a minute portion of the housing stock.

Tax Policies

Taxes play a very important part in the housing sector in most countries. The tax structure is generally not neutral with regard to housing but rather is used to influence the type of tenure, the amount of housing consumed, and the price of housing. Although countries will tend to differ in the kinds of tax preferences granted to housing, most will usually give housing some kind of special treatment not afforded to the consumption and production of other goods.

Some nations allow the deductibility for income-tax purposes of the interest expense on a mortgage and of local property taxes. The major differences among nations are not in whether or not these deductions are allowed but in whether there are dollar limits on them and whether or not these deductions are merely offsets to imputed rental income.

In Canada, the United Kingdom, Germany, and France, there are monetary limits placed on the amount of interest that may be deducted from income. However, the limits are set so that approximately 80 percent of home buyers can deduct all of their interest payments. The reason for ceilings is the policy that such relief should go to the middle class, not to the rich. Therefore, only a reasonable amount should be deducted. For example, in the United Kingdom home owners are limited to deductibility of the first £25,000 of mortgage; interest on amounts in excess of that cannot be deducted. The United States has no such limits on the amount of interest that can be deducted for tax purposes.

The Scandinavian countries, Germany, and Switzerland require that interest and local taxes can only be deducted as offsets against the imputed rental income of the house, what economists consider to be the value of the rent that could have been obtained in the market. The concept of imputed rent is alien to most noneconomists. The idea that the occupancy of one's own house could be subject to taxation is no doubt repugnant to most people. Yet respectable economic arguments can be put forward to support the proposition that the imputed rent on an owner-occupied house should be counted as taxable income. Against such imputed income are deductions for maintenance, interest, and depreciation to reduce the amount of taxable income.

Where imputed rental income is declared, it is usually taken as an arbitrary percentage of the house value, between 1 and 4 percent. After all the deductions for interest, maintenance, and depreciation are taken, the net income may often be negative so that no taxes may actually have to be paid. In Sweden and Denmark a negative income, or loss, is allowed against income. But in Germany a loss on owner occupation is not allowed.

In lieu of the usual interest deductability, Germany allows a generous allowance to be taken: 5 percent a year for the first eight years. This deduction is comparable to the size of deduction a home owner would declare in the United States or the United Kingdom.

Housing, especially an owner-occupied principal residence, is usually given preferential treatment for capital gains. Most countries either have no tax on the profit on sale of a principal residence or have a low tax at about half the ordinary-income rate. Canada, France, and the United Kingdom have no capital-gains tax on a residence. In the United States, Germany, and Sweden, the capital-gains tax is less than the tax on ordinary income. However, in Switzerland there is no significant advantage afforded to profits on sale of a house; but tax rates in that country are low.

Tax concessions are criticized on the grounds that they are expensive and are inefficient in terms of helping those that actually need the assistance. They are also vulnerable to the charge of not being progressive because they give a subsidy to a class that does not need housing assistance. Since the value of the tax incentives depends on the marginal tax bracket of the individual, those in the highest brackets receive the greatest benefit. Since these are also the people with the highest incomes, they thus receive a subsidy that is not based on need. These are valid criticisms that are not unique to any particular country. These arguments are presented in every debate on taxation in almost every country. Politically, however, the removal of tax preferences on housing is taboo in most market-economy countries.

Inflation and Housing Investment

In the market economies inflation has a disproportionate impact on housing. (Figure 4-1 shows inflation rates for various countries.) During periods of inflation opposing forces are set in motion in the housing sector. On the one hand, the higher interest rates that accompany inflation tend to drive down values, all other things being equal. Also, higher interest rates on mortgages raise the monthly cost of occupying a house, which in turn means that people will be able to afford less-expensive housing, further depressing the market. However, opposing these effects is the fact the inflationary expectations lead people to buy housing immediately, in expectation of further price increases. Real estate is frequently viewed as one of the few

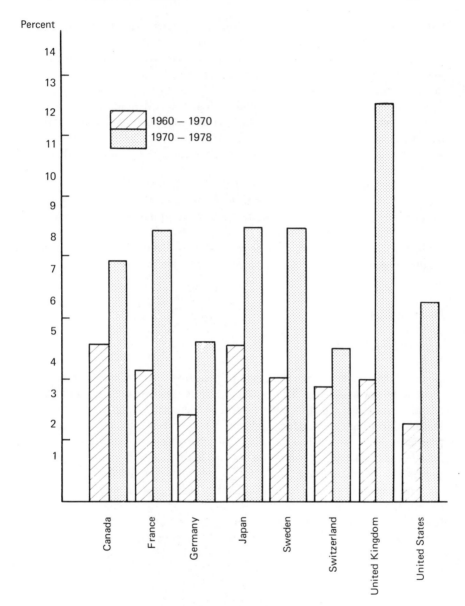

Source: International Monetary Fund, *International Financial Statistics.*
Figure 4-1. Rate of Increase in Cost of Living, 1960 to 1970 and 1970 to 1978

inflation-proof commodities around, since the rate of appreciation in house prices has exceeded the rise in the general price level.

Therefore, people tend to invest their money in housing rather than in other goods or financial assets, which drives up the price of housing. On balance, then, the inflationary forces that tend to drive up the price of housing are stronger than those that would drive it down.

Inflation tends to increase the demand for real assets as ways of escaping the depreciating currency. Housing tends to be the current choice for most people as the real asset they would like to hold while currency is depreciating. Governments also tend to foster this demand by the use of various methods to encourage owner occupation, such as preferential tax treatment and indirect subsidies. Most countries in North America and Western Europe have some forms of preferential fiscal policies that aid home owners.

In times of inflation the relative advantage is toward home owners. As the value of housing increases because of inflation, the owner, as opposed to the renter, is made relatively better off. Housing has become the favorite investment of moderate-income families attempting to preserve capital against inflation. Equity in a house is usually the largest component of their wealth. (See table 4-2 for a comparison of average prices and rents.)

Housing Costs

Affordability Burden

In an international comparison, one of the most interesting questions concerns how housing costs differ among nations. This is not only intriguing but also quite difficult to answer, because there are so many complicating factors. Housing types differ, as do methods of financing and government policies, all of which affect housing costs. Nevertheless, despite all the difficulties encountered in a comparison across national boundaries, such a comparison is possible (see table 4-3).

The important factor in determining housing costs is not the price per se, but the affordability burden faced by the occupant (see table 4-4). Affordability refers to the interaction of several factors: the cost of the house itself, the terms of financing, governmental policies such as preferential tax treatments, and the income of the person purchasing the house. Some combination of all four of these factors determines the relative affordability burden.

Housing Prices

Housing prices differ enormously around the globe, making it difficult to establish typical housing prices. The problem can be seen with reference to the United States, where there is a tremendous regional variation in house

Table 4-2
Average Prices and Rents, 1976

Country	Rent Per Month (dollars)[a]	Prices[b] Condominium (thousands of dollars)	Single House (thousands of dollars)
Austria	200	37-69	52-82
Belgium	217	46-57	63-89
Canada	285	NA	40
Denmark	197	34-47	50-59
Finland	125	29-36	42-66
France	255	66-81	80-90
Germany	235	28-41	77-135
Ireland	177	13-20	12-16
Italy	175	14-24	37-67
Japan	151	50-56	89
Netherlands	157	26-53	49-68
Norway	255	33-37	40-51
Sweden	193	26-35	46-53
Switzerland	180	74-150	130-185
United Kingdom	100	42-52	52-63
United States	299	NA	44-52

[a]Union Bank of Switzerland, "Prices and Earnings Around the Globe."
[b]Eugene Conser, *European Real Estate* (New York: Exposition Press, 1976).

prices. However, despite the problems, there is sufficient information on which to base a reasonable comparison of housing prices across nations. One of the most thorough international comparisons was made by Conser, who analyzed European housing costs for the period around 1976.[3] His observations were for the typical urban house of decent quality. These data have the virtue of consistency in that they represent one person's viewpoint. In addition, information from Japan is made available by the Japan Housing Loan Corporation, and information on Canadian and United States housing is widely available in published statistics. Based on these data, table 4-1 contains the best estimates of what a typical urban house in 1976 would cost in the various countries. It can be seen that there is a wide range of prices, with Canada at the low end and Japan, Germany, and Switzerland at the high end.

Taking the estimated house prices and financing them utilizing common techniques for each of the countries produces a range of monthly payments.

Taxes

Some nations allow preferential tax benefits that affect the occupancy cost of housing. Tax deductibility of mortgage interest, common in the United

Table 4-3
**Comparison of Housing Costs and Average Incomes in Selected Countries,
1976-1977**

Country	Income	Rent as a Percentage of Income	Price as Number of Years Earnings Condominium	Single House
Canada (Montreal)				
School teacher	$14,517	23.5	NA	2.76
Construction worker	15,595	21.9	NA	2.56
Manager	28,052	12.2	NA	1.42
France (Paris)				
School teacher	$ 8,047	38.0	9.18	10.65
Construction worker	3,487	87.7	21.12	24.27
Manager	21,267	14.1	3.45	3.99
Germany (Dusseldorf)				
School teacher	$12,797	22.0	2.69	8.28
Construction worker	7,358	38.3	4.66	14.40
Manager	23,628	11.9	1.46	4.49
Japan (Tokyo)				
School teacher	$11,235	16.1	4.73	7.94
Construction worker	6,372	28.4	8.49	10.48
Manager	23,961	7.6	2.23	3.72
Sweden (Stockholm)				
School teacher	$12,784	18.1	2.38	3.87
Construction worker	12,965	17.8	2.35	3.81
Manager	22,666	10.2	1.34	2.18
Switzerland (Zurich)				
School teacher	$20,333	10.6	5.50	7.47
Construction worker	10,771	21.4	10.47	14.62
Manager	26,125	8.3	4.28	6.03
United Kingdom (London)				
School teacher	$ 8,079	14.8	5.87	7.19
Construction worker	5,769	20.7	8.11	9.91
Manager	10,868	11.1	4.35	5.27
United States (Chicago)				
School teacher	$18,425	19.5	NA	2.60
Construction worker	17,050	21.1	NA	2.81
Manager	28,513	12.6	NA	1.68

States, can be a significant factor. However, it is not ubiquitous; among the countries listed, only three allow deductibility of mortgage interest. (Canada, it should be noted, has now changed its laws to allow deductibility, but had not done so at the time of this analysis, about 1976.) Utilizing the best estimates of the likely tax rates that would be applicable, the impact of taxes is deducted from the monthly payment to arrive at a net payment for the housing burden. This also tends to shift the ranking by significantly lowering cost for those countries that admit the tax benefits.

Table 4-4
Comparative Housing Affordability

	Canada	France	Germany	Japan	Sweden	Switzerland	United Kingdom	United States
House price (dollars)[a]	40,000	85,000	100,000	100,000	50,000	150,000	55,000	48,000
Down payment	8,000	34,000	30,000	40,000	25,000	45,000	11,000	4,800
Financing[b]								
Mortgage	32,000	51,000	70,000	60,000	47,500	105,000	44,000	43,200
Interest rate (%)	10	10	5-7	9.5	10-5.5	6	10	9
Term (years)	30	20	10-33	35	60	—	30	30
Monthly payment[c]	280	492	586	493	357	837	386	340
Tax benefits								
Interest deductibility	—	106	—	—	—	—	138	90
Other	—	—	104	—	—	—	—	—
Payment net of taxes[d]	280	386	482	493	357	837	249	250
Income, school teacher (month)	1,209	671	1,066	936	1,065	1,694	673	1,535
Percentage of income	23	58	45	53	33	59	37	16
Income, manager (month)	3,448	1,772	1,968	1,996	1,888	2,177	905	2,376
Percentage of income	12	22	24	25	19	38	28	11
Rate—overall affordability[e]	2	6	4	8	3	7	5	1

Table 4-4 (continued)

[a]Prices for France, Germany, Sweden, Switzerland, and the United Kingdom are from Eugene Conser, *European Real Estate* (New York: Exposition-Banner Press, 1976); prices for Japan are from information supplied by the Ministry of Construction; for Canada, from *Canadian Housing Statistics* (Canada Housing and Mortgage Corporation, 1978); for the United States, *Statistical Yearbook* (U.S. Department of Housing and Urban Development).

[b]Financing terms were based upon an assumption that the customary methods would be used and that lenders would use common loan-to-value requirements, and so forth.

[c]Only three of the countries allowed interest deductibility at that time, about 1976. Canada began to allow tax deductibility of mortgage interest in 1979. Germany does not allow tax deductibility of interest, but does allow a tax deduction of 5 percent of the sale price to be deducted for the first eight years. France allows deductibility of interest for the first ten years after purchase. The United Kingdom allows tax deductibility of interest on the first £25,000 of principal.

[d]All income data are from Union Bank of Switzerland, "Price and Earnings Around the Globe" (1976).

[e]The overall rank is subjective, although based primarily on the percentages of income devoted to housing. Japan was ranked eighth because of housing-quality considerations as well as the income and cost data.

[f]In Germany it is customary to have two mortgages. In this example the first mortgage was for 40 percent of value at 7 percent for thirty-three years. The second, from a *Bausparkassen*, was for 30 percent of value at 5.5 percent for ten years.

[g]In Sweden, two loans are customary. A first mortgage is for 70 percent of value at 10 percent for sixty years. The second mortgage, from the state, is for 25 percent of value, at 5.5 percent initially (increasing by 0.335 percent per year for twelve years) for sixty years.

[h]In the German-speaking countries it is common to have an unamortized first mortgage that never comes due.

Income

Incomes vary widely among nations. The results of a survey conducted by
the Union Bank of Switzerland give some impression of what incomes are
like.[4] The bank periodically reviews prices and wages from around the
world. Rather than using the mythical average or median income, it has
determined incomes for various occupational categories. This is a better
method than mythical income averages by which to represent housing
burden. The data also have the virtue of being for the same period—around
1976—as Conser's housing data. Two income categories have been used for
the analysis; the salary paid to a school teacher and the earnings of a
business manager, both in major urban areas.

The after-tax housing-cost burden can now be compared with the incomes of both the teacher and the manager as the basis for a comparison of
affordability. The ranking is then computed using a composite mean of the
two occupational categories.

The analysis shows that the United States and Canada are consistently
the lowest in housing costs. The housing-cost burden, considering all factors, is lower in North America than elsewhere. In Europe the Swiss have by
far the greatest housing-cost burden, considering all factors. However, this
is somewhat mitigated by the fact that incomes are correspondingly high.
Sweden has the lowest housing burden compared with other countries.

Japan has a very high housing burden compared with other countries.
The price of housing in Japan is high, and there are no special tax incentives
to lower the cost. One caveat is in order, however. The cost of housing may
be much higher than for any of the other countries when quality is taken into consideration. Japanese houses tend to be smaller and are often built at
great distances from the central city. There is much consumer dissatisfaction with housing conditions in Japan, higher than that found in other
countries.

Conclusions

Why is housing in terms of its affordability burden much cheaper in the
United States and Canada than in Europe? Some of the reasons are
straightforward, such as the fact that the price of the housing unit itself is
cheaper. This has much to to with the cost of land, which is a major portion
of housing costs. Land in the United States tends to be plentiful and is
reasonably cheap, especially compared with land in the urban areas of
Japan, Germany, and Switzerland. Financing terms in the United States
and Canada are somewhat lenient but not uniquely so, since lenient financing schemes are also found in Europe and Japan. Tax deductibility is also

an important component, especially in the United States where it is perhaps the most significant external factor in lowering housing costs.

An anomaly in this analysis is presented by the United Kingdom. Most of the ingredients for low relative housing costs are present, save one. In the United Kingdom the price of housing is low, the method of financing is lenient, and the taxation system has significant preferences for home ownership. However, incomes in the United Kingdom also tend to be low, offsetting these positive factors, so that in terms of overall affordability the United Kingdom ranks lower than might be apparent at first glance.

Sweden, which is not generally known as a place for cost bargains, ranks just behind the United States and Canada in housing affordability. There are several interesting reasons for this. The system of development in Sweden places very severe restrictions on land speculation, which have the effect of reducing the price of land. Thus land prices are low for new housing. Mortgage-interest terms are quite lenient, with long repayment periods and below-market interest rates for second mortgages. These all tend to lower the cost of housing despite the fact that there are no tax preferences. In fact, in Sweden the imputed rental income of housing must be included in calculating taxable income.

The foregoing analysis was concerned with the price of home ownership. In some countries, such as the United States and Canada, home ownership is within the reach of most working families, as can be seen by the relatively modest housing burden placed on an average schoolteacher. It is not surprising, then, that the rate of home ownership is high in North America. On the other hand, Switzerland, Germany, and France stand out as examples of countries that place high burdens on home owners. Thus it is not surprising that home ownership is relatively limited in those countries. The Swiss and the Germans have the lowest rate of home ownership among countries in the world, and no doubt one of the reasons is the tremendous burden placed on working families by the cost of owning a house. But it must also be said that in Germany, Switzerland, and France there is a viable rental-housing sector. Given the adequacy of the rental-housing stock and the high cost of owning property, most families in the urban areas tend to be renters.

Rental Housing

For every unit of rental housing there is an economic or break-even amount of rent required to cover: (1) amortization of the capital cost, (2) the operating expenses or running costs, (3) property taxes, (4) depreciation on the property, (5) a reserve for replacement and vacancies, and (6) a return on the equity capital invested. This particular formula holds true regardless of whether the developer is a state-owned enterprise, a nonprofit cooperative, or a private investor motivated by profit. All the components must be covered or accounted for in some way.

In market economies almost all of the economic costs are covered by the rent charged to the tenants. Rent can of course be lowered by the administration of government subsidies. But direct subsidies do not alter the economic rent, only who pays it. The level of rents in market economies tends to be set in the market by the interaction of the supply of units provided by investors and the demand for units by tenants. The United States provides the classic example of a rental-housing system, free of state controls, in which rents are set in the market.

In socialist countries the rent charged in publicly owned dwellings falls far short of the economic rent. For example, it does not reflect the amortization of capital cost. Rent is usually set high enough to cover operating costs, but sometimes even lower than that. It may often be set at what is considered to be a reasonable proportion of income. In Eastern Europe roughly 4 to 5 percent of wages is considered reasonable. In the market economies, on the other hand, rent is set at a rate to cover all costs and provide a return on the investment. When rent is kept below a break-even level, it has to be made up with subsidies, as in the centrally planned countries, or out of the equity of the property under rent control in the absence of state subsidies.

In Western Europe rent policy has gone through three distinct phases: (1) rent control after the war, (2) decontrol of rents after 1960, and (3) efforts to stabilize rents after 1970.[5] There has also been an accompanying tendency for governments to institute housing-allowance programs to ease the rent burden on low- and moderate-income families and the elderly.

Every country in Europe, North America, and Japan imposed rent controls during World War II. In Europe there was also á legacy of rent controls stemming from World War I in France, Britain, and Germany. During the interwar years the controls had not entirely been lifted, although there were pressures to eliminate them gradually. However, the dire economic conditions of the 1920s and 1930s led to political support for continuation of the earlier controls. Thus at the beginning of World War II rent controls were still in place in much of Europe. Immediately after the war there was fear that widespread housing shortages would lead to extremely high rents if the market were left alone to ration the available housing. Therefore, controls remained in place after the war and were lifted only slowly.

A second phase of European rent policy emerged after 1960 with the gradual decontrol of rents. However, it proved far easier for governments to establish controls than to remove them. As might be expected, when controls were lifted rents tended to rise. With rising rents came demands from citizens used to low rents for the reimposition of controls, regardless of the consequences. As a result the process of decontrolling rents in Europe was not altogether smooth. By the 1960s the worst shortages were over in most countries because of the large amount of house construction during the 1950s. Since the emergency was over, there was no technical reason to maintain the rent controls; but politics dictated otherwise.

By 1970 the emergency nature of the housing shortage was clearly no longer evident, although political pressures remained to keep rents artificially low. Emphasis in most countries had shifted from attempts to control rents to programs to stabilize them. The distinction between control and stabilization may be a fine one, but it does mark some difference in policy. For example, in the United Kingdom the stabilized rent is what is called a "fair rent," which has substantially replaced rent control. Fair rent is defined as the rent that a unit would command in the market in the absence of a scarcity factor. Theoretically, if there were absolutely no scarcity the rent would be zero. The market rent of any commodity is an indication of its relative scarcity. It is not surprising that in the face of this basic contradiction, the United Kingdom has indeed found it difficult to make the system operational.

Germany, Switzerland, and Sweden have substituted forms of rent arbitration for rent control. Rent increases may be challenged by tenants in special courts. These countries and others also have strong security-of-tenure laws that make evictions extremely difficult, if not impossible. A quid pro quo has developed. Investors are free from onerous rent-control laws. Tenants have considerable security of tenure and are provided guarantees against immediate harm from rent increases. The governments have inaugurated measures to stimulate investment in rental property by means of tax incentives and financial assistance. Also, low-income renters are given subsidies so that they can pay the market rate.

Analyses of rent control shows that it affects both producers and consumers.[6] On the production side, rent control reduces the incentives for private persons to hold rental housing for profit. This is especially true in the United Kingdom, where fifty years of rent control have virtually driven the private rental sector into extinction. Even in the United States, where rent control is not common, experience shows that where it has been imposed it has tended to reduce investment in rental housing.

On the consumption side, the effect of rent control is quite interesting. Rent control reduces the willingness of consumers to pay market rates for rent, especially for newly constructed housing. Under rent control a large body of older apartment buildings will have low rents that were mandated by the rent-control law. Having been built at lower historic costs, the older stock would normally have lower rents than new units anyway; but rents are kept artificially low by rent control. To counteract the negative incentives to build under rent control, new construction is usually offered some kind of

exemption or partial exemption from full controls. But when the new housing comes on the market, the rents, which reflect current construction costs,
are higher than those for the old stock. The gap between the rents required
for new construction and for the older dwellings is substantial, and this
creates a reluctance on the part of consumers to rent the newer stock.

Differences in rents between older and newer dwellings create tremendous problems in the administration of rent controls. In the absence of controls the market tends to take care of these differences. But where rent controls have been in existence, the state is called on to do something to level
the disparities. Otherwise new housing will stand vacant even while there are
waiting lists for older housing, a situation that occurred in Germany and
Sweden. The likely answer is government intervention in the market with
subsidies that try to even out the rents between new and old dwellings.
Housing allowances and interest-rate subsidies for production of housing
have been used to bridge this gap.

Housing Subsidies

Since the turn of the century governments of the industrial countries have
enacted welfare measures to house the poor and upgrade the housing of
workers. Although early efforts were manifestations of private philanthropy, the function eventually was assumed by the state. State housing subsidies are essentially of three types: (1) capital-cost subsidies to lower the
cost of building housing, (2) operating-cost subsidies which tend to lower
the cost of occupancy, and (3) direct assistance to individuals with what are
typically called housing allowances. The first two measures are aids to
public or private housing investors, who pass on the cost reductions as
lower rents to tenants. The third is assistance tailored to the individual
needs of the families involved and passed on indirectly to the investors.

Assistance to Builders

In order to reduce the cost of housing, either the capital costs, the cost of
financing, the cost of the land, or the operating expenses must be lowered.
Although only a few methods exist by which to lower these costs, there are
nevertheless a variety of different combinations.

Capital costs can be lowered by etablishing below-market land costs
through subsidies or grants. Financing charges can be lowered by the use of
lenient terms or by subsidizing the rate of interest. Operating costs can be
reduced by means of the government directly contributing some part of the
maintenance, materials, utilities, or insurance. Although there are a variety

of programs and many national approaches, there are only a few generic ways to get the job done.

Some of the major subsidy programs used in various countries can be compared on the basis of how they affect the rent to the tenant. Such a review is presented in table 4-5, an analysis of the variety of methods used in the United States, Europe, and Japan to lower the capital, financing, or operating costs of housing. These subsidies are typically available to government entities, nonprofits, and profit-making enterprises, depending on the policies of the government involved.

The deepest form of subsidy is the capital subsidy, where the government in effect takes care of the cost of construction. Public housing in the United States, Canada, and Japan is subsidized in this way. Other forms of subsidy, such as interest-rate subsidies, are not as effective as the capital subsidy in reducing the cost. Although reductions from interest-rate subsidies are significant, they still result in relatively high rents for new construction.

Many countries are no longer solely dependent on builder-subsidy schemes such as those identified in table 4-5 to provide housing for the needy. Rather, these builder schemes may be supplemented by individual or personalized housing assistance in the form of some type of housing allowance. For example, in public housing in England, tenants who are unable to pay the rent established by the local councils receive rent rebates that depend on their individual needs.

France has moved aggressively toward a housing-allowance system and therefore does not depend only on the production of subsidized housing with below-market interest rates to HLMs and others. Rather, those who need additional assistance above the modest subsidies provided in the assisted housing programs receive it in the form of family allowances. Sweden is almost completely reliant on housing allowances to take care of the needy. Their building-subsidy programs via state second mortgages do not offer a deep subsidy and do not result in any significant reduction in rents. The same situation holds true for Germany, Switzerland, and Japan. In fact, all the European countries, as well as Japan, are placing increased reliance on individual subsidies through housing and family allowances rather than on deep subsidies to builders.

The deep subsidies to builders, although on the wane in Western Europe, are still operating in the United States. The public-housing program in the United States contains very deep subsidies on the construction side in order to produce low rents. The other housing program in the United States for rental assistance (known as Section 8) also provides large subsidies to builders. However, arguments continue to be put forward in the United States in favor of the European path toward individual-family assistance and away from indiscriminate builder subsidies.

Table 4-5
Major Features of Housing-Production Subsidy Programs in Selected Countries

	United States, Canada, and Japan	France	Germany	United Kingdom	Switzerland
Type of program	Low-rent public housing	Rental-housing assistance (*prets locatifs aides*, or PLA)	Rental-housing assistance	Local-authority housing	Rental-housing assistance
Qualified owners	Local housing authorities (public)	HLM bodies (semipublic), private developers	Private nonprofit and limited-profit groups and individuals	Local housing authorities (public)	Private limited-profit groups and individuals
Form of subsidy	Capital-cost subsidy (100 percent in United States and Canada and 50-75 percent in Japan), plus some operating-expense assistance	Interest-rate subsidy plus capital grant up to 20 percent of development cost	Interest-rate subsidy, which declines over a twelve-year term	Interest-rate plus supplementary subsidies for some operating expenses	Interest-rate subsidy, which decreases over a ten-year period, plus small capital grant
Tenant rent as percentage of economic rent	32 percent and possibly lower	60 percent initially, but subsidy decreases over thirty years	70 percent initially, but subsidy decreases over twelve years	55-60 percent	76 percent initially, but subsidy decreases over ten years
Other subsidies available	Welfare assistance	Family housing allowances	Family housing allowances	Rebate of portion of rent charged	Family housing allowances

In the Eastern European countries, rents are not established at break-even levels. Rather, there are deep capital subsidies: the land is donated free, and the buildings are constructed utilizing funds appropriated from the central government or from the funds of nationally owned enterprises. Rent is kept artificially low because maintenance costs are largely assumed by the state; when interest is charged, it is at a very low, below-market rate.

In Brazil there are no housing-subsidy programs like those found in Europe, the United States, and Canada. Rental housing is not relied on as a means of subsidizing the poor. In Brazil and most other developing countries, the primary emphasis is on enabling the poor somehow to own their own homes, either through the construction of minimal-standard dwellings or "sites and services" self-help schemes. Poor countries feel that they cannot afford the enormous fiscal burden of continuing housing subsidies.

Housing Allowances

Most nations have tended to move toward systems of housing allowances that provide individual assistance, as opposed to the system of subsidizing construction. The rationale is succinctly stated by Hallett:

> The argument for individual subsidization starts from the assumption that the aim of the subsidy policy should be to help those in need. This is most effectively achieved by paying them money and leaving them to choose the most convenient housing.[7]

The greatest drawback to a system of housing allowances is the fear and suspicion that unrestricted cash payments to families would be used to purchase things other than housing. This is probably true, as consumers have many needs. Although this is a paternalistic view, it has restricted the acceptance of housing allowances in the United States and Canada.

A further argument against housing allowances is that the payments themselves do not guarantee that additional housing gets built. In theory, the additional money that goes into the housing market by way of the allowances should provide an incentive for owners to build new housing to accommodate this increased demand. However, the United States' experience tends to show that such allowances do not necessarily provide an incentive for new construction.[8] Allowances do result in upgrading of the existing housing stock because landlords, assured of their rent, will spend money to improve individual housing units. Thus the allowances are indeed incentives to rehabilitation and maintenance, although not necessarily to new construction.

Notes

1. Secretary of State for the Environment, *Housing Policy: A Consultative Document* (London: Her Majesty's Stationery Office, 1977).
2. Ibid.
3. Eugene Conser, *European Real Estate* (New York: Exposition Press, 1976).
4. Union Bank of Switzerland, "Prices and Earnings Around the Globe" (Zurich, 1978).
5. For a more complete discussion of European rent control, refer to Joel F. Brenner and Herbert M. Franklin, *Rent Control in North America and Four European Countries* (Washington, D.C.: Potomac Institute, 1977).
6. Graham Hallett, *Housing and Land Policies in West Germany and Britain: A Record of Success & Failure* (London: Macmillan and New York: Holmes and Meier, 1977).
7. Hallett, *Housing and Land Policies.*
8. U.S. Department of Housing and Urban Development, *Experimental Housing Allowance Program: A 1979 Report* (Washington, D.C., 1979).

References

1. Joel F. Brenner and Herbert M. Franklin, *Rent Control in North America and Four European Countries* (Washington, D.C.: Potomac Institute, 1977).
2. Eugene P. Conser, *Real Estate—European Style* (New York, Exposition-Banner, 1976).
3. The Financial Times, "Housing Finance in Western Europe," *European Trends*, no. 51 (May 1977).
4. E. Jay Howenstine, "Innovations in European Home Ownership Policy," *Construction Review* (April 1975).
5. E. Jay Howenstine, "European Experience with Rent Controls," *Monthly Labor Review* (June 1977).
6. Carroll R. Melton, *Housing Finance and Homeownership: Public Policy Initiatives in Selected Countries* (Chicago: International Union of Building Societies and Savings Associations, 1978).
7. Mortgage Bankers Association of America, *Selected Aspects of European Housing Finance* (May 1974).
8. Stanley E. Smigel, "Trends and Problems in European Housing

Finance," *HUD International*, Information Series 26 (Washington, D.C.: U.S. Department of Housing and Urban Development, 1974).

9. Morris L. Sweet and S. George Walters, *Mandatory Housing Finance Programs: A Comparative International Analysis* (New York: Praeger, 1976).

10. Union Bank of Switzerland, "Prices and Earnings Around the Globe" (Zurich, 1976).

11. United Nations, Economic Commission for Europe, *Annual Bulletin of Housing and Building Statistics for Europe* (1977).

12. United Nations, Economic Commission for Europe, Committee on Housing, Building and Planning, *Financing of Housing in the Countries of Southern Europe* (HBP/GE. 2/R.3, March 4, 1976).

13. United Nations, Economic Commission for Europe, *Human Settlements in Europe: Postwar Trends and Policies* (ECE/HBP/18, 1976).

14. United Nations, Economic Commission for Europe, Committee on Housing, Building and Planning, *Study of Major Trends in Housing Policies in ECE Countries* (HBP/SEM.15/PM/R.8/Add. 1, December 13, 1976).

15. United Nations, *World Housing Survey* (1974).

16. U.S. Department of Housing and Urban Development, *European Housing Subsidy Systems: An American Perspective* (Washington, D.C., 1972).

17. George Vernez, "Savings and Loan Societies for Low Income Urban Families," *Development Digest* 14, no. 4 (October 1976).

Part II
Highlights of Individual Countries

5 Housing in the United States

Housing Policy

Private Enterprise and Government Support

Housing policy in the United States, as revealed through the operation of the housing sector since the turn of the century, emphasizes the role of private enterprise in providing housing for nearly all citizens, in amount and quality consistent with household budgets. The entire housing-delivery system, from design, construction, and financing, places primary reliance on the private sector with a minimum of direct government involvement. Production of housing is largely in the hands of thousands of individual entrepreneurs who build housing in localized markets. Individual households are free to select their housing in accordance with their own tastes and budgets. Housing finance is made available by private financial intermediaries such as banks, savings-and-loan associations, and other thrift institutions.

Although the government is not directly involved in the production, financing, or consumption of housing, it would be a serious mistake to think that the U.S. government plays an insignificant role in the housing sector. At almost every stage of the housing-delivery process government is present, although often in an indirect role. The role of government in the housing sector, as it has evolved since the 1930s, is to support the private institutions that are involved directly. This indirect governmental role utilizes such measures as regulation of financial institutions, influence on interest rates, provision of guarantees and insurance, subsidies for low-income families, and maintenance of a preferential system of taxation for housing consumption and investment.

Government and Land Development

At the local level the municipalities control the permit process for land development. Development can occur only where the local authorities have given their permission and where the plans for housing construction are in accordance with local zoning ordinances, subdivision regulations, and environmental-protection measures.

Land policy developed during colonial times ensures that government should control only that land which it needs, the rest to be sold or ceded to individuals for their private use. The Homestead Acts and the Southwest and Northwest Ordinances laid down the basic underpinning of private land ownership in the United States. However, as the nation expanded westward, the federal government came into control of vast amounts of land that could not be efficiently given over to private utilization. Furthermore, much of the land under government ownership is not suitable for urban use, although it may be valuable for mineral extraction, grazing, farmland, or watershed. Ownership rights have been retained by the government, although use by private persons can be obtained through mining permits and grazing rights.

It would be wrong to categorize the land-development policies of the United States as completely laissez-faire, since there is considerable government intervention into the land market. Environmental protection has been one avenue by which the government has become increasingly involved in land-use decisions. The National Environmental Policy Act of 1970 provides the government with great powers to regulate uses, since any land uses that tend to degrade the environment come under its purview. Furthermore, the Clean Air and Clean Water Acts, which require strict standards for ambient-air quality and local water supplies, provide for further government intrusion into private land-use decisions. It is no longer possible to build any project—residential, commercial, or industrial—of any significant magnitude that does not have to go through multiple reviews at both the local and the regional levels for conformance to a variety of laws. The large number of reviews and permits required for any substantial development indicates that the government is deeply involved in the land-development process.

Planning in the Housing Sector

Prior to the Depression of the 1930s, governments at all levels took little interest in the provision of housing, which was seen at that time as a purely private matter. However, after the Depression, which hit the housing sector particularly hard, the government's recovery measures included several programs to assist in housing provision. These efforts have been long lasting, and have shaped the character of the housing market. This is especially true of housing finance. The 1930s produced the private mortgage insured by an agency of the government, which remains one of the most influential housing innovations of that period. Since that time have come housing-subsidy programs to assist families of low and moderate income. Subsidy programs are, however, not entirely in the government sector since they usually depend on private investment, albeit with subsidies from the federal government. Public housing under direct government ownership constitutes less than 2 percent of the housing stock.

There is no central economic-planning mechanism in the United States, nor is there a central housing ministry with the power to determine the level of housing production and the resources that go into the housing sector. The market performs this resource-allocation function. Accordingly, the level of housing production will fluctuate from year to year since the demand, prices, and availability of credit all are independently determined in the marketplace. Housing is comparable to all other items in the economy, having the market set the price and level of production.

The Department of Housing and Urban Development (HUD), the cabinet-level agency responsible for housing, does not have powers to allocate resources into that sector. Rather, it depends on its ability to work in tandem with the private sector and to assist in indirect ways, through low-income subsidies, research, advocacy, promulgation of standards, and persuasion. Since 1968 annual housing-production targets have been set by HUD, as required by housing legislation enacted in that year. The targets are merely the secretary's estimates of likely housing production, taking into consideration housing privately financed as well as that subsidized by the federal government. Such targets have no weight in themselves except as indications of a desired level of housing production. Thus it is not surprising that actual production deviates considerably from the production targets.

U.S. Housing Problems

The United States is a well-housed nation by almost any standard, in terms of housing condition, levels of housing satisfaction, and the extent of home ownership. The Annual Housing Survey reported in 1976 that 88 percent of those interviewed expressed satisfaction with their house and neighborhood. Only 5 percent of households expressed deep dissatisfaction with either their present housing unit or neighborhood. The census also reports that 93 percent of all housing units were complete, with all the required plumbing, and in good condition, with only 8 percent of the housing stock deemed to have serious defects. The rate of home ownership is quite high, at 64 percent, and continues to increase each year. Thus the picture that emerges from an overview of the U.S. housing stock is that the nation is well housed and that most households are reasonably well satisfied with their accommodations.

Despite the generally good condition and high level of consumer satisfaction, it would be a mistake to think that housing problems do not exist in the United States. In the United States the housing problem takes on several dimensions. Most obvious are those affordability aspects of housing consumption that leave many low-income families unable to secure adequate accommodations at prices or rents that represent a reasonable portion of the family budget. As many as 11 percent of all households are below the poverty level and face severe problems in securing adequate housing that they can afford. Low-income, female-headed households are those least able to find adequate shelter at an affordable price. The government has developed programs that attempt to address this imbalance by building low-income housing and general-welfare programs for medical, food, and rental assistance.

There is also the problem of young households being able to afford their first house at prevailing market prices. The secular rise in house prices and the propensity of housing prices to outstrip increases in incomes have made housing relatively more expensive than other goods. The affordability problem has been partially addressed through the provision of lenient financing, with graduated-payment mortgages and low-down-payment schemes. These have been successful in opening up home ownership to some households entering the market for the first time. However, there are limits to the amount of assistance that can be afforded by these schemes alone; as the price of housing continues to increase, such would-be first-time home purchasers continue to face a difficult problem for which no answer has been found.

Another aspect of the housing problem is the deplorable condition found in many older inner-city neighborhoods. Much of the housing stock in core cities has been aging and deteriorating through lack of maintenance and rehabilitation. Housing policy is seen as one way of upgrading such deteriorated neighborhoods through programs of general assistance to cities and specific federally funded subsidized programs for urban renewal and revitalization. Since 1949 there has been a concerted effort to channel federal funds into cities to stem the decay and to revitalize neighborhoods as well as city centers. This effort has had mixed results; many urban centers have been revitalized, but success in uplifting deteriorated neighborhoods has not been comparable. The problems of revitalizing neighborhoods are closely linked to the changing demographic profile of urban areas. As more affluent households have left for the suburbs, the residual population is poorer and cannot support the housing inventory at its former level of maintenance. In addition to decline and decay there has been some abandonment of housing in many of the large urban areas, a situation that has tended to exacerbate greatly the problems associated with renewal of older core areas.

In spite of the obvious achievements of the United States in providing a decent level of accommodation to the overwhelming majority of its citizens, serious problems in the housing sector remain. For solution to these problems, primary reliance is still placed on the private sector, although there is a growing awareness that the intractable nature of the problems requires considerable public and private cooperation for their eventual solution.

Such cooperation comes in the form of increased public assistance, especially to low-income households; the use of financial incentives to private-sector entrepreneurs to provide housing and associated development; and also more stringent regulations.

Housing Production

Housing and the Economy

The amount of resources going into housing expressed as a percentage of the gross national product (GNP) has been on a secular decline since the beginning of the twentieth century. Since the end of World War II the relative decline in the housing sector has been noticeable (see figure 5-1 and table 5-1). The high point was in 1950, a record production year for new housing, when 5.5 percent of GNP went into the housing sector. Since then the low has been 2.2 percent in 1975, a particularly bad year for the housing sector; and the average has been somewhere in the neighborhood of 3.5 percent. The decrease in the amount of GNP going into housing is explained more in terms of the adequacy of the present housing stock rather than by any turning away from housing as an investment. The housing shortages that were apparent during and immediately after World War II have been alleviated, and there is less need to devote as much of the national income to the housing sector.

Housing expressed in terms of population, as new units per 1,000 inhabitants, has been approximately 7.5 since the end of World War II. Such a rate of building is moderate in terms of the effort put forward by other industrial countries.

One unique feature of American housing production that should not be overlooked is the annual production of mobile homes, which accounts for as much as 20 percent of the total. Mobile homes are outgrowths of travel trailers, which became popular in the 1940s as appurtenances that could be hitched to the back of an automobile and carried from place to place. However, today most mobile homes are never moved once they have been delivered to a site. They bear little resemblance to the former travel trailers used for recreational purposes.

Housing Prices

The prices of both new and existing houses have been rising every year since World War II. In 1977 the median price of a house stood at $48,000, up substantially from the 1947 price of only $18,000. The same trend has been evident for the prices of existing housing, which have also moved in tandem with the price of a new house (see table 5-2).

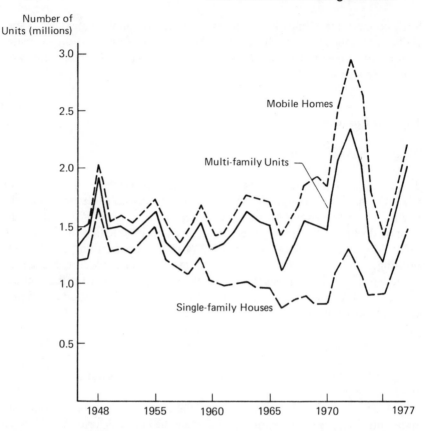

Source: U.S. Bureau of the Census, *Current Construction Reports: Housing Starts* (annual).
Figure 5-1. Total Housing Starts by Type of Structure, United States,
1948-1977

The rise in the price of a new house has two primary ingredients. Over the years the standard house has tended to change, since newer models are increasingly larger and contain more amenities. For example, the house in 1977 was considerably larger than houses built immediately after the war. It also had more bedrooms and baths, both indicators of the greater level of amenities contained in newer houses. The percentage of new houses with two or more baths increased from 53 percent in 1965 to 69 percent in 1977. Also, the size of a typical house increased; in 1977 such a house would be likely to be 1,720 square feet (159.8 square meters) and to have three bedrooms, two and one-half baths, and one kitchen.

It has been estimated that these changes in quality have accounted for 27 percent of the increase in house prices, with the remaining 73 percent to

Table 5-1
United States: Selected Housing-Production Statistics, 1953-1977

Housing Activities	1953	1960	1965	1970	1977
Dwellings started (thousands)	1,103.0	1,296.0	—	1,233.5	1,636.3
Dwellings per 1,000 population	8.1	7.2	7.8	7.1	7.6
Housing construction as a percentage of gross domestic product	4.1	4.5	4.1	3.2	4.7
Percentage of total by type of investor					
Public authorities	3.3	3.4	2.4	2.3	0.1
Private	96.7	96.6	97.6	97.7	99.9

Source: United Nations, *Annual Bulletin of Housing and Building Statistics for Europe.*

be accounted for by other factors [2]. Indeed, the price of housing has tended to rise 20 percent faster than the level of general prices, as measured by the consumer-price index. Inflation in house prices has placed a greater burden on those attempting to purchase a house for the first time. For this reason, first-time home buyers are unlikely to be in a position to purchase a new house, but must instead purchase a small house in the existing house market. Almost two-thirds of all first-time home buyers purchase existing houses rather than new ones.

Cyclical Behavior of Home Building

Since the end of World War II the annual volume of house building has been characterized by sharp year-to-year fluctuations. There have been

Table 5-2
Median Prices for Both New and Existing Houses in Selected Years, 1965-1977

Year	Median Price of a New Existing House	Median Price of an Existing House
1970	$23,400	$23,000
1975	39,300	35,300
1977	48,800	42,900

Source: U.S. League of Savings Associations, *Fact Book* (annual).

seven major downturns in house construction since 1945. There are two reasons for such sharp cyclical behavior in the housing sector. First, there are the effects of the business cycle, where housing decline tends to precede a period of recession and conversely to increase at the low point of the recession and lead in the way to recovery. The second cause of instability relates to the absence of adequate mortgage money when competition for investment funds becomes intense, with mortgage rates rising as the thrift associations experience an outflow of deposits.

Structure of the Housing-Finance Sector

Mobilization of Savings

The bulk of the funds in the mortgage market come from mobilization of the savings of individual households (see figure 5-2). In 1977 individual household savings amounted to 5.0 percent of personal disposable income. This rate of savings is not especially high by world standards; it is three to four times lower than that of the Germans and Japanese. The institutions that collect individual savings, through over-the-counter time accounts and savings accounts, are commercial banks, savings-and-loan associations, mutual savings banks, and industrial credit unions. In addition, other savings are garnered by the usual array of institutions such as pension funds, insurance companies, government bonds, and corporate bonds and equities. In 1977, the $108.9 billion invested in savings accounts was deposited as follows:

	Amount (Billions)	*Percentage*
Savings- and-loan associations	$ 51.1	46.9
Mutual savings banks	11.0	10.2
Commercial banks	39.2	36.0
Other	7.6	6.9
	$108.9	100.0

The safety of savings is guaranteed by the Federal Deposit Insurance Corporation (FDIC) for commercial banks and mutual savings banks and by the Federal Savings and Loan Insurance Corporation, an arm of the Federal Home Loan Bank Board (FHLBB), for the savings-and-loan associations. Individual savings accounts are insured up to $40,000 each, with no limit on the number of accounts a household may possess. Institutions pay a small insurance premium on their deposit balances. Should an institution become insolvent for any reason, the federal insurance agencies will in-

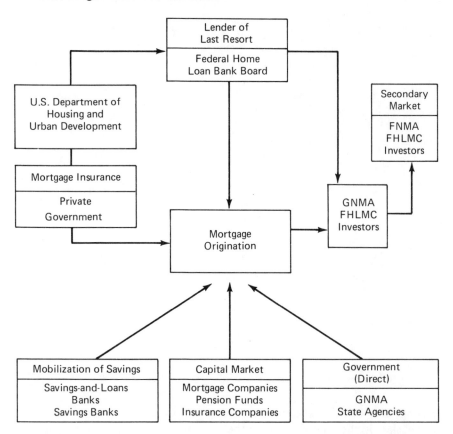

Figure 5-2. United States: Structure of the Housing-Finance Sector

tercede to guarantee the value of accounts. The confidence-building nature of this government guarantee cannot be underestimated in its importance to the structure of the entire banking and saving system. Many people still remember the 1930s, when half the nation's banks failed.

Lending Institutions

Thrift associations provide the bulk of all money for mortgages (see figure 5-3). Savings-and-loan associations, mutual savings banks, and the savings departments of commercial banks are the key thrift institutions. They all accept deposits from individuals and pay interest on their accounts at the market rate, and also make long-term mortgage loans at a rate consistent with that of other long-term instruments.

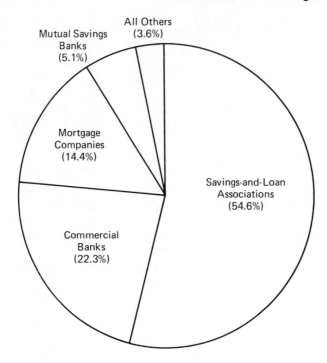

Figure 5-3. Residential Mortgage Loans by Originator, 1977

Savings-and-Loan Associations. Savings-and-loan associations were first established in the United States in the late nineteenth century, on the model of the building societies in England. They were then small, not-for-profit mutual associations whose primary purpose was the accumulation of savings for house purchase. The savings-and-loan industry has grown enormously over time, especially in the period immediately after World War II. In 1945 savings-and-loan assets stood at $45 billion; by 1978 they had grown to $523 billion.

Savings-and-loan associations are chartered to do business either by the state in which they are located or by the Federal Home Loan Bank Board. Regardless of their charter savings-and-loans can operate only within the state in which they are founded. The prohibition of nationwide branching or operation across state lines tends to limit the ultimate size of such associations. Similar restrictions apply to commercial banks and mutual savings banks. Approximately two-thirds of all savings-and-loans are mutual companies, and only one-third have stock ownership.

State-chartered savings-and-loan associations can be members of the Federal Home Loan Bank System and participate in federal deposit insurance. In 1978 there were 4,723 such associations, of which 2,000 were federally chartered. Almost all associations belonged to the Federal Home Loan Bank Board system, and 99 percent had federal deposit insurance.

Mutual Savings Banks. Mutual savings banks are quite similar in form and function to the savings-and-loan associations. They were originally founded as close-knit societies to encourage thrift among workers. Today there are 467 of them located in the eastern part of the country.

All mutual savings banks are without stock ownership. Savings-and-loan associations, on the other hand, may be either mutual or stock companies. Money on account in a mutual savings bank (MSB) is a deposit rather than a share. There is one major difference between savings-and-loans and mutual savings banks, since the latter can issue third-party obligations (checks) known as negotiated orders of withdrawal. The growth in this aspect of their business will tend over time to blur the distinction between mutual savings banks and commercial banks.

Commercial Banks. As a rule, commercial banks are not significantly mortgage lenders, preferring to concentrate on short-term loans to businesses and consumers. In 1978 commercial banks held 18 percent of the outstanding mortgages on single-family homes. Although commercial banks generally tend not to engage in residential mortgage lending, there are many notable exceptions. Commercial banks in the western United States have traditionally made mortgage loans. For example, the Bank of America in California, the nation's largest bank, is the single largest mortgage holder among all lending institutions. The extent of commercial-bank activity in mortgage lending depends on the tradition of individual banks in a given region of the country.

Taxes on Savings Institutions. Savings associations benefit from preferential tax policies that allow 40 percent of their net income to be counted as loss reserves, thus reducing their effective rate of taxation from 48 percent to about 25 percent. For an institution to qualify, 82 percent of its assets must be invested in housing. This is an indirect benefit to borrowers, since savings-and-loans' costs are lower than they would be without the tax benefit. This arrangement is a quid pro quo to the institutions in return for their restriction to the mortgage market.

Interest on Savings Deposits. All interest earned on savings deposits is taxed as ordinary income. Interest income is reported to the Internal Revenue Service (IRS), and the individual is liable for payment of taxes due. There are no preferences on earned interest income, no matter what the purpose is for saving. There are no savings schemes that offer bonuses to persons saving money for housing, as is common in Europe.

Capital-Market Resources

There is no extensive involvement of capital-market resources in the primary mortgage market. Institutional investors do not use their funds to make direct mortgages. However, some will make money available to intermediaries who will issue mortgages.

Mortgage Bankers. Capital-market resources are mobilized for issuance for mortgages through mortgage bankers. The term "mortgage banker" is somewhat misleading, since these are not depository institutions but ones that perform a middleman function in the mortgage area. Essentially, their operation consists of borrowing short-term money, usually from commercial banks, and originating mortgage loans. These loans are held for a short period; this is called "warehousing." They are then sold to the ultimate investor. The bulk of the business of mortgage bankers has traditionally been with government-insured or -guaranteed loans of the Federal Housing Administration and the Veterans Administration. Such loans are sold to investors that wish to hold mortgages in their portfolios: insurance companies, mutual savings banks, pension funds, and the federal agencies in the mortgage market.

Over the years subtle changes have occurred in mortgage banking, as mortgage-banking concerns have become subsidiaries of commerical banks, large financial companies, and savings-and-loan associations. It is profitable for these financial institutions to perform the middleman function and to mobilize other people's funds in the credit market. The enterprise makes its profit from the fees charged for origination and servicing of the loan over the life of the mortgage.

Insurance Companies. Until the 1950s insurance companies were significant lenders on residential mortgages, but since then the proportion of their assets in mortgages—especially single-family houses—has declined. Their participation is more likely to be found in commercial mortgages on large apartment projects and nonresidential real estate. The specific reasons for their abandonment of residential real estate are not entirely clear, but apparently the yields on long-term government and corporate bonds and commercial mortgages are more attractive to them.

Pension Funds. Pension funds, although enormous repositories of cash, are not major factors in the mortgage market. The real-estate industry has for years coveted these funds, but so far no blandishments have been sufficient to get them into the mortgage market in a significant way.

Credit Unions. Credit unions do not as a rule make mortgages; rather, they are oriented toward consumer loans, especially automobile finance.

However, they do provide significant funds to the housing sector for repair, renovation, and home-improvement loans.

Direct Lending by Government

In the United States, neither federal nor state governments generally make direct loans for housing. Government involvement is more likely to take the form of insurance and guarantees. Even housing-subsidy programs for the poor depend on government guarantees and insurance, with the actual money for building coming from the private sector. Direct provision of mortgage loans by government is very slight. However, indirect subsidies such as tax policies have an enormous impact.

Mortgage Instruments

In 1978 the average mortgage loan was made for 76.1 percent of the value of the property. The balance was provided by the borrower either from savings or from the equity value in a currently owned house.

Many families have paid off their mortgages and thus own their houses outright. In 1976 only 63.5 percent of all owner-occupied houses had mortgages. It is interesting to note that families that own their houses without mortgages tend to be older and often retired from the labor force, and that the houses tend to be of lower value. Most mortgaged houses have only one mortgage. Only 5.4 percent of owners had more than one mortgage, according to the 1970 census.

The most common type of mortgage is the fixed-rate, level-payment, amortized loan. The interest is fixed for the term of the loan, which may be from twenty to thirty years. The loan is self-amortizing, and the payment made each month is constant. More than 95 percent of all mortgage loans are of this type.

The United States is one of the few countries in which the source of mortgage lending is a savings system and in which the mortgage interest rate is fixed for the term. This situation is workable only under conditions of stability and reasonable certainty. In retrospect this was the pattern of most of the postwar experience in the United States, when the inflation rate (from 1945 to 1965) was extremely low. During those years the rate of inflation averaged less than 3 percent per year. However, since 1965 the rate of inflation has increased dramatically; the resultant rise in interest rates has threatened the system of fixed rates for mortgages (see figure 5-4). There has been a growing interest in the use of variable-rate mortgages. In California, for example, the variable-rate mortgage has proved to be extremely popular with both savings-and-loan associations and banks. This phenom-

Percent

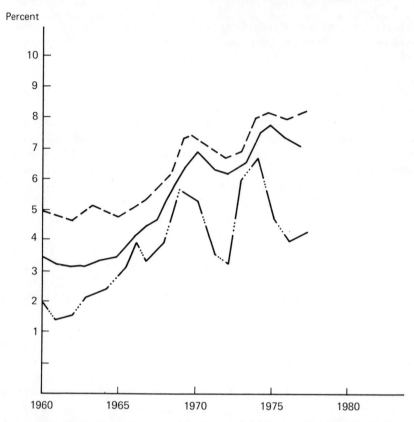

Source: Organization for Economic Cooperation and Development, *General Statistics Bulletin*.
Figure 5-4. Interest Rates in the United States, 1960-1977

enon is likely to spread. Since 1975 alternative types of mortgage loans have
been introduced in some of the states. The legal basis for mortgage lending
is controlled by the individual states, and most states have restrictions on
changing interest rates on existing mortgages. But there is increasing acceptance of variable-rate instruments, which tie the rate to the movement of interest rates in the economy.

There is also a new program of graduated-payment mortgages (GPMs),
where the interest rate and number of years to maturity are fixed, but where
the payments made in the first five to seven years are low, gradually increasing to a fixed level at the end of this period. The GPM is beneficial to young
households that can look forward to increases in income over the years.

Mortgage Insurance

Some mortgage loans are insured by policies that indemnify the lender in
case of default. Down-payment requirements are lower if the mortgage is

insured or guaranteed. The Federal Housing Administration (FHA), which pioneered the concept in the United States, charges a fee of 0.5 percent of the loan balance, used for an insurance reserve fund to pay for any losses and for the operating costs of the agency. There are also private mortgage-insurance companies that insure loans for a fee of 0.25 percent. The Veterans Administration operates a guaranty program for qualified veterans of military service, and the Farmers Home Administration has a comparable program for homes in rural areas (see table 5-3). Technically, these are not insurance schemes but simple guarantees. With mortgage in-surance or guarantees the ratio of the loan to property value can be greater than 90 percent. For conventional loans (without insurance or guarantee) the loan-to-value ratio will seldom exceed 75 or 80 percent.

Secondary-Market Operations

In the United States as many as one-third of the mortgages originated by savings associations, banks, and others will be resold to investors in what is known as a secondary market (see table 5-4). There is an active market among the investors and institutions that find the high yields on mortgages attractive, since these rates are typically 1 to 1.5 percentage points over the rate for corporate bonds.

The Federal National Mortgage Association (FNMA) is the largest pur-chaser of mortgages in the secondary market. FNMA is a unique corpora-tion, which, although privately held, is assisted by the government to perform a public purpose. Originally, in 1934, FNMA was created as a government corporation. Then it became part of the Department of Hous-ing and Urban Development; still later, in 1968, it spun off from the federal government. Of its fifteen directors, five are chosen by the president and ten by the stockholders.

Table 5-3
Value of Mortgage Originations by Insurance Status for the United States, 1977

Type of Insurance	Amount (billions of dollars)	Percentage
Conventional (without insurance or guarantees)	124.4	7.8
Private mortgage insurance	21.6	12.5
Federal Housing Administration	10.0	8.0
Veterans Administration	14.8	8.6
Total	172.8	100.0

Source: U.S. Department of Housing and Urban Development, *Statistical Yearbook*. (annual)

Table 5-4
Summary of Secondary-Mortgage-Market Activities by Type of Institution for the United States, 1977

	Transactions (billions of dollars)		
Institutions	Loan Originations	Loan Sales	Loan Purchases
Commercial banks	35.2	5.8	1.8
Mutual savings banks	8.1	0.3	3.3
Savings-and-loan associations	86.1	13.5	13.9
Mortgage companies	22.8	23.8	3.3
Federal credit agencies	3.0	8.9	9.7
Mortgage pools	—	1.5	24.9
All others	2.1	0.5	2.1
Total	157.8	54.3	59.0

Source: U.S. Department of Housing and Urban Development, *Statistical Yearbook*. (annual)

FNMA borrows money in the capital markets as a federal agency, thereby obtaining a favorable rate. Proceeds from bond sales are used to purchase eligible mortgages (both government insured/guaranteed or conventional) from primary lenders. Its profitability depends on the spread between interest income on its mortgage portfolio and its cost of borrowing. Its charter provides a reserve commitment from the U.S. Treasury of $2.25 billion, should the need ever arise. In 1978 FNMA's portfolio of mortgages stood at $45 billion.

Other government-supported agencies in the secondary market are the Government National Mortgage Association (GNMA) and the Federal Home Loan Mortgage Corporation (FHLMC). Both GNMA and FHLMC will guarantee large pools of mortgages that are originated by savings associations and mortgage bankers and are then sold to investors. The guarantees of the payment of principal and interest and the quality of the mortgages in the pool makes this an attractive form of long-term investment.

The secondary mortgage market is increasingly being dominated by the trading of large pools of mortgages guaranteed by GNMA and FHLMC. The mechanics of these operations are not difficult to understand. Lenders are able to accumulate mortgages, which are usually insured by either federal or private insurance, and to aggregate the mortgage loans into an investment package of at least $1 million. For example, it would take an average of thirty mortgages to aggregate to $1 million. Based on these mortgages in the pool, the institutions, such as savings-and-loans, will issue a certificate and sell the entire pool or participations in the pool to investors. These packages or pools of mortgages, if they meet certain conditions, can be guaranteed by GNMA or FHLMC. What is being guaranteed is that the principal and interest will be passed through to the investor, with the risk of default assumed by GNMA and FHLMC. These guarantees make the pools eminently salable in the capital market. Yields on these mortgage-pool participations tend to be high, at least 1 to 1.5 points above the going rate for many high-grade corporate bonds.

The way the pass-through works is that each month investors receive both principal and interest due on the underlying mortgages. Thus the cash flow, since it contains an amortization component, is quite high in relation to alternative investments like bonds, which yield only the interest. Should any of the mortgages in the pool be terminated because of sale or default, the proceeds are immediately disbursed on a pro rata basis to the investors and the size of the pool is correspondingly reduced.

In 1976 these mortgage pools represented more than 50 percent of all secondary-market activity, a trend that seems likely to continue. It has been beneficial to the mortgage market because it has helped to tap a previously underutilized source of funds in the capital markets.

Lender of Last Resort

The lender of last resort is the Federal Home Loan Bank Board (FHLBB). More than any other institution, it tends to serve this particular function. Although the FHLBB has jurisdiction only over the savings-and-loans, it effectively is lender of last resort to approximately one-half of the mortgage market, the rest being split among commercial banks and other institutions.

The FHLBB makes advances to its members, particularly in times of credit stringency, by borrowing in the capital market and lending to its member institutions. During the credit crunches of 1966, 1969, and 1973 (times of sudden outflow of funds from thrift institutions), the FHLBB was instrumental in infusing funds into the savings-and-loan sector, providing mortgage money when traditional sources went dry.

In addition, the FHLBB has a regulatory role over the nation's savings-and-loan associations. Although its legal influence is limited to savings-and-loans, its influence in the housing market extends beyond that through its directorship of the Federal Home Loan Mortgage Corporation (FHLMC) and its promulgations of standards for mortgage lending.

The Department of Housing and Urban Development (HUD) is a contender for the lender-of-last-resort designation, largely through its Government National Mortgage Association. GNMA, acting with appropriations from Congress, can provide primary lenders a market for mortgages as it did under the Emergency Home Finance Act of 1970. The potential exists for GNMA to act should Congress appropriate the funds for it to do so.

Interest Rates and Mortgage Rates

The mortgage market in the United States is highly specialized. Since the end of World War II, the savings-and-loan associations and other lenders have developed considerable expertise in underwriting mortgages. In addition, the development of an extensive secondary market has made the mortgage a desirable investment instrument. Because of those developments the risk usually associated with investing in mortgages has decreased considerably. Although investors have a variety of alternatives, mortgages are finding increasing acceptance. The yield on mortgages has been higher than that on high-grade corporate bonds. However, since the end of the war the traditional spread between the yields on high-grade corporate bonds and on mortgages has tended to decline, which is an indication of the investor's perception of the decrease in the risk of holding mortgages.

Interest-rate ceilings, which limit the amount banks and savings institutions can pay depositors, are determined by actions of the Federal Reserve system. Thrift institutions (savings-and-loan associations and mutual savings banks) may pay a premium above the limit imposed on banks. The premium is currently 0.25 percent, which is considered sufficient to keep the thrift institutions competitive with the banks.

Some states have usury laws that provide interest ceilings on mortgages. In 1978, twenty-five states had some type of interest-rate usury ceiling. Furthermore, the Federal Housing Administration and Veteran's Administration maintain interest-rate ceilings on their programs that contribute to the stickiness of interest rates.

The effects of usury laws and rate ceilings have been undermined by the fact that mortgage lending terminates when the market rate exceeds the ceilings. Whenever this has persisted over a sustained period, statutory ceilings have invariably been raised or eliminated. Yet despite the futility of interest-rate ceilings, they remain as symbolic instruments that politicians use for their own purposes.

Financing an Individual House

In the United States, $50,000 was the average cost of a new house in 1977 (see table 5-5). This figure does not mean that one could have bought housing in every market in the United States for that price. In the Washington, D.C. metropolitan area, $50,000 would not have bought much of a house,

Table 5-5
United States: An Illustrative Example of Financing the Purchase of an Individual House

1. Value of house: $50,000
2. Mortgage terms:
   a. 80% of value = $40,000
   b. 9% per annum interest (fixed)
   c. 30-year term to maturity
   d. Payment = $321.85 per month
   e. Owner's equity = $10,000
3. Variations:
   a. High-value insured/guaranteed loan of 95% of value (FHA, VA, PMI), or $7,500 principal amount

      Payment = $382.20 per month
   b. Variable-rate mortgage—when rate increases after 2 years to 10% per year

      Outstanding balance at end of 2 years = $39,450

      New payments over 28 years at 10% = $350.30/month

and certainly not the average one. It would also not have purchased much housing in Los Angeles or in some other markets in the country. The family purchasing the house would likely approach a savings-and-loan, mortgage banker, or commercial bank for a loan of 80 percent of the value, or $40,000. The rate of interest is assumed to be 9 percent per annum (the rate in 1977) with a fixed term of thirty years to maturity. The interest rate would not vary over that time. The resultant mortgage payment would be $321.85 per month. To this payment would have to be added other occupancy costs, which include local property taxes of approximately 1 percent of the market value, casualty insurance, and maintenance expenses including utilities.

The family seeking the mortgage would ordinarily have to approach only one institution. Second mortgages are somewhat rare; they are found on only 5 percent of the mortgaged properties in the United States.

A mortgage of 80 percent of value would not be sufficient if the family did not have the savings of $10,000. This is especially true of young families forming their first household in the early stages of the life cycle. In the United States, high-value mortgages—up to 95 percent—are available; but they usually require some form of mortgage insurance or guarantee. The FHA issues mortgage insurance for a fee of 0.5 percent of the loan. Private mortgage insurance is also available, and the fee is usually 0.25 percent on a top slice of 20 to 25 percent of the mortgage amount.

With a high-value, 95-percent mortgage, the household will only need an equity of $2,500. Payment on the high-value mortgage will amount to $382.20 per month (at the same interest rate), an increase of slightly more than $60 per month over the payment on the 80-percent mortgage.

With the advent of sustained inflation, variable-rate mortgages are becoming more popular in the United States as lenders look to match their cash flows more evenly. In the preceding example, assume that a variable-rate mortgage had been written, and that after two years there had been an increase in the interest rate from 9 percent to 10 percent. Accordingly, the terms of the mortgage would then be revised. The mechanics of the revision are not difficult to comprehend. At the end of two years the outstanding balance on the mortgage would be $39,450. The method used in the United States to adjust the interest rate under a variable-rate contract is to amortize the outstanding balance at the new rate. In this case, amortization of the $39,450 balance over the remaining twenty-eight years at 10 percent would require a new payment of $350.30 per month, an increase of 8.8 percent over the original payment.

Housing Consumption

Housing and the Family Budget

Housing is the largest single item in the average family's budget (see table 5-6). The Bureau of Labor Statistics has estimated that the American family of moderate means spends approximately 23.5 percent of its income on housing. This housing figure includes not only the amount spent on rent or mortgage payments, but also such items as insurance, heat, utilities, and other expenses.

Table 5-6
Average Budget of a Hypothetical Moderate-Income Family by Expenditure-Categories for the United States, 1977

Expenditure Categories	Amount (dollars)	Percentage
Food	4,818	24.0
Housing	4,719	23.5
Transportation	1,727	8.6
Clothing, personal care	1,827	9.1
Medical care	1,165	5.8
Other	1,064	5.3
Total consumption	15,300	76.2
Other items	904	4.5
Social security	1,124	5.6
Personal income taxes	2,750	13.7
Total	20,079	100.0

Source: U.S. Bureau of Labor Statistics. Autumn Urban Family Budget and Comparative Indexes for Selected Urban Areas (annual).

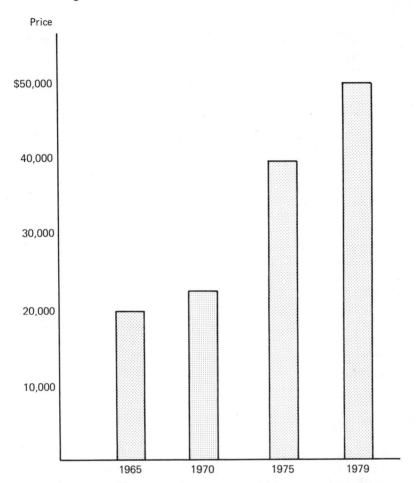

Source: U.S. Department of Housing and Urban Development and Bureau of the Census, "New One Family Houses Sold and For Sale," Construction Report C-25.

Figure 5-5. Median Price of a New House in the United States

Income is the most important determinant of ability to purchase and finance a house. In 1977 the price of a new house was 3.0 times the median family income (see figure 5-5). This particular ratio has been relatively stable for two decades, varying between 2.8 and 3.1 (see table 5-7). Historical statistics indicate that at the turn of the century, approximately ten years' earnings were needed to purchase a house. This ratio fell steadily until World War II, when it stabilized at a ratio approaching 3.0 times annual income. To put this figure in perspective, it is common for housing to cost at least 4 times the average income in Europe and 8 or 9 times average

Table 5-7
Ratio of Median Home-Sales Prices (for New Construction) to Family
Income in the United States, Selected Years, 1950-1975

Year	Median Family Income (dollars)	Median Sales Price (dollars)	Ratio, Sales Price to Income
1950	3,107	8,800	2.8
1955	4,421	13,700	3.1
1960	5,417	15,200	2.8
1965	6,957	20,000	2.9
1970	9,867	23,400	2.4
1975	13,700	39,700	2.9

Source: U.S. Bureau of the Census, *Census Of Housing* (1950 and 1960), and U.S. Department of Housing and Urban Development, *Statistical Yearbook* (annual).

income in Japan. Thus, in terms of average income, the price of an American house tends to be somewhat lower than that found in other advanced countries.

Persons of lower income, especially young families buying their first house, tend to buy existing houses, which are cheaper. In 1977, two-thirds of all first-time purchasers bought an existing house. The existing-house market is not restricted to first-time buyers. Each year, the number of existing houses sold exceeds the amount of new construction by a factor of 3.

Home Ownership

Owning one's own house is the most popular form of tenure, with almost two-thirds of the population exercising this option. The rate of home ownership has been steadily increasing each year. Home ownership is not necessarily related to income. In the United States one-half of the people who are under the poverty line are home owners. However, home ownership among the poor is largely a rural phenomenon, as the urban poor tend to rent.

The reasons for home ownership are many, but the most prominent are (1) an efficient real estate market and (2) preferential taxation.

Efficient Real-Estate Market. In the United States a good deal of the real-estate activity takes place because of the mobility of the population. Year in and year out, almost 20 percent of the population tends to move, thus necessitating numerous real-estate transactions. Such activity is necessarily within the existing-real-estate sector because it is so much larger than the amount of new construction each year. As people move they tend to upgrade their housing, as their incomes and life-styles may have changed during the interval.

Accommodation of the approximately 15 million annual real-estate transactions requires the service of more than 500,000 persons employed directly in selling and leasing homes. Although the real-estate industry is fragmented, it has proved quite efficient in handling the enormous annual volume of transactions.

Preferential Taxation. Favorable tax policies for owner occupants are important incentives to housing consumption and production. Home owners can deduct the interest paid on mortgages in calculating federal and state income taxes. Also deductible for federal tax purposes is the amount paid as property taxes to the local government. These two deductions significantly reduce the after-tax cost of housing, sometimes by as much as 20 percent or even more, depending on the tax bracket of the individual. There is no imputed rental income from housing recognized for tax purposes in the United States, although interest and property-tax offsets to income are allowed.

Owner-occupied housing held for more than one year and then sold qualifies as a capital gain and is taxed at a rate less than one-half that for ordinary income. A person selling a principal residence and investing the proceeds in another house within two years can escape the tax on any capital gain that may have occurred.

Rental Housing

Although the majority of the housing units built in the United States are single-unit structures for owner occupancy, units built as apartments (in multiunit structures) have tended to average approximately 25 percent of the total (see table 5-8). More than one-third of all households rent their dwellings. Despite increasing rates of home ownership, the absolute number of rental accommodations has been increasing.

Table 5-8
Total Housing Starts by Expected Tenure in the United States, Selected Years, 1950-1977

Year	Single Units for Owner Occupancy		Multiple Units for Rental Occupancy		Total Housing Units
	Number	Percentage	Number	Percentage	
1950	1,692	88.7	216	11.3	1,908
1955	1,499	92.1	128	7.9	1,627
1960	995	79.5	257	20.5	1,252
1965	964	65.4	509	34.6	1,473
1970	813	56.7	621	43.3	1,434
1975	892	76.9	268	23.1	1,160
1977	1,451	73.1	535	26.9	1,986

An examination of the characteristics of renter households reveals that their income tends to be lower than that of owners. Most other indicators confirm a generally lower socioeconomic status. Although some families have opted for rental tenure out of personal choice, most renters have no option because their incomes are too low for home ownership.

Rents have traditionally been set by market forces. During both world wars rent controls were enacted, but these were later lifted. Also, during the brief period of price controls under the Nixon administration in 1971, rent was controlled along with other goods and services.

Power to control rents has been exercised by local units of government. The majority of local governments have refrained from the imposition of peacetime rent controls. There are notable exceptions: New York City; Boston; Washington, D.C.; and several smaller cities on the east and west coasts. Nonetheless, the subject of rent control remains a sharp political issue in inflationary times.

For privately owned rental housing, depreciation for tax purposes is allowed. An owner of residential property that is rented can deduct an amount of from 2 to 5 percent of the structure value each year against income as a legitimate cost of business operation. Thus depreciation allowances tend indirectly to lower the effective rent to tenants by increasing the after-tax return to the investors.

Housing Subsidies

Direct government subsidies for housing are restricted to the poor, or more specifically to families with incomes that do not exceed 80 percent of the median income. Subsidy schemes tend to be complicated in their actual operation, and they are frequently changed by the Congress. In essence, however, there are two direct-subsidy schemes in operation in the United States.

Local-Authority Housing. Public housing for poor families is operated by housing authorities created by local governments. The federal government reimburses local authorities for the capital costs and supplements the operating expenses. Therefore, the local authority can charge the tenants a low rent, which by law cannot exceed 25 percent of their income.

Housing authorities generally set rents to break even, meaning that rents should equal maintenance costs. Capital costs need not be recovered by the local authority and therefore need not figure into the rent setting. Neither does the local authority pay property taxes, so rents can be set lower by that amount.

Subsidy Schemes. In an attempt to analyze housing-subsidy schemes, consider a development with the following characteristics: 100 units of housing, and a total development cost of $3 million, which includes land, materials, labor, and all fees and financing costs.

Assume that the development has a mortgage of 80 percent of value at a rate of 10 percent. If such a project were privately owned by profit-motivated investors who had invested $600,000 in equity, then, given the development costs, debt structure, and all expenses, the economic rent to break even is $395.00 per month per unit.

A rental-assistance program for low- and moderate-income families, authorized by Congress in 1974, is also operated by local authorities with federal subsidies. Private builders will construct housing and be guaranteed 75 percent of the required rent. On the strength of the federal guarantee, for thirty years, the private builder will develop rental housing with private financing. As part of the same program, low-income families can find their own dwellings in the private market and have the federal government pay up to 75 percent of the rent. To qualify for participation in this program, a family must have income not exceeding 80 percent of the median income.

Table 5-9 is an analysis of the housing-subsidy schemes. Compared with

Table 5-9
United States: example of a Typical Housing-Subsidy Scheme with Unsubsidized Development

	Nonsubsidized Prototype	Low-Rent Public Housing	Comments
Development costs	$3,000,000	$3,000,000	Assuming no difference in actual costs of construction
Mortgage	$2,400,000	None	Government subsidy is in an amount to retire debt for the capital costs
Investor equity	$600,000	None	Subsidy equals what would normally be required for debt retirement
Operating costs	$180,000	$150,000	Local authorities pay no local property tax
Return on equity	$40,000	None	Local authorities are nonprofit
Breakeven rent	$395/month	$127/month	
Actual rent to tenant	$395/month	$127/month	Rent need only cover operating costs
Amount of subsidy	—	$268	
Subsidized rent as percentage of economic rent	—	32%	

unsubsidized housing, public housing reduces rent by 68 percent or even more, depending on tenant income.

References

1. Federal National Mortgage Association, *Guide to Fannie Mae* (Washington, D.C., 1979).
2. U.S. Department of Commerce, U.S. Bureau of the Census, *Current Housing Reports*, Series H-150-74F, Annual Housing Survey, "Financial Characteristics by Indications of Housing and Neighborhood Quality for the United States and Regions" (Washington, D.C.: U.S. Government Printing Office, 1978).
3. U.S. Department of Housing and Urban Development, *Statistical Yearbook* (annual).
4. U.S. League of Savings Association, *Fact Book* (annual).

6 Housing in Canada

Housing Policy

As might be expected, there are far more similarities than differences between the housing sectors of Canada and of the United States. The common border, similar pattern of historical development, and overlapping cultures of these two countries make it unsurprising that their major economic institutions would develop in tandem. However, a survey of Canadian housing institutions and practices reveals some significant and interesting differences in both their form and their range of activity. In this section some of the highlights of Canadian housing policies and institutional practices will be highlighted and compared with the corresponding U.S. activities.

Private Enterprise and Government Support

Canadian housing-sector activities are dominated by private enterprise in both the production and the financing phases. Housing activities are not centrally planned or directed, nor is the direct involvement of the government a dominant factor in the allocation of housing resources. Like the United States, Canada has elected to have the government fill the important role of assistance to the private institutions involved in housing provision. The Canadian provinces are more heavily involved in housing than are the individual states. Under the confederation system the provinces have more discretionary power than do states in the United States, and this is reflected in housing and many other social sectors.

Although direct responsibilities for production and financing of housing reside in the private sector, the central government has assumed very important roles in housing finance and land development and in providing housing subsidies for low-income families.

Perception of the Housing Problem

By world standards, the quality of housing in Canada is quite high. According to indicators of housing quality such as the percentage of owner-occupied dwellings, the number of units lacking plumbing, and the size of housing units, Canada compares favorably to the United States and other nations. In 1971 less than 10 percent of Canada's dwelling units could be considered crowded, and only 8 percent lacked essential plumbing. By almost any objective standard, Canada has some of the best-housed people in the world. Only an extremely small number of Canadian dwellings lack facilities or are substandard in other ways. Yet housing remains, as it has long been, an extremely contentious issue. One reason for this is inflation in the housing sector, because of which many people consider the price of housing and rents to be going beyond the means of the average citizen. Although this is not entirely clear from empirical evidence, the perception exists that there is a serious crisis in housing in Canada. The Canadian National Monograph for Habitat states the following contradictions:

> There is a housing shortage, yet all but a relatively small number of unattached individuals have accommodation; at least 20% of the households have substantially more than they can really use. The price of home ownership has skyrocketed, yet, the majority of the population who have joined the ownership "club" have no desire to see the value of their dwellings level off, much less fall; prices in the new housing market often reflect the rapid growth of these existing values. Rents are too high, yet, rents have generally risen more slowly than incomes over the past decade and investors are finding it less and less worthwhile to engage in rental housing production, compared to other options. A surplus of serviced land would bring prices down, yet the demand of established neighborhoods when faced with specific land development proposals is frequently that the "surplus" be created somewhere else, not next door. It is becoming more difficult for young couples starting out to acquire their own (single-detached) house—the best they can afford is a row house or apartment. . . . While this is widely perceived as a problem, the high cost of low density settlement, longer travel time from outlying suburbs to work, the need for better community ammenities, and the growing burden of municipal taxes for services are all issues as well. [1]

Thus paradoxes abound when one considers the idea of the "housing problem" as such, and Canada is no exception in this respect.

Housing Production

Canada utilizes a somewhat larger percentage of its gross domestic product (GDP) for housing than does the United States (see table 6-1). In 1978 Canada devoted 5.7 percent of its GDP to housing, as opposed to 4.4 percent for the United States. In terms of population, new-dwelling construction in Canada registered 10.5 units per 1,000 inhabitants, a quite impressive level of production.

Private investors account for almost all new housing. Although the figure for the percentage of public as opposed to private investment has

Table 6-1
Canada: Selected Housing-Production Statistics, 1950-1978

Housing Activities	1950	1960	1965	1970	1978
Dwellings completed (thousands)	89.0	123.8	153.0	175.8	246.5
Dwellings per 1,000 population	6.5	6.9	7.8	8.2	10.5
Housing construction as a percentage of gross domestic product	—	4.7	4.8	4.1	5.7
Percentage of total by type of investor					
Direct government	—	—	0.6	0.9	0.9
Public assisted	—	—	19.0	30.3	6.5
Private	—	—	80.4	68.8	92.6

Source: Canada Mortgage and Housing Corporation, *Canadian Housing Statistics.* (annual)

fluctuated, the trend has been in the direction of an even greater percentage of private housing development.

The level of annual housing starts has not been as volatile as in the United States, although the performance of the Canadian housing industry has certainly not been even. Since the economies of the United States and Canada are so closely linked, it is not surprising that cycles in the U.S. economy are matched by similar performance in the Canadian economy. Figure 6-1 shows the relationship of annual housing starts for the United States and for Canada. Canada has approximately one-tenth the population of the United States, and when the performances are scaled accordingly it can readily be seen that historically there has not been that much difference in the pattern of cyclical annual fluctuations in the housing sector, although the swings have not been as exaggerated on the Canadian side.

Structure of the Housing-Finance Sector

Mobilization of Savings

The basic depository institutions oriented to household savings in Canada are the chartered banks, trust companies, and credit unions (*caisses populaire*).

Chartered Banks. One of the most striking differences between the financial structure of the United States and that of Canada is that in Canada financial intermediaries tend to be much larger in terms of their assets. The

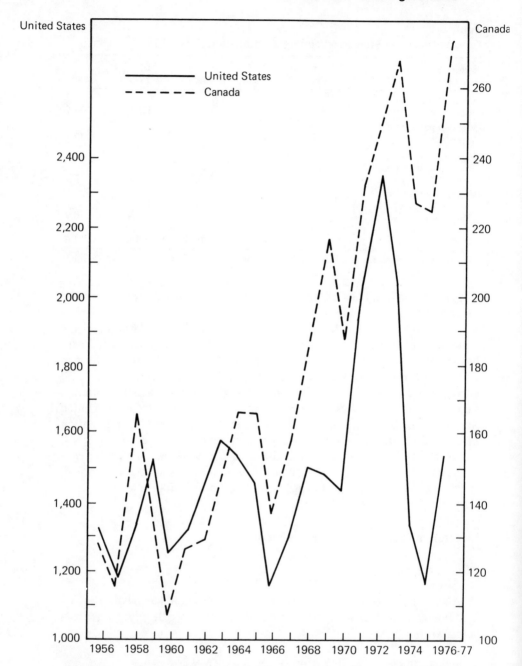

Figure 6-1. Annual Housing Starts, United States and Canada (in Thousands of Units)

banks, savings-and-loans, and other financial institutions in the United States tend to be local, with severe restrictions on their ability to establish branches or to conduct banking activities across state lines. This is not the case in Canada, where financial institutions can operate nationwide. For example, there are only thirteen chartered banks in Canada; but because they have extensive branching throughout the country, they may be of great size. In the United States, on the other hand, although there are over 15,000 banks, they are restricted from operating outside their own state boundaries. As a result, banking in Canada is quite concentrated, wtih a handful of banks completely dominating the entire banking field: five banks account for 85 percent of all assets. The same is true of the other financial intermediaries, such as trust and mortgage-loan companies, which also do business nationwide.

Like their counterparts throughout the world, the commercial banks in Canada have an asset structure heavily weighted with business loans and government securities. Mortgages accounted for only 8 percent of total bank assets in 1977. But the significant feature of bank activity is that mortgage lending has increased sharply, especially since 1970. In 1966 chartered banks had 2.8 percent of their assets in mortgages, with a dollar value of $788 million; by 1978 this figure had grown to $5.6 billion. The upsurge in bank mortgage activity is demonstrated by the fact that in 1978 banks accounted for 31 percent of all mortgage loans approved by lending institutions. See figures 6-2 and 6-3 for the structure of the Canadian mortgage market and the amount of all mortgage loans outstanding.

Trust Companies. Trust companies are nonbank thrift institutions that accept household savings. As their name implies, they also engage in trust activities, as well as offering other services, such as passbook savings and checking accounts. The bulk of their lendable funds comes from time deposits with terms of up to five years.

There are over sixty trust companies with branches all over Canada and total assets of more than $24 billion. Trust companies have tended to specialize in mortgages, which represented approximately 75 percent of their assets in 1978.

Loan Companies. Savings-and-loan associations as such do not exist in Canada. The building-society movement did take hold in Canada during the nineteenth century, when savings associations on the model of the British societies were established. However, these institutions faded from the scene toward the end of the nineteenth century and were replaced by loan companies. The early loan companies raised their funds in the bond market and were not depository institutions. However, in 1921 Canadian laws were changed so that the loan companies could accept deposits; they then began to function as traditional savings banks.

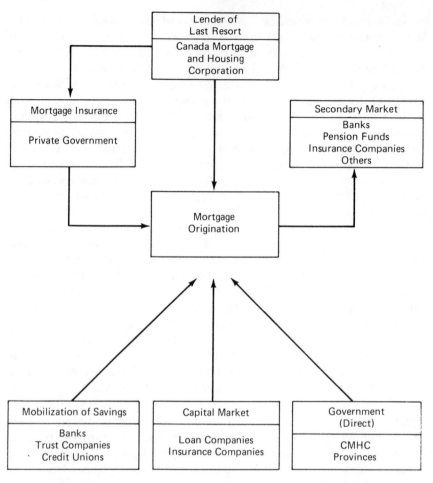

Figure 6-2. Structure of the Canadian Mortgage Market

Mortgage-loan companies tend to be stock companies that are frequently subsidiaries of commercial banks. They accept term deposits but also issue their own bonds in the market. In 1978 there were twenty-eight mortgage-loan companies doing business across Canada. Approximately 80 percent of their assets are in mortgages.

Credit Unions (*Caisses Populaire*). The credit-union movement is well represented in Canada, with more than 4,000 such institutions doing business. In 1978 they had assets of more than $12 billion. Unlike their counterparts in the United States, Canadian credit unions are very active in residential mortgages. In 1977, 46 percent of their assets were in mortgages, almost entirely for individual home ownership.

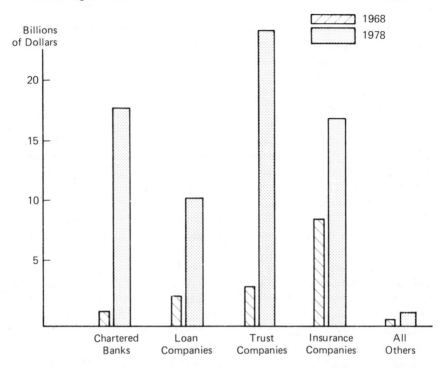

Source: Central Mortgage and Housing Corporation, *Canadian Housing Statistics* (annual).
Figure 6-3. Amount of All Mortgage Loans Outstanding, 1968-1978

Capital-Market Resources

In the Canadian housing-finance system, the capital market plays a more significant role in mortgage origination than it does in the United States. The trust and mortage-loan companies obtain the bulk of their funds by soliciting term deposits, known as guaranteed-investment certificates for the trust companies and debentures for the loan companies. Technically they are closer to capital-market instruments than to over-the-counter passbook savings. These instruments are competitive with low-denomination bonds and bank certificates of deposit.

Direct Lending by Government

There is some direct government lending through the Canada Mortgage and Housing Corporation (CMHC), which has the power to make direct loans when required for housing-subsidy programs, lending in rural areas or in places of capital deficiency. However, other than the occasional provision of CMHC loans, there is little direct government intervention in the mortgage market. Each province has a housing entity, but these do not directly provide much in the way of housing finance.

The Renewable Mortgage

The standard Canadian mortgage instrument is unique. It has often been described as a rollover mortgage, but it is more properly a renewable mortgage. It has a short maturity of from one to five years, although it is usually amortized over a twenty-five to thirty year period.

Renewable mortgages became popular in the late 1960s and are now the dominant form of mortgage loan, accounting for more than 90 percent of residential lending. The renewable mortgage owes its origination partly to necessity and partly to unique features in the Canadian banking laws. Deposit insurance on savings is available in Canada, but only for deposits that have maturities of five years or less. As a result of this feature of the law, lending institutions began accepting term deposits for periods not to exceed five years, in order to be eligible for the coverage. Coincidentally, the ability to renew a loan periodically is beneficial to the lending institution during periods of sustained inflation. Thus the popularity of this form of mortgage is largely due to the fact that it does alow the financial institutions to obtain a better match of assets and liabilities.

At the end of the term, the mortgage is up for renewal at the current market rate, which may be higher or lower than the original contract amount. The lender is under no contractual obligation to renew the mortgage loan. It is within the lender's right to terminate the loan, and it is likewise the right of the borrower not to renew. Experience has been that, for one reason or another, one out of every four loans will not be renewed. It is, however, in the interest of the lender to renew since the loan is now "seasoned" and less risky as an investment than a new loan with less equity and no proven repayment history.

At the end of the one- to five-year term, no new closing costs are imposed when the loan is renewed, unless the borrower decides to change lenders. However, making a switch in lenders is apt to be expensive, since closing costs can then be imposed that will negate any benefits from the switch.

It is interesting to note that in Canada there is greater participation by chartered banks in mortgage lending than there is among commercial banks in the United States. This is because the Canadian renewable mortgage allows better matching of assets and liabilities, making mortgages attractive to commercial banks.

The renewable mortgage is used almost exclusively for single-family houses or small rental units. Most large multifamily projects continue to be financed with fixed-term mortgages.

Mortgage Insurance

Mortgage insurance (see table 6-2) was initially introduced by the government in 1935 in the Dominion Housing Act, one year after the Federal Housing Administration (FHA) program was established in the United States. The mortgage-insurance program under the aegis of the Canada Mortgage and Housing Corporation is commonly known as NHA insurance since the passing of the National Housing Act of 1954. NHA-insured loans are typically for 90 to 95 percent of value for terms up to forty years. The policy fee of 0.875 percent of the principal is added to the loan and amortized over the life of the mortgage.

Private mortgage insurance is also available. High-valued houses are more likely to have private mortgage insurance than NHA since NHA is deliberately targeted to the middle of the value spectrum.

Almost three out of every four mortgages underwritten is insured, in contrast with the situation in the United States, where mortgage insurance, both private and public, is written on less than one-third of all transactions.

Secondary Mortgage Market

There is a secondary mortgage market in Canada, which tended to develop after the establishment of the NHA mortgage-insurance program in 1955 (see table 6-3). However, in Canada the secondary mortgage market is quite small compared with that in the United States. The Canadian secondary market encompasses less than 5 percent of mortgage originations, compared with 33 percent in the United States.

The structure of the housing-finance sector in Canada explains why a large secondary market has not developed. In Canada the major institutions are nationwide. One of the functions of a secondary market is to arbitrage

Table 6-2
Percentage Distribution of Mortgage Insurance in Canada, 1977

	Percentage
FHA insured	43
Private mortgage insurance	30
Uninsured	27

Source: Canada Mortgage and Housing Corporation, *Canadian Housing Statistics.* (annnual)

Table 6-3
Sales and Purchases of Insured NHA Mortgages, 1957-1978
(millions of dollars)

Lending Institution Making Sale		Sales to Other Firms and Institutions							
	Chartered Banks	Life-Insurance Companies	Trust Companies	Loan and Other Companies	CMHC	Pension Funds	Corporate[a]	Unincorporated	Total
Chartered banks	4.6	2.4	8.4	51.7	—	75.7	25.8	1.6	170.2
Life-insurance companies	—	7.1	—	—	—	—	—	—	7.1
Trust companies	24.9	54.5	81.0	20.4	—	57.5	45.4	107.8	391.5
Loan and other companies	2.4	0.5	7.5	13.0	—	15.1	0.8	—	39.3
CMHC	55.2	5.6	100.6	54.1	—	—	39.8	—	255.3
Other firms and institutions	—	1.9	25.9	2.0	—	—	3.1	—	32.9
Total	87.1	72.0	223.4	141.2	—	148.3	114.9	109.4	896.3

Source: Canada Mortgage and Housing Corporation, (annual) *Canadian Housing Statistics.*

funds from one section of the country to another. The secondary market does this by utilizing funds in excess regions to purchase mortgages in regions where there is a shortage of mortgage money. However, in Canada this can be done by the financial institutions themselves, since they have national branches and can internally arbitrage mortgage money. There are also only a few large institutions in Canada, as opposed to the numerous small institutions in the United States.

One aspect of secondary-market operation in Canada is significantly different from the United States experience. The Canadian renewable mortgage has been salable in international money markets. Because of its relatively short term, investors are not locked into Canadian mortgages for a long commitment. Canadian interest rates have also been high by international standards, making them attractive investments, especially since the mortgages themselves are insured. In the United States mortgages are typically not sold in the international arena.

Over the years there has been talk of developing a larger secondary mortgage market, but little has come of it. In 1973 a secondary-market entity known as the Federal Mortgage Exchange Company was established, but by 1979 it had not yet gone into operation.

Lender of Last Resort

The lender of last resort for housing in Canada is the Canada Mortgage and Housing Corporation (formerly Central Mortgage and Housing Corporation). It has a dominant role in the Canadian system, and combines the functions of the FHA and the FHLBB in the United States. It has far greater powers than does either of its U.S. counterparts. In addition to its mortgage-insurance program, it administers housing programs and can also make direct loans in capital-deficient areas and for special programs.

Financing an Individual House

To observe the operation of the housing-finance system from another level consider the purchase of a house with a value of $50,000 (see table 6-4). The home purchaser would likely obtain a mortgage of 80 percent of value from a single institution, such as a commercial bank or a trust company. The maturity would be thirty years and would be either insured with NHA mortgage insurance or a conventional loan. In any case the mortgage would likely be 1 percentage point higher than would be true in the United States, at least by historical standards.

The significant and unusual features in the Canadian mortgage system

Table 6-4

Canada: An Illustrative Example of Financing the Purchase of an Individual House

1. Value of house: U.S. $50,000
2. Mortgage terms:
   A. 80% of value = $40,000
   B. Annual interest of 10% per annum with 5-year renewable (rollover) provision
   C. Amortized over 30 years
   D. Monthly payment of U.S $351.02
3. Variation: the interest rate rises to 11% after the first 5-year term, and the mortgage is renewed at that rate
   A. Balance on loan after 5 years = U.S. $38,515
   B. Terms of new mortgage to amortize balance of US $38,515 over remaining 25 years = U.S. $371.49 per month

is the almost exclusive use of the five-year renewable mortgage for residential loans. Every five years the terms of the loan are rewritten to reflect mortgage-market conditions. The rate can go either up or down, depending on conditions in the market at that time. To understand this system, let us use the illustration wherein the mortgage interest rate rises from 10 percent to 11 percent after the first five-year term. At the time for renegotiation of the mortgage, the outstanding balance is $38,515. Thus a new mortgage written over the remaining twenty-five-year term at 11-percent interest would be for $371.49 per month, which is approximately $20 per month higher than the payment during the first five years. However, for the second five-year term the mortgage holder would be locked into that particular interest rate. Holders of NHA mortgages have the option of extending the terms of the mortgage in order to keep the mortgage payment constant.

Housing Consumption

Home Ownership

Home-ownership rates in Canada remain quite high, although the percentage has tended to decrease over the past few decades. Whereas 65.6 percent of all households owned their own houses in 1951, two decades later that proportion had decreased to 60.3 percent. Canada is a highly urban nation, and increased urbanization since World War II has brought greater numbers of people into the cities. To accommodate this inflow, large numbers of apartments have been built, so that the ratio of home ownership has slowly tended to subside (see table 6-5).

As in the United States, the price of housing in Canada has been rising dramatically for the past decade. The rise has been greater than the in-

Table 6-5
Summary of Housing Characteristics

Item	1951	1961	1971	Percentage Increase 1951-1961	1961-1971
Total occupied dwellings	3,409,295	4,554,493	6,034,510	33.6	32.5
	100.0%	100.0%	100.0%	—	—
Type of dwelling[b]					
Single detached	2,275,615	2,978,501	3,591,770	30.9	20.6
	66.7%	65.4%	59.5%	—	—
Single attached	237,655	404,933	679,590	70.4	67.8
	7.0%	8.9%	11.3%	—	—
Apartments and flats	885,565	1,151,098	1,699,045	30.0	47.6
	26.0%	25.3%	28.2%	—	—
Tenure					
Owned	2,236,955	3,005,587	3,636,925	34.4	21.0
	65.5%	66.0%	60.3%	—	—
Rented	1,172,340	1,548,906	2,397,585	32.1	54.8
	34.4%	34.0%	39.7%	—	—
Size of dwelling					
Average rooms per dwelling	5.3	5.3	5.4	—	—
Crowded dwellings[c]	641,820	750,942	569,495	17.0	−24.2
	18.8%	16.5%	9.4%	—	—

Source: Canada Year Book (1974).
[a]Excludes the Yukon Territory and Northwest Territories.
[b]Excludes mobile dwellings.
[c]Dwellings in which the number of persons exceeds the number of rooms.

creases in personal disposable income and in the general price level. This rapid increase in house prices may be responsible for the decrease in the rate of home ownership. The Canadian housing sector has been afflicted not only by inflation in the cost of construction, but also by rises in land prices and steep increases in mortgage rates. All these have combined to raise the price of housing greatly and to create a particular burden for those of moderate income and for new potential home purchasers.

Shelter costs in Canada are roughly consistent with those in the United States. Few Canadians spend more than 25 percent of their gross income for shelter, as the average expenditure for shelter is less than 20 percent (see table 6-6).

Tax Policies Affecting Housing

Canada has not had the favorable tax measures for housing that have characterized the United States. One of the most prominent features of the U.S. housing market has been the tax deductibility for home interest, a

Table 6-6
Patterns of Family Expenditures by Income Quintiles (1972 Survey Data in Eight Cities)

Item	Lowest Quintile	Mid Quintile	Highest Quintile
Family characteristics			
Average net inco (pretax)	$5,358	$11,789	$22,992
Homeowners (%)	34.2	55.7	72.6
Wife works full time (%)	3.9	17.6	31.6
Average total expenditure	$5,685	$11,543	$20,556
Food (%)	24.3	17.4	14.1
Shelter (%)	22.9	15.9	12.8
Clothing (%)	6.6	7.2	7.4
Travel and transportation (%)	9.5	13.8	11.7
Personal taxes (%)	6.8	15.6	23.5
All other current expenditures (%)	29.8	30.1	30.5

Source: Adapted from *Canada Year Book* (1974).

feature that had been lacking in the Canadian tax structure until 1979. However, despite the lack of income-tax deductibility, home ownership in Canada is at almost as high a level as in the United States. Beginning in 1980 there has been a national program of tax deductibility for mortgage interest, like that in the United States, which will be phased in gradually and eventually will allow complete deductibility of mortgage interest on owner-occupied houses.

Has there been a difference in housing consumption, especially home ownership, as a result of Canada's lack of the income-tax deductibility feature? An answer is probably revealed in the statistics on home ownership since the end of World War II, which show home ownership steadily increasing in the United States and decreasing in Canada. It is probably not coincidental that the period of increasing inflation since the late 1950s has driven many households in the United States to invest in housing as a hedge. The income-tax deductibility of mortgage interest rates in the United States has made housing an increasingly attractive alternative for investment and has made renting far less attractive. Without the income-tax deductibility for mortgage interest rates, housing as an investment is less attractive. Canadians have more freely chosen their tenure without blandishments of income-tax considerations, which affected the large number of apartments built in Canada in the 1960 and 1970s.

However, the sustained inflation in the Canadian economy has had political ramifications in the housing sector as both renters and owners have clamored for relief. It is only natural that owners should desire relief in the form of deductibility of interest in the manner of their U.S. neighbors. This became a volatile political issue in the 1979 national elections, and agitation led to adoption of preferential tax treatment of owner-occupied housing.

On the savings side, the government adopted two measures in 1977 to stimulate savings for housing purchases. The first $1,000 of interest received on bank deposits, government bonds, and certificates held in trust and mortgage-loan companies is exempt from income taxation. Also, for those who aspire to home ownership, $1,000 per year may be deposited in a home-purchase fund for up to ten years with all the interest earned tax free if the proceeds are used ultimately for home purchase.

Rental Housing

Most rental housing in Canada is privately owned with private entrepreneurs controlling 89 percent of the rental market. About 5 percent of the rental stock is in the hands of nonprofit corporations financed by direct loans from the Canada Mortgage and Housing Corporation. The remainder of the stock, approximately 6 percent, is owned by the municipal, provincial, and federal governments. Almost all of this government housing is for low-income renters.

Inflation has also led renters to demand political relief through the imposition of rent control. In Canada the control of rents is under the authority of the provinces. All the provinces have been exploring the issue of rent control, but not all have adopted comprehensive ordinances. The exception is British Columbia, which adopted a rent control ordinance in 1974.

Housing Subsidies

There is a Canadian public-housing program that operates in much the same way as the United States program. The central government provides loans to provinces and municipalities for the capital costs of providing rental housing, up to 90 percent of the total value. Operating costs are shared by the federal and municipal governments. Rents in public housing are set depending on income. Public housing is intended to serve the lowest one-third of the income distribution in each locality.

References

1. Canadian Habitat Secretariat, Minister of State for Urban Affairs, "Where Are We Headed?: A Discussion Paper on Human Settlements in Canada" (Ottawa, 1976).
2. Central Mortgage and Housing Corporation, *Canadian Housing Statistics 1978* (Ottawa, 1979).
3. Carroll R. Melton, "The Canadian Mortgage Market," Chicago, Inter-

national Union of Building Societies and Savings Associations, July
   1979.
4. Michael L. Unger, "The Canadian Mortgage Market and the
   Renegotiable Term Mortgage," Federal Home Loan Bank Board,
   Washington, D.C., 1977, mimeographed.
5. Ministry of State for Urban Affairs, Canada, *Human Settlement in
   Canada* (Ottawa, 1976).
6. United Nations, Economic and Social Council, Economic Commission
   for Europe, "Financing of Housing: Monograph prepared by Central
   Mortgage Housing Corporation CMHC (Canada)" (April 1979).

7

Housing in the United Kingdom

Housing Policy

Public and Private Participation

Housing is more of a political issue in the United Kingdom than in almost any other advanced industrial country. Controversies over the roles of public and private investment in housing have been raging since the turn of the century. Housing policy has evolved over the years as an extremely political issue and the divisions have been sharply drawn along the philosophical lines of the major parties. The two main political parties, Conservative and Labor, have housing policies as distinct as their political and economic philosophies.

The major contention between opposing philisophical (and political) camps is the role of private-sector investment in the provision of housing, especially housing for rent. The Labor party, having no faith in the private sector, has over the years enacted a series of stern measures to control rents and guarantee security of tenure, which have severely curtailed the ability of private investors to provide rental housing. The Conservatives, on the other hand, although not especially hostile to the private rented sector, have turned their attention to owner occupancy, to the neglect of the private rented sector. As a result, the stock of private rented housing in the United Kingdom has decreased every year and now shows signs of impending extinction.

The void caused by the enfeeblement of the private rented sector has been filled by public housing, which was for many years the dominant housing sector. Council housing continues to account for almost half the housing in Britain.

The practical result of the lack of a viable private rental-housing sector is that newly formed households, or those households that have to move for job-related or other reasons, have little alternative other than to attempt to purchase housing. There are long waiting lists for council housing, and eligibility depends on one's having resided in the particular jurisdiction for a certain period. Since there is little choice in tenure, the housing market as a whole has tended to operate in a manner that promotes the preference for owner occupation. This is no doubt one of the reasons for the sustained growth in the owner-occupied housing sector.

115

Housing policy in the United Kingdom as revealed by actions taken since the end of World War II, consists of three distinct thrusts:

1. Publicly owned housing, especially what is known as council housing, is to be the vehicle for social housing.
2. Tenants are to be protected with elaborate security-of-tenure provisions, and rent control will be used to keep down the level of rents.
3. Owner occupation of housing will be encouraged and accorded special tax dispensations and incentives.

Land Development

Historically, the process of land development in the United Kingdom has been dominated by the philosophy that private persons should not be able to receive personal financial advantage from profits in land values that accrue through the normal course of land development. The idea that the unearned increment in land development should at least be taxed away has its intellectual roots in Ricardo and Mill. Development value, the difference between agricultural and urban land prices, is considered fortuitous, resulting from decisions of local authorities, which grant permission to develop the land and which often provide public roads and utilities. Profits that may accrue from such permissions and betterments should go not to a private party but to the community as a whole, through a "betterment levy" on the profits.

The United Kingdom had been moving toward a system of land-use regulation at the local level patterned after the Swedish model. Essentially, it has sought to have the public authority purchase all land that is to be put to an urban use. The purchase would be at current use value, probably the agricultural value; land would then eventually be resold to private developers at the low agricultural value, thereby eliminating speculative land profits.

In 1967 the Land Commission Act was passed, which laid the groundwork for steep taxes on land-development profits. The incremental development value was taxed at 40 percent, and this was subsequently raised to 80 percent.

In 1974 the Labor government passed the Community Land Act, which obligated local authorities to purchase land in anticipation of development. However, very little money was appropriated from the Exchecquer for this purpose, and implementation therefore languished. When the Conservatives came to power in 1979, they quickly repealed the law because of their philosophical opposition to this level of public involvement in development. This on-again-off-again history of housing and development measures has recurred as governments have changed.

*Perception of the Housing Problems
in the United Kingdom*

In 1951 the housing deficiency was over one million units, with the number of households greatly exceeding the number of existing housing units. By 1977 there was rough parity between the number of households and the number of housing units: a population of approximately 20 million and a housing stock of almost 21 million units. Although there is now numerical parity between houses and households, these figures conceal many serious local problems, particularly in the inner cities. The industrial sections in the Midlands and the North, and particularly in Scotland, continue to have a large proportion of unsatisfactory housing.

By all objective standards, the citizens of the United Kingdom are reasonably well housed. Despite this fact, housing remains a volatile social issue, a fact that was acknowledged in the introduction to the Green Paper on Housing Policy:

> Some people consider that the housing situation today is paradoxical. Housing in England and Wales appears to compare reasonably well in terms of basic ammenities and space with countries in both Western Europe and North America. We have more and better houses in relation to the number of households than ever before. Nevertheless, despite a sharp rise in total housing expenditures in recent years, the problems persist. Housing is sometimes discussed as though little has been achieved and things are getting worse. The explanation of the paradox may lie in the widening gap between the majority living in housing of good standards and the substantial but diminishing number living in poor conditions: and in the fact that the equation of recent years resulted in increases in average payments by householders in line with or faster than prices—though normally as much as earnings—despite big increases in general assistance. [6]

Housing Production

The effort expended in the housing sector in the United Kingdom has been modest in comparison with that in other European nations. Over the postwar period United Kingdom expenditures for new housing construction have utilized roughly 3 percent of gross domestic product (GDP), about on a par with the figure for the United States. Measured in terms of population, the rate of building has averaged slightly above 6 new dwellings per 1,000 population (see table 7-1).

The demand for new housing continues to be strong. Even though the United Kingdom has a static population, it is showing an increase of 145,000 new households per year because of declining household size. In the United Kingdom the demand for housing is being propelled by this increase

Table 7-1
United Kingdom: Selected Housing-Production Statistics, 1953-1977

Housing Activities	1953	1960	1965	1970	1977
Dwellings completed (thousands)	330.4	307.3	325.7	368.2	322.6
Dwellings per 1,000 population	6.5	5.9	7.2	6.6	5.8
Housing construction as a percentage of gross domestic product	3.7	3.0	3.6	2.9	3.3
Percentage of total by type of investor					
Local authorities	74.2	42.2	41.7	48.6	45.2
Other authorities	5.2	1.5	2.3	3.3	9.6
Private person, unaided	20.6	54.7	54.6	46.4	44.1
Private person, aided	—	1.6	1.4	1.7	1.1

Source: United Nations, *Annual Bulletin of Housing and Building Statistics for Europe* (annual).

in the number of households plus a continuing demand for replacement of some of the older existing stock. Therefore, a static or even a declining population does not necessarily mean that the demand for housing will decline in the near future.

In the United Kingdom the government housing sector is very large, accounting for almost half the total number of units built. Local authorities that are adjuncts of the local council government build housing with government interest-rate subsidies. There have also been nonprofit housing associations in operation since the 1960s, which develop housing with direct government subsidies.

Housing built by private persons is for owner occupation. Virtually no new private housing is constructed for rental purposes. In the United Kingdom private investment in rental housing has been discouraged by public actions. The objective of the left has been, unabashedly, to eliminate the private rented sector.

> Whereas other European countries have treated the landlords as an instrument rather than a victim of public policy, the British, depending on the party in power, have alternatively suppressed and relieved landlords in a myopic and doctrinaire fashion. Their reaction has been to get out of the market. [7]

Rented housing in Britain is not the recipient of the kinds of subsidies and treatments that are prevalent in the United States, Germany, and other countries. For example, depreciation cannot be taken on rented housing. In the United States and in Germany depreciation allowances provide a large portion of the rate of return to investors and provide an indispensable incentive.

Structure of the Housing-Finance Sector

The structure of the housing-finance sector in the United Kingdom is not as complicated as that of most other countries because of the almost complete domination of the private sector by one institution—the building society (see figure 7-1). Most of the raising of funds for housing, the issuance of mortgages, and even regulation as such are confined to building societies. On the other hand, public-sector involvement in housing is represented by the local authorities. Thus these two institutions, building societies and local authorities, dominate the United Kingdom's housing sector.

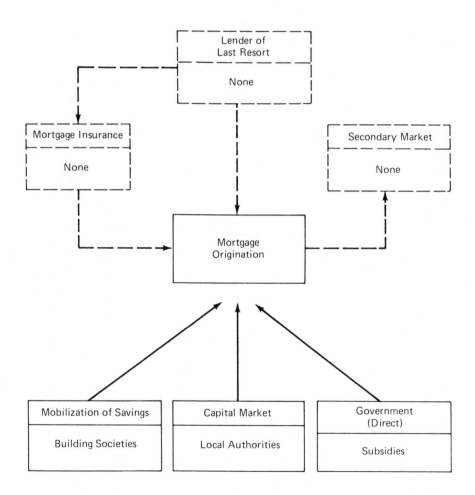

Figure 7-1. Structure of the Mortgage Market in the United Kingdom

Building Societies

Modern housing finance originated in England with the building societies. The first building society was started in Birmingham, England in 1781. Since then building societies have been established throughout the United Kingdom, and institutions based on the building-society principle now flourish throughout the world. In the United Kingdom there are now 400 societies with total assets of $300 billion.

Many cultures have so-called rotating-credit societies, of which the building society is an example. These societies have been known to exist in China, Japan, and in parts of Africa. The principle is one of compulsory periodic contributions from everyone and benefits that accrue to members one at a time. For example, such a rotating-credit system enabled the Oriental immigrants to the United States to establish their own small businesses.

Early building societies operated by having members make regular contributions, from which loans were made to the members one at a time. The first building societies were called "terminating" societies because once all the members had obtained their own houses, the society disbanded or terminated. Later, permanent societies were established, which continued to lend even after they had taken care of the original members.

All the terminating associations eventually evolved into continuous or permanent associations, with the emphasis on saving for its own sake. All such associations in Britain are mutual societies owned by the contributors. Building societies proliferated across Europe, although they have never been as popular in other countries as in the United Kingdom.

The U.K. building societies specialize completely in mortgage lending and, in fact, do very little other lending. They are unique in that they completely dominate mortgage lending within the United Kingdom, with more than 80 percent of all mortgage originations. No other single kind of institution can claim that type of dominant position in any other Western society.

Building societies in the United Kingdom have grown rapidly since World War II. In this sense they are much like the savings-and-loans in the United States, which also had phenomenal growth in the postwar period.

Mobilization of Savings. Building societies have been taking an increasing share of the market for personal savings. Their share of personal savings went from 9 percent in 1950 to 47 percent in 1977. During this same time the share of personal savings going to the national savings banks and to the commercial banks had decreased proportionally. Correspondingly, the share of all household financial assets represented by building societies has also more than doubled (see table 7-2). Certainly one of the reasons that the building societies have been so successful in attracting personal savings is the nature of the taxation on interest earned on building-society shares.

Table 7-2
Shares of Short-Term Household Financial Assets

Year	Building Societies (%)	Banks (%)	National Savings (%)	Notes and Coins (%)	Other (%)
1966	24	30	34	9	3
1967	26	31	32	9	2
1968	28	32	30	8	2
1969	30	31	28	9	2
1970	32	31	26	9	2
1971	34	30	26	8	2
1972	35	31	24	8	1
1973	35	34	22	8	1
1974	35	36	19	8	1
1975	39	33	19	9	1
1976	41	31	18	9	—
1977	43	29	19	8	—

Source: Building Societies Association, "Evidence Submitted by the Building Societies Association to the Committee to Review the Functioning of Financial Institutions" (October 1978).

The interest to savers is taxed at a rate that is somewhat less than the average, giving the societies a small but significant advantage over the banks.

In addition to regular passbook deposits, the building societies have increasingly been attracting term shares, analogous to the certificates of deposit that have become common in the United States. Term shares are not exactly new to British societies, since they have been around for many years. However, after the early 1970s the building societies turned to term shares to raise additional capital. Term shares pay an additional 0.25- to 0.5-percent interest over ordinary shares and are held for a minimum period of from one to four years. Their popularity came about because of heavy outflows from building societies in the early 1970s due to the volatility of short-term interest rates. To counter this outflow and to become more competitive with other financial institutions, building societies promoted fixed-term shares. In 1978 such shares represented almost 10 percent of deposit balances in building societies, compared with 60 percent term deposits in U.S. savings-and-loans.

Building-society accounts are quite widespread. In 1977, 36 percent of the adult population had building-society accounts, representing a significant penetration of the savings market. Such accounts are typically small, with 90 percent of them amounting to less than £2,500.

The building societies' greatest competition for small savings comes from the government itself. Since there is not much of an industrial-bond market in Britain, the market for medium- and long-term funds is dominated by government issues, which are at yields that are quoted net of all taxes. At Britain's high rates of taxation on investment income, which go up to 98 percent, the investment in tax-free government issues is extremely attractive for high-bracket taxpayers.

The building societies themselves tend to be quite concentrated. Although there are more than three hundred of them, the largest five societies have more than half of all the assets, and the largest twenty-five control almost 90 percent of all assets. There are no restrictions on branching, so the societies are national institutions.

Building societies are highly specialized, devoting almost all their efforts to lending on housing. This intense specialization has tended to mean that they can exist on a narrow spread. Typically the spread between what they pay savers and what they lend for mortgages is 1.5 percent, which is somewhat lower than that for American savings-and-loans.

Building societies have no explicit requirements that borrowers must first have been savers. It is true that in times of credit shortages, preferences go first to shareholders, but this is not a hard and fast rule.

Taxation of Building Societies. Interest paid to shareholders in building societies is net of taxes, so that individuals do not usually have to report what they receive as interest income from money on deposit. Rather, the society pays the taxes at the "composite" rate, which tends to be somewhat lower than the average rate that would be personally applicable to those individuals who have funds on deposit (see figure 7-2). This tax incentive encourages depositors to put money into building societies, since they can obtain a higher rate after taxes from building society shares than they could on most other investments.

As an example, in 1976 the basic tax rate in Britain was approximately 35 percent. However, the composite rate for the building societies was 27.75 percent. A 7-percent share-rate tax paid is worth 10.77 percent gross to the taxpaying investor. But with the composite rate at only 27.75 percent, lower than the 35-percent basic rate, the cost of the money to the society was only 9.69 percent, thus enabling the society to charge a lower rate for mortgages than would otherwise be possible. Another way of describing the relationship is that since interest is quoted on a tax-paid basis, the gross rate before taxes is about one-third higher than the net. Thus for a 7-percent after-tax rate, the gross rate would be in the neighborhood of 10 percent. Adding to that the society's markup, the mortgage rate would then be in the neighborhood of 11 percent, given a 7 percent net-of-tax return on shares.

Regulation of Building Societies. In the area of housing finance, there are few formal controls in the form of written regulations. Rather, the British style is for the building societies (see table 7-3) to work very closely with the

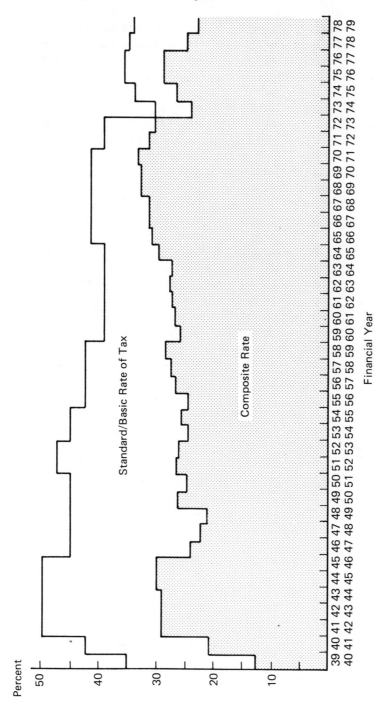

Source: The Building Societies Association, *BSA Bulletin* (No. 17 January 1979).

Figure 7-2. The Gap Between the Composite Rate and the Standard/Basic Rate

government, primarily through the medium of the Joint Advisory Committee on Mortgage Finance. The Building Societies Association, the cartel that dominates the building societies, and the government have agreed by memorandum that their common objectives are to:

1. Support the growth of owner occupation.
2. Produce and maintain a flow of mortgage funds to enable the house-building industry to plan for a high and stable level of house building for sale.
3. Contribute toward the stabilization of house prices.
4. Maintain an orderly housing market in which, subject to the three points just mentioned, sufficient mortgage funds are available to allow purchasers a reasonable opportunity to own the sort of house they want.

Mortgage Lending. A building society typically will issue a loan for 80 percent of value, although in some cases it will go as far as 95 percent if there is an accompanying guarantee by a life-insurance company. In the United Kingdom second mortgages are rare because the building societies are prepared to make high-value loans. However, as much as 5 percent of mortgages are second mortgages known as "topping up loans."

Building societies first set the rate of interest that they will pay to savers; then the mortgage market rate is set by adding on a margin, a practice of

Table 7-3
Share of Total Assets, End of 1977

Societies in Rank Order by Size	Total Assets (£)[a]	Share of Total (%)	Cumulative Total Assets (£)	Cumulative Share of Total (%)
Largest 5	18,391	53.6	18,391	53.6
6-10	5,324	15.5	23,715	69.2
11-15	2,968	8.7	26,683	77.8
16-20	1,887	5.5	28,570	83.3
21-25	982	2.9	29,552	86.2
26-30	727	2.1	30,279	88.3
31-35	539	1.6	30,818	89.9
36-40	426	1.2	31,244	91.1
41-45	389	1.1	31,633	92.3
46-50	324	0.9	31,957	93.2
51-55	285	0.8	32,242	94.0
56-60	253	0.7	32,495	94.8

Source: Building Societies Association, "Evidence Submitted by the Building Societies Association to the Committee to Review the Functioning of Financial Institutions" (October 1978).

cost-plus pricing. There is no conscious attempt by the building societies to set a rate that will clear the market. Considerable political pressure exists to keep mortgage rates low.

> Building societies have always been slow to change rates of interest; they are reluctant to raise rates because they regard themselves as providing a public service and they are reluctant to lower rates for what may turn out to be a short while. [1]

Rates tend to be set by the Council of Building Societies Association, which recommends to members the rates of interest they should pay investors and the rates they should charge for mortgages. Although the recommendations are not binding, they are generally taken. They tend to become minimum rates, as some societies charge somewhat higher rates on mortgages and offer more favorable terms to savers.

All mortgages written by building societies have a variable interest rate tied to money-market movement, which can be adjusted periodically as market conditions warrant. In order to cushion the blow of rising interest rates, societies will often increase the number of years of amortization in order to keep the payment level.

Since 1945 building societies have charged a variable rate of interest. Building-society assets and liabilities are more closely matched through the use of the variable-rate mortgage. In fact, the term "variable-rate mortgage" is virtually unknown in Britain, since the ability to vary mortgage rates with changes in market conditions is considered natural. Rates can be varied at any time with no real limits on how much or how fast the society can change them. However, the borrower is free to redeem the loan without penalty if desired.

The volatility of the mortgage rate can be seen with reference to the period 1973-1974, when, because of capital-market conditions, the mortgage rate went from 8.5 percent to 11 percent within a period of nine months. Between April and October 1976 there was a 6-percentage-point swing in the lending rate, up to 12.25 percent. However, during the decade of the 1970s there have been decreases that have been just as dramatic as the increases; under the variable-rate scheme, the mortgage holders are given the benefit of decreases in a timely manner.

Building societies have proved that with a variable-rate instrument it is possible to do what all bankers seek to avoid, borrow short and lend long, since the variable rate provides a measure of safety. The money in the building society is short term since it is there on demand, with less than 10 percent of total funds in term accounts.

Interest Rates. Interest rates in the United Kingdom have been extremely volatile (see figure 7-3). The minimum lending rate of the commercial banks

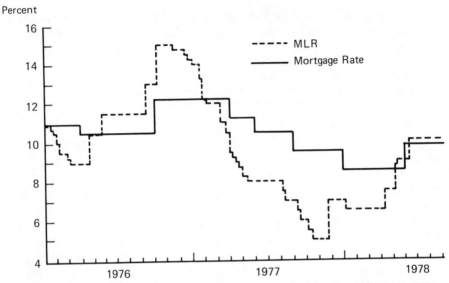

Source: Building Societies Association, "Evidence Submitted by the Building Societies Association to the Committee to Review the Functioning of Financial Institutions," October 1978.

Figure 7-3. Rates of Interest

changed 54 times between 1975 and 1978, for example. Building societies also have to adjust their interest rates periodically in order to remain competitive and to take cognizance of interest changes in the money market in general. However, changes by the building societies in mortgage rates and rates paid to depositors are much less frequent and less dramatic than the changes in the commercial-bank lending and saving rates. The philosophy of the building societies is to steer a steady course in rate changes and to make as few changes in rates as possible. Accordingly, building societies will often stand fast in a fluctuating market when they believe that such movements are temporary. Only when they believe that interest shifts are likely to last for a considerable period of time will they follow suit and either raise or lower their minimum recommended interest rates. The interest rates are set by an action of the Building Societies Association, which recommends interest rates to its members. Such rates are advisory only, although they are obligatory on the largest eighteen associations.

Much emphasis has been placed on the fact that the interest rates charged by the building societies are consistently below the market clearing rate or the rate that would prevail if it were not for the action of the cartel in establishing a lower rate. This has been expressed by the building societies themselves as follows:

Because building societies are non-profit making, they do not seek to maximize the difference between the rate of interest paid to investors and that charged to borrowers. If the practice of making recommendations were discontinued there would be a strong tendency for the mortgage rate of some societies to rise when marketing conditions permitted, especially if mortgage funds were in short supply. [1]

One reason for this is undoubtedly political, as politicians have an interest in keeping mortgage rates low in order to keep their constituents satisfied.

Mortgage rates tend to be political sacred cows. There is considerable public concern over the level of mortgage interest rates, and the building societies keep this uppermost in their minds. Mortgage interest rates tend to be quite sticky since there is a considerable social pressure to keep them as low as possible. Building societies consider themselves to be in existence for public purposes and do not wish to raise interest rates. Since politicians also do not wish them to raise interest rates, their rates tend to be sluggish in the upward direction. This is abetted by the method of establishing mortgage interest rates, which is essentially to establish a rate paid to savers first and then add a margin to it. Since the societies are reluctant to change the rate that they pay savers, they are correspondingly reluctant to raise mortgage interest rates.

In return for the cartel setting the mortgage interest rate at somewhat below the market rate, the societies are relatively free from government regulation and are given a preferential rate of taxation. Savers accept a lower coupon rate on deposits because their after-tax rate is considerably higher because of the preferential taxation on building societies' share accounts. This is a quid pro quo arrangement between the building-society cartel and the government.

Building societies do not have a system of deposit insurance on savings accounts such as exists in the United States and Canada. In their opinion such a system is not necessary because the depositors are protected primarily by prudent lending policies. Further, their ability to vary rates as conditions warrant gives them protection against serious deposit outflows.

In summary, it can be seen that building societies enjoy three privileges that have been essential to their dynamic growth. The first of these is that the rate that depositors are paid is net of tax, and that that rate of taxation is essentially below the basic rate of income tax that most depositors would ordinarily have had to pay. The second privilege is that the interest that borrowers pay is deductible from income taxes, thus lowering the occupancy costs of home ownershilp. Third, building societies have been exempted from rigid credit restrictions on their operations and instead work through an informal network with the government. Banks and insurance companies are under no such lenient regulatory situation.

Insurance Companies

Insurance companies issue mortgage loans, usually on high-priced houses, but do so in such a manner as to sell endowment policies. Payments that are made are really insurance premiums plus interest on the loan. The insurance policy runs concurrent with the term of the mortgage, and when the policy has matured the proceeds from the policy go to repay the principal outstanding on the loan. This is a rather complicated way of financing housing that is not used very extensively.

Local Authorities

The capital market as such is not a very large factor in the private housing market in the United Kingdom. However, local authorities do issue bonds to finance council housing and also do some lending under special circumstances. Local authorities will sometimes make mortgage loans, especially to first-time home buyers and for redevelopment projects.

Most local-authority borrowing is on a fairly short-term basis; approximately 30 percent of gross borrowing is for less than one year, and 38 percent is for a term of one to five years. The term of borrowing is based on the authority's determination of what debt structure will give it the best terms overall. What in fact happens is that the entire pool of borrowed funds has an average interest rate, or pool rate, which is the relevant rate of interest for the local authority's operation. For purposes of establishing rents, the loans of housing authorities are amortized over a sixty-year period and internal charges are made accordingly.

Mortgage Insurance

There is no system of mortgage insurance comparable to those found in the United States and Canada. For some high-value mortgages the building societies will require that the individual take out an endowment life-insurance policy that would serve the same effect as mortgage insurance should something happen to the individual. But this use of insurance is not comparable to the usual systems of mortgage insurance.

Secondary Mortgage Market

In the United Kingdom there is no secondary market as such. The loans originated by the building societies remain in their portfolios. There is no active trading of mortgages, nor any on mortgage-backed bonds or mortgage participations. The U.K. system is almost exclusively a savings-bank system, and there is very little mortgage-trading activity at either the primary or the secondary level. Since the individual building societies are quite large institutions and operate nationwide, there is no need for an external arbitraging function, which a secondary market would provide.

Lender of Last Resort

There is no lender of last resort in the United Kingdom; no analog to the Federal Home Loan Bank exists. There is, however, considerable cooperation between the government and the Building Societies Association, so that government policy in the mortgage market is translated via this mechanism. This is effective since there are relatively few building societies that dominate private lending in the United Kingdom.

There has been considerable discussion, as appeared in the Green Paper, of the creation of some type of lender-of-last-resort mechanism. What has been discussed appears to be similar to the Federal National Mortgage Association or the Federal Home Loan Mortgage Corporation: some mechanism to increase the liquidity of the mortgage system and to tap the capital markets. Fears of instability in the mortgage market have kindled interest in the desirability of some entity that goes beyond the activities of the Building Societies Association.

Purchasing and Financing an Individual House

A house purchaser would go directly to a building society to finance his house (see table 7-4). Mortgage loans would be available for 80 percent of value for a maturity of up to thirty years; this is similar to what a purchaser would experience in the United States or Canada. For the United Kingdom, let us consider an interest rate of 10 percent (on a $50,000 house), since historically U.K. interest rates have been at least 1 percentage point higher than those in the United States.

Assume that the intereste rate rises at some time during the holding period of the mortgage. In the United Kingdom the mortgage with a variable rate is routinely issued by building societies. However, it is common to have the payment remain constant even when the rate is raised and merely to extend the term to maturity. Let us see how this works in practice.

Assume that the mortgage rate increases from 10 to 10.25 percent after two years. The outstanding balance after two years is $39,489 and the original payment is $351.02 per month. The original payment can be maintained if the term to maturity is lengthened to 381 months, an increase of 45 months.

Assume a second variation in this case: an increase to 10.5 percent after

Table 7-4
United Kingdom: An Illustrative Example of Financing the Purchase of an Individual House

1. Value of house: U.S. $50,000 (£25,000)

2. Mortgage terms:
   a. 80% of value
   b. 10% per annum
   c. 30-year term to maturity
   d. Payment = $351.02 (£175) per month

3. Variations:
   a. Mortgage-rate increase to 10.25% after 2 years, leaving mortgage payment constant. The balance of $39,489 (£19,750) is financed at a constant payment of $351.06 (£175), and the term to maturity is lengthened to 381 months, an increase of 45 months.
   b. Mortgage rate increases to 10.50% after 2 years, leaving mortgage payment constant. To amortize the remaining balance of $39,489 (£19,750) requires lengthening of the maturity to 477 months. an increase of 141 months.

Note: The limit on lengthening the term is reached at a mortgage interest rate of 10.60%, when the interest due will equal the payment of $351.02 (£175), leaving no surplus for amortization.

two years, adjusting the term to leave the payment constant. In this example, to amortize the remaining balance of $39,489 requires lengthening of the mortgage term to 477 months, an increase of 141 months.

Although it is possible to lengthen the terms of the mortgage in order to keep the payment constant, at high rates of interest it is hardly worth the effort. There is a break-even point at which, given a level payment, the installment will not equal the interest due. In this case the break-even point is at 10.66 percent, when the original payment is only sufficient to pay the interest, leaving nothing for amortization.

Lengthening the term to keep the payment constant is only useful when mortgage rates are low, in the neighborhood of 5 to 7 percent. Once mortgages get up in the range of 9 percent or more, the mere lengthening of terms adds an intolerable burden to the mortgage borrower while giving very little benefit to the lender.

Housing Consumption

Home Ownership

Home ownership is increasingly popular among the younger generations in the United Kingdom, as can be seen in table 4-3. The highest rates of home ownership are in the age group from 25 to 44, precisely those who were forming households in the years after World War II. Thus as this group and those following them work their way through the population, home ownership will undoubtedly become even more common. Table 7-5 and figure 7-4 show percentages of owner occupation in the United Kingdom.

Home purchase is partly impelled by the lack of rental accommodation available to young households. The statistics bear this out, showing the highest rates of home ownership in the younger age cohorts, a situation considerably at variance with that in the United States.

First-Time Buyers. The percentage of building-society loans that go to first-time purchasers has been quite impressive (see table 7-6). In 1970 more than 60 percent of all loans for both new and existing houses went to first-time buyers. In 1978 this had fallen to 47 percent. This contrasts sharply with the U.S. savings-and-loan associations, which in 1977 did only 36 percent of their lending to first-time buyers. Again, the preponderance of first-time buyers in the housing market does tend to reflect the lack of choice of tenure for many new households who are unable to secure either satisfactory rental accommodations in the shrinking private market or local-authority housing.

Sales of Existing Housing. The resale of existing houses is the dominant housing activity in the United Kingdom. The ratio of building-society advances on existing as opposed to new houses increased from 3 to 1 in 1967 to approximately 4 to 1 in 1977. This experience is consistent with that of the United States, where sales of existing housing exceed sales of new housing by approximately the same ratio.

Table 7-5
United Kingdom: Owner-Occupied Dwellings as a Percentage of All Dwellings, 1914-1974

Year	Percentage of Owner-Occupied Dwellings
1914	10.6
1950	29.5
1961	43.0
1965	46.6
1966	47.2
1967	48.0
1968	48.8
1969	49.4
1970	50.0
1971	50.5
1972	51.4
1973	52.2
1974	52.5

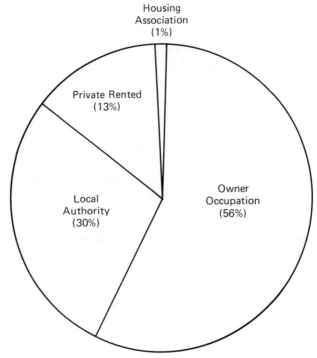

Source: National Dwelling and Housing Survey, Department of the Environment.
Figure 7-4. Housing Tenure in England, 1977

House Prices. Over time, the ratio of new-house prices to income has tended to rise slightly. In 1956 a new house cost approximately 3.1 times average earnings. This has tended to increase steadily, so that by 1979 the ratio stood at 3.69. This is a slightly higher ratio than that found in the United States. Over the period from 1956 to 1978, the price of a new house tended to increase slightly faster than average earnings. The figure has not been steady but has tended to fluctuate especially with the dramatic inflation in prices of houses that occurred between 1972 and 1974.

Tax Benefits. The income tax initially enacted in 1799 to finance the Napoleonic Wars provided tax relief on interest payments. The present tax system grew from this over the years and continued to permit interest deductions. However, the Finance Act of 1974 put restrictions on the amount to tax relief for house interest and restricted tax deductability for interest only to mortgages. As stated in the Green Paper:

> Tax relief on mortgage interest grew from being an ordinary part of the tax system, not a deliberately designed special relief to encourage owner occupa-

Table 7-6
Building-Society Loans to First-Time Buyers and Former Owner Occupants, 1969-1977

Period	Number of Loans (thousands)	Percentage of all Mortgages	Average Dwelling Price (£)	Average Advance (£)	Average Income (£)	Average Percentage Advance	Average Advance/ Average Income
First-time buyers							
1969	290	63.0	4,097	3,240	1,617	79.1	2.00
1970	329	61.0	4,330	3,464	1,766	80.0	1.96
1971	394	60.4	4,838	3,914	1,996	80.9	1.96
1972	394	57.9	6,085	4,954	2,281	81.4	2.17
1973	283	51.9	7,908	6,115	2,734	77.3	2.24
1974	220	50.8	9,037	6,568	3,231	72.7	2.03
1975	306	47.0	9,549	7,292	3,753	76.4	1.94
1976	352	49.2	10,181	8,073	4,285	79.3	1.88
1977	355	48.2	10,857	8,515	4,800	78.4	1.77
Former owner-occupiers							
1969	170	37.0	5,148	3,460	1,987	63.9	1.74
1970	211	39.0	5,838	3,854	2,168	66.0	1.78
1971	259	39.6	6,666	4,407	2,466	66.1	1.79
1972	287	42.1	8,965	5,538	2,748	61.8	2.02
1973	262	48.1	11,900	6,273	3,118	52.7	2.01
1974	213	49.2	13,049	6,577	3,618	50.4	1.82
1975	345	53.0	13,813	7,409	4,299	53.6	1.72
1976	363	50.8	15,160	8,509	4,997	56.1	1.70
1977	382	51.8	16,246	9,101	5,558	56.0	1.64

Source: Building Societies Association, *BSA Bulletin* no. 17 January 1979.

tion. It came to be a benefit to an increasing proportion of mortgages. The value of the relief was increased by increases in tax rates, and its cost by the growth of the number of owner occupiers, increasing mortgage debt and rising mortgage interest rates. [5]

There is tax relief on mortgage interest up to the first £25,000. Any amount over £25,000 is not exempt. It is interesting to note that the only interest that is deductible for income-tax purposes is that on an owner-occupied house. Interest payments on consumer loans and other debt are not deductible from income taxation.

There is no capital-gains tax on the sale of a principal residence in the United Kingdom. This is certainly one of the favorable aspects of housing ownership in the United Kingdom and is undoubtedly one of the factors motivating households to invest their money in housing rather than in some other asset.

In the United Kingdom there was once a tax on imputed rental income, but this was eliminated in 1963. It was declared on the infamous Schedule A, a very controversial feature of the tax code. This tax was eliminated because of its great unpopularity. The concept of imputed income from housing is based on the assumption that an owner-occupied house yields a stream of housing services over time that have a cash value equivalent to what they would cost in the market if the house were rented.

Other Special Benefits. There is a savings bonus scheme in operation in the United Kingdom. If a person saves every month for five years, he or she is eligible for a government bonus equal to one year's savings, on which no tax is paid. If this bonus is left undisturbed for two additional years, it is doubled. This is a significant inducement to save for home ownership.

There is also what is known as an option mortgage scheme, in which the building societies will grant mortgage loans a full 2 percent below the going market rate. Those eligible to receive mortgage-rate reductions are households that forego the normal tax deductibility of interest to which they would be entitled. This is especially good for households with relatively low incomes, for whom the tax advantages do not amount to very much. The interest rate is subsidized directly by the government, and the savings are passed on to the individual household.

Rental Housing

Rent Control. Rent controls date from World War I; they were first installed in 1915. As with all such measures, they were intended to be temporary. However, over the years the controls have become permanent features of the housing market. Some measures were taken to decontrol rented housing after World War I, but controls were reintroduced in 1939 with the advent of World War II. Despite frequent changes in government after the war, rent controls were never rescinded—even when the Conservatives were in power.

Almost all rental housing is under some form of control, with the exception of some very expensive housing at the upper end of the spectrum. Under a complex system of classification, dwellings are either rent controlled or rent regulated. Essentially, the controlled rents are set lower than the regulated rents. Controlled units can be redesignated as regulated on termination of tenancy (often by death of the tenant) or substantial rehabilitation of the building. A regulated unit is entitled to "fair rent," which is deemed to be that rent that would be obtained for the unit in the absence of any scarcity in the rental market. The bias in the administration assumes that rents are higher than they ought to be because there is a scarcity, which tends to be self-fulfilling in the long run.

Despite the shift to partial decontrol, the private sector in rental housing continues its steep decline. Not much of a private market in rental housing remains. The decline in private rental housing has been quite large, at the rate of 100,000 units per year. In general, corporate owners and large-scale ownership of housing are now gone. Most of the current landlords in the private sector are elderly, and they are in fact a vanishing breed (see figure 7-5).

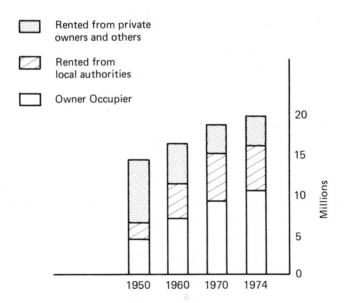

Source: Central Statistical Office, *Social Trends* (1975).

Figure 7-5. Stock of Dwellings by Tenure, United Kingdom, 1950-1974

Some of the decline in private rental housing has been the result of its sale for owner occupancy. There are firms that specialize in converting large estates. In addition, some of the older stock has been demolished in various urban-redevelopment and slum-clearance programs.

Fair rents still tend to be below what would be considered economic market rents. Although fair rent is defined as that which would be obtained in a competitive, fully supplied market, research shows that such fair rents are substantially below break-even levels. Thus the private rental stock continues to decline as no new private rental housing is built and age takes its toll on the stock that remains [6].

Housing Associations. It has been hoped that nonprofit housing associations will be able to fill the void caused by the decline of the private rental sector. Housing associations can borrow money from local authorities to build housing. However, they are also eligible for direct subsidies from the Department of the Environment. Rents charged by housing associations are "fair" rents; the subsidy is the different between the "fair" rent and the "cost" rent, which is the economic rent required to break even. The subsidy to the housing associations is one they request; receipt of the subsidy, however, is not a matter of right but is dependent on the state of the budget at the time.

Local-Authority Housing. In the United Kingdom public housing is built and managed by local authorities, which are part of the local council governments. These authorities borrow money at below-market interest rates from the central government. In addition, there are government subsidies to the local authorities to help them with operating expenses. The rents are set correspondingly lower than market because of the low interest rate and other subsidies.

In the United Kingdom public housing reaches a wide income spectrum; it is not just housing for the poor. On ideological grounds, there are no means tests for admission to public housing. Therefore, it is not surprising to find large numbers of middle-income families living in public housing. There is a significant overlap between the income and occupational characteristics of those in council housing and those who are home owners. In order to provide for low-income council tenants, an additional subsidy is necessary. Rent rebates, which reduce the rent below the general level, are financed by subsidies from the central government.

By law, local authorities must make "reasonable charges" for all their rented housing. Although the authorities have considerable discretion as to the level of rent they charge, they must set rents so that their housing-revenue account is in fiscal balance, considering all the expenditures that must be made and also taking into account subsidies from the government.

The housing-revenue account is kept for all the properties within an authority, which means that the usual practice is to pool all rents so that the level of rents does not depend on individual buildings and capital costs for any particular structure, but rather on an overall level to balance the account.

Rent policy for council housing calls for the pooling of rents in all the buildings owned by a local authority. This tends to keep down the rents of newly constructed dwellings, which otherwise would be quite high because of escalating building costs. Since the bulk of the existing stock was built in the past at lower cost, its economic rents tend to be lower. Pooling rents produces slightly higher rents for the older units but much lower rents on the newly constructed dwellings.

Once the average rents for the authority are set, rebates are given to low-income tenants. The shortfall caused by the rebates is made up from government subsidies. Council-housing rents tend to be quite low; thus there is no incentive for tenants to leave, even when they can afford to do so.

The rent in local-authority housing is heavily subsidized, as can be seen by the figures in table 7-7. The various subsidies to local-authority housing account for more than half of the total cost of operation. The amount of contribution from rents has fallen significantly. Whereas net rent in 1960 accounted for more than 70 percent of total operating costs, by 1976 that figure had fallen to 45 percent. The decrease in the contribution of rents toward local-authority operation is primarily due to inflation. Costs of operating, especially the cost of utilities, as well as other costs have increased significantly. In an attempt to mitigate the effects of inflation on a sizable section of the population, the government has not allowed rents to rise as fast as the price level and has made up the difference with subsidies. The result has been sharply decreasing contributions of rent toward total operations.

Illustrative Example of Local-Authority Housing

In Britain the subsidized housing-production schemes involve the local housing authorities building public housing. A hypothetical housing development can be used to illustrate the depth of subsidy resulting from council housing. Assuming that our prototype development of 100 units was built by a local authority, it would then be able to take advantage of the interest-rate subsidy provided by the central government. Local authorities can obtain subsidies that make their effective rate of borrowing 4 percent, amortized over sixty years. According to this formula the annual debt service is $133,000, as shown in table 7-7. Local-tax exemption further reduces

Table 7-7
United Kingdom: Example of a Typical Housing-Subsidy Scheme
Compared with Unsubsidized Development

	Nonsubsidized Prototype	Local-Authority Housing	Comments
Development costs	$3,000,000	$3,000,000	Assuming comparable costs
Mortgage	$2,400,000	$3,000,000	Local-authority bonds cover entire capital cost
Investor equity	$600,000	None required	
Debt service	$255,000	$133,000	Amortization; 60 years, 4%
Operating costs	$180,000	$150,000	No local taxes paid
Return on equity	$40,000	None required	Local authorities are non-profit
Break-even rent	$395/month		
Actual rent to tenant	$395/month	$200/month	The tenant's rent is based on pooling all properties owned by the local authority and bears no direct relationship to actual development costs; actual rent would be half the break-even rent
Amount of subsidy	—	$195	

operating costs. Since the authorities are nonprofit institutions, there would be no requirement for a profit. As a result the local council housing in this case could have a break-even rent of $236.00 per month, which is 60 percent lower than the required level in the absence of all subsidies.

However, rents are not based on actual capital costs but are calculated by pooling costs. Since our prototype is a new unit, it would have a higher break-even rent than would older housing stock. Pooling rents causes the actual rent charged by the housing authority to be substantially lower. In general, housing-authority rents cover only 50 percent of their costs, so we can expect that the rent actually charged to tenants would be much lower than the $236.00 per month because of the pooling arrangement.

References

1. The Building Societies Association, "Evidence Submitted by the Building Societies Association to the Committee to Review the Functioning of Financial Institutions" (London, 1978).
2. The Building Societies Association, "Facts About Building Societies" (London, 1979).

3. The Building Societies Association, *BSA Bulletin* (quarterly).
4. The Building Societies Association, "The Housing Policy Review and the Role of Building Societies" (London, 1978).
5. Department of the Environment, "United Kingdom Monograph on Current Trends and Policies in the Fields of Housing, Building and Planning" (presented to the United Nations, Economic Commission for Europe, Committee on Housing, Building and Planning, May 1978).
6. Department of the Environment, *Housing Policy*, Technical volumes I-III (London: Her Majesty's Stationery Office, 1977).
7. Secretary of State for the Environment, *Housing Policy: A Consultative Document* (London: Her Majesty's Stationery Office, 1977).
8. Graham Hallett, *Housing and Land Policies in West Germany and Britain: A Record of Success and Failure* (London: Macmillan, and New York: Holmes and Meier, 1977).

8

Housing in the Federal Republic of Germany

Housing Policy

Public and Private Cooperation

Germany faced a severe housing crisis after World War II. As a principal combatant and theater of conflict, it experienced extensive devastation to its housing stock as well as to the industrial infrastructure. Germany emerged from the war with half the housing in its major cities either destroyed or damaged so extensively as to be uninhabitable. The task of providing shelter for millions of homeless people was indeed staggering.

The first priority was obviously to eliminate the housing shortage both by building as many new units as possible and by managing the habitable housing stock that was left standing, and to control rent in order to reduce price gouging as a result of the acute shortages.

The government elected to encourage a high level of housing construction by offering incentives and subsidies to the private sector. Generous assistance was given to nonprofit enterprises to construct rental housing for moderate-income families. Later, similar incentives were given to private builders. Such incentives were well received by thousands of individuals who constructed small rental units of two to six dwellings each, with the owner usually occupying one unit. The building effort was successful in the sense that, by 1974, 14 million housing units had been built, providing equality between the number of households and the number of dwellings. The severe wartime shortage had come to an end.

The private market accounts for most of the housing in Germany as a consequence of policies that have evolved steadily over the years. In the 1950s the German emphasis was on direct state aid to repair the war damage and increase the housing stock. However, by the 1960s that emphasis had shifted toward a dependence on the private capital market and on private developers.

The Essence of Housing Policy

The essence of housing policy as revealed by the Federal Republic of Germany (FRG) since World War II has three parts:

1. Government (both federal and state) will assist the private sector to build and maintain rental housing through favorable tax incentives, grants, and subsidies.
2. Government will provide personalized assistance to families whose incomes are too low to obtain decent housing through a housing allowance.
3. Home ownership will be encouraged through tax preferences on owner occupation, and bonuses for saving for home ownership.

Contemporary Housing Problems

Although in a numerical sense the housing shortage has ended, considerable work remains if the FRG is to create a satisfactory housing situation. Despite the large numbers of housing units built since 1949, much of the prewar stock needs repair or replacement. Much of the older housing consists of tenements in inner-city areas, many of them lacking essential facilities. Approximately 40 percent of the housing stock in the FRG was built before 1939, and 25 percent before 1918.

Housing cost for owner occupation continues to be a problem. The high cost of housing as a result of high costs for land and construction is a significant barrier for workers who aspire to home ownership.

Housing Production

Housing and the Economy

The postwar rate of dwelling construction in the FRG has been high in comparison with that in other European countries and North America (see table 8-1). During the 1950s and 1960s the rate of building per 1,000 inhabitants exceeded 10. In terms of the level of resources devoted to housing, however, FRG performance had been moderate, averaging just over 5 percent of gross domestic product (GDP).

Housing Production

Housing activities in the Federal Republic of Germany correspond more closely to those of the United States than to those of any other country in Europe. As a rule, the government per se neither builds nor owns housing, much as in the United States. Even what is considered social housing is owned

Table 8-1
Federal Republic of Germany: Selected Housing-Production Statistics, 1953-1976

Housing Activities	1953	1960	1965	1970	1976
Dwellings completed (thousands)	—	574.4	591.9	478.1	392.4
Dwellings per 1,000 population	10.5	10.4	10.0	8.1	6.4
Housing construction as a percentage of gross domestic product	5.1	5.4	5.2	5.4	5.5
Percentage of total by type of investor					
Public-housing authorities	4.9	2.7	3.2	2.3	3.1
Housing associations and cooperatives	38.9	26.1	25.4	18.5	13.1
Private	56.2	71.2	71.4	79.3	83.8
Individuals	50.2	62.4	58.8	58.7	64.0
Housing corporations	3.0	4.3	5.6	11.2	11.4
Enterprises	3.0	4.5	7.0	9.4	8.4

Source: United Nations, *Annual Bulletin of Housing and Building Statistics for Europe.*

privately by either profit or nonprofit entities. There is an extensive system of subsidies that enables the private sector to carry out public purposes.

Nonprofit entities play a major role in providing housing for both rental and owner occupancy. The large nonprofit housing enterprises do not undertake actual construction; in fact, they are prevented from doing so. Some of the nonprofit entities receive their seed money from labor unions, churches, and even state bodies. However, their major financial requirements for the actual building of housing are obtained privately in the capital market.

Nonprofits have a long history in Germany, having begun before the turn of the twentieth century. They originated primarily as a protest movement against the kind of worker housing that was being built at the time. Nonprofits were created in order to counteract what was considered exploitation of workers by profit-motivated owners.

Neue Heimat, the largest nonprofit builder in all of Western Europe, is sponsored by a group of trade unions. As an example of its prodigious activity, in 1974 it owned 268,000 rental units and had also been responsible for building more than 200,000 units that had been sold for owner occupation.

In 1976 the German nonprofit housing sector numbered 1,960 housing associations distributed as follows: 1,311 cooperatives, 555 limited-dividend corporations, 61 joint-stock companies, and 33 other enterprises. They collectively owned approximately 18 percent of the entire German housing stock, down from the more than 30-percent ownership they had had in 1955. The share of nonprofit housing has declined since the 1950s. Reasons for this have included increasing owner occupation and competition from other private, profit-motivated developers. Today the nonprofit sponsors put more emphasis on providing housing for special groups such as the elderly, young families starting out, and very large families, sectors of the market not as well served by other developers.

Private investors had been encouraged to develop rental housing using limited-dividend corporations. One of the incentives is that accelerated depreciation is available for such investment; 40 percent of the investment can be written off over eight years. In order to qualify, rents must be limited to what is "responsible," based on cost.

Structure of the Housing-Finance Sector

Mobilization of Savings

The institutional facilities for obtaining household savings to finance housing are the 771 savings banks, the 26 public-statutory credit institutions, the 97 private life-insurance companies, the 22 carriers of social insurance, and the 16 private and 12 public-statutory building-and-loan associations (see figures 8-1 and 8-2, and table 8-2).

Savings Banks. Savings banks have provided between 13 and 17 percent of the financing for the construction of housing. Savings banks are overwhelmingly nonprofit establishments with a public-statutory character; as a rule, their local facilities and operations are limited to the area of the appropriate municipality. Savings banks can convert up to 60 percent of their savings reserves into long-term loans.

Buildings-and-Loan Associations (*Bausparkasse*). Building-and-loan ations (*Bausparkasse*) function as specific capital-accumulation institutions for the financing of housing construction. There are two types of building-and-loan associations differentiated by legal status, namely, private and public. Private building-and-loan associations are corporations that operate on a regional basis. The public building-and-loan associations, on the other hand, are usually legally dependent divisions of the savings banks and are therefore bounded as to their area of business. Just as in the case of savings banks and the other public-chartered credit institutions, the liability for their obligations is guaranteed through their public character.

The objective of their operations is collective savings by persons associated by contract with the building-and-loan association. Contrary to normal lending practices in which the circles of people taking loans and of those saving do not coincide, in this case borrowers are required to have saved a certain amount with an association before a loan can be granted

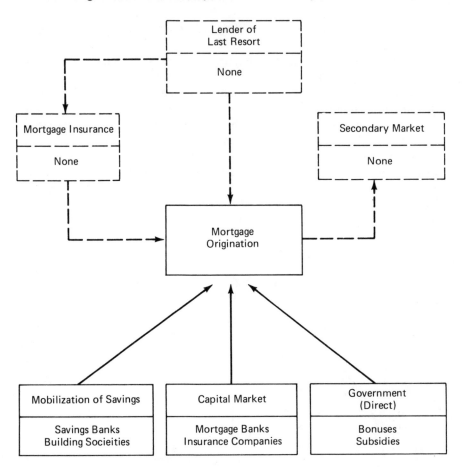

Figure 8-1. Structure of the Mortgage Market in the Federal Republic of Germany

This practice results in three essential peculiarities. For a person saving for housing construction, it is not the rate of interest on the savings that is of primary importance, but rather the claim to a loan at an advantageous interest rate. The savings interest rate is usually between 2.5 and 3 percent and the loan rate between 4.5 and 5 percent. Because of these nonfluctuating loan rates, it is also understandable that savings/construction involvement has risen from year to year. Whereas in 1952 the building-and-loan associations participated in the financing of 6.4 percent of housing construction, their share in 1972 was 23.7 percent (including amounts saved), and in 1978 about one-third.

The building-and-loan associations grant loans, usually without security other than the property, for 60 to 65 percent of the total cost of construction as a second mortgage. Such lending is facilitated by the fact that loans have to be liquidated within seven to fourteen years.

Collective saving of the type described presumes a mutual contract between the saver and the building-and-loan association on the basis of which the saver is committed to deposit regular savings and the building-and-loan association is committed to grant a loan. The object of the contract is the saving of an agreed-on amount and the obligation of the association to lend the difference between the contract amount and the savings at maturity of the commitment. The allocation occurs only after the minimum savings period of one to two years has elapsed and a minimum savings of, at the most, 40 percent of the contract amount has been saved. Along with the loan interest there is also a so-called finalization fee, normally 1 percent of the contract, to cover the closing costs, and a loan fee of 1 to 3 percent for processing.

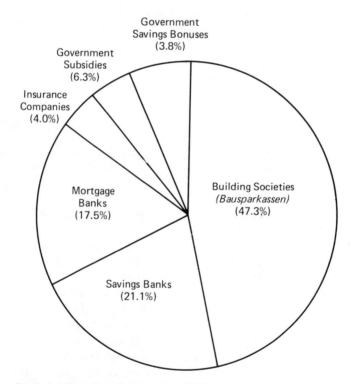

Source: Bundesbaublatt, *Der Woknungsbau* (1977).

Note: Does not include household equity.

Figure 8-2. Institutional Housing Finance by Source of Funds, Federal Republic of Germany, 1977

Table 8-2

Participation of Housing-Finance Institutions, Federal Republic of Germany, 1977

	Amount (million DM)	Percentage
Savings banks	10,175	114.5
Mortgage banks	8,416	12.0
Insurance companies	1,959	2.8
Building societies (*Bausparkassen*)	22,691	32.5
Total private institutions	43,241	61.8
Government subsidies	3,039	4.3
Government savings bonuses	1,853	2.6
Total government	4,892	6.9
Total institutional finance	48,241	68.7
Household equity	21,699	31.3
Total housing investment	69,940	100.0

Source: Bundesbaubbtt, *Der Wohnongsbau* (1977).

Because there usually arise considerable time differences between the allocation of a contract amount and the actual claim to the commitments, the building-and-loan associations enjoy the availability of considerable liquid funds, which can partially be used—at normal market interest rates—for other lending.

Persons who save with a building-and-loan association are given a generous bonus of 25 to 35 percent of the sum saved, up to a maximum of DM 400 per annum (DM 800 for a couple) if income is within certain limits. These bonuses are tax free.

Building-society loans accounted for only a small fraction of loans in 1960, but they now figure in more than 60 percent of the loans for single-family housing. This system is much like the savings schemes in France, since it divorces the process from market rates. The second mortgage from the building society can be at a much lower rate than the first mortgage obtained from traditional sources.

Bond Institutions

An important part of housing finance, 14.5 percent on the average, is supplied by the private- and publicly chartered mortgage banks that are bond institutions.

Securities (bonds) carrying the name of the owner are traded in the stock exchanges. The mortgage bonds issued must be covered to the same nominal amount by mortgages. The bond holders thereby obtain a direct right of foreclosure in case of default. The interest rate and interest-payment conditions are mentioned in the text of the security. Payment occurs either by redemption or by open-market purchase by the institution. The owner of the bond, on the other hand, does not have a right to give notice of cancellation; but the bond is exchangeable at a bank for up to 75 percent of its exchange value. The configuration of new bonds to be issued must correspond to the general condition of the capital market and interest rates at the time of issuance.

In practice, the interest rate for the borrower (including the current administrative-cost rate for the bond institution) is measured at an additional 0.5 to 1 percent on top of the nominal interest rate paid by the institution to the purchaser of the bond. Furthermore, the mortgage loan is paid out at a discount. The builder has a commitment for a firm rate for a certain time.

Having both depository and bond institutions in the housing sector is advantageous because swings in the national economy tend to be offsetting. As interest rates increase and funds tend to slacken at depository institutions, money can still be raised in the bond market. Should bond rates fall, there will be subsequent inflows of funds to savings institutions. A shift from one will benefit the other, thus offsetting the negative effects.

Mortgages

In the German system a home purchaser is likely to have to put down 20 to 25 percent in cash. He would then obtain a first-mortgage loan of perhaps up to 40 to 50 percent of the value for a period of as long as 30 years. The first mortgage is likely to come from a mortgage bank or savings bank. A second mortgage would frequently be obtained from a building-and-loan association *(Bausparkasse)* for the balance at a lower interest rate. Usually a second mortgage is at a higher interest rate, but in this case the interest rate on the second mortgage is lower than that on the first. Most home purchasers have to have more than one mortgage because the first mortgages are typically for no more than 50 percent. The combination of two or three mortgages will usually produce a package in which the total loans-to-value ratio is in the neighborhood of 85 percent.

The interest rate on a first mortgage from a savings bank will be written at a variable rate. A mortgage from a mortgage bank, however, will be for a fixed rate of interest. The interest rate on the second mortgage from a building-and-loan *(Bausparkasse)* under a savings contract will also be fixed.

Mortgage Insurance

There is no system of mortgage insurance comparable to that found in the United States and Canada.

Secondary Mortgage Market

There is also no secondary market for mortgage loans. A portion of the mortgages are originated by mortgage bankers that issue their own securities. These mortgage loans are kept in the bank's portfolio in order to meet the amortization requirements of the bonds; thus they are not traded. Savings banks are also under no apparent pressure to sell off any meaningful quantity of their loans. Therefore, a secondary market as such has not developed in German mortgages.

Lender of Last Resort

In the German system there is no lender of last resort. There is no single dominant entity in the mortgage market that tends to set the pace and the tone for mortgage lending, as there is in some other countries. There is no entity that corresponds to the Federal Home Loan Bank Board in the United States or to the Canada Housing and Mortgage Corporation.

Taxes

Savings institutions engaged in financing housing receive preferential rates of taxation. In the FRG the corporate income-tax rate is 56 percent. However, the effective rate is lowered to 46 percent for building-and-loan associations and credit cooperatives. Insurance companies and banks are accorded the lower rate on that portion of their profit derived from real estate. Building-and-loan associations that are publicly chartered pay taxes at the corporate rate of 44 percent.

Interest earned on savings accounts is normally taxed as income from capital. However, the first DM 400 is tax free (DM 800 for a couple) for savers with incomes of DM 24,000 (DM 48,000 for a couple). For the elderly, over age 64, an amount of interest earned not to exceed DM 3,000 is free from taxation.

Interest Rates

Because the rate of inflation in postwar Germany has been low in comparison with that in other nations, interest rates have been low. Mortgage bond rates and mortgage rates from savings banks have moved in tandem. During the 1960s, mortgage rates were typically less than 6.5 percent; during the 1970s, they fluctuated between 6 and 10 percent. In the FRG there is essentially no spread, or risk premium, between the rate on industrial bonds and mortgage rates.

Table 8-3
Germany: An Illustrative Example of Financing the Purchase of an Individual House

---

1. Value of house: U.S. $50,000 (DM 90,000)

2. Mortgage terms:
   a. First mortgage
      1. 50% of value
      2. 8% interest for 33 years
      3. Monthly payment = U.S. $179.65 (DM 323)
   b. Second mortgage (from *Bausparkassen*)
      1. 30% of value
      2. 4.5% interest for 10 years
      3. Monthly payment = U.S. $155.45 (DM 280)
   c. Owner's equity = 20% (U.S. $10,000, DM 18,000)

3. Total monthly repayment = U.S. $335.05 (DM 603)

Note: Under the special savings scheme, the contractual amount with the *Bausparkassen* is for U.S. $25,000 (DM 45,000): 40% is saved through periodic deposits and forms the down payment or equity. The balance of the contracted amount, 60%, or U.S. $15,000 (DM 27,000) is issued as the second mortgage.

Financing an Individual House

Germany is of special interest because of its unique bonus plan for savings for housing, which is a very important feature in financing home ownership.

In Germany more than one mortgage is usually necessary, sometimes as many as three. In this illustration (see table 8-3) we will assume that a first-mortgage loan is obtained from a savings bank or mortgage bank, and a second-mortgage loan from a *Bausparkasse* or building-and-loan association. Even with the two mortgages, it is customary to have a considerable owner's equity.

In this case assume that a first mortgage can be obtained for 50 percent of value, for a term of thirty-three years, at a rate of 8 percent per annum. (An 8-percent rate of interest was used since the mortgage interest rates in Germany have typically been somewhat lower than those in the United States.)

Of particular interest is the second mortgage, which is obtained from the *Bausparkasse* and is usually for around 30 percent of value, for a term of ten years, at a low 4.5-percent interest rate.

The second loan was obtained because of a contractual savings agreement. Originally the saver contracted with the *Bausparkasse* for $25,000. Of that amount, 40 percent is saved by the individual and hence becomes the equity; and 60 percent is borrowed after the agreed amount of savings has been accumulated. There are also bonuses available to aid in the accumulation of the required amount. Once the $10,000 has been accumulated in the savings account, the individual is eligible for a loan of $15,000 at a low interest rate.

Now let us see how well these loans combine and what the effects are. The first mortgage requires a repayment of $179.60 per month and the second $155.45 per month. This produces a total payment of $335.05 per month over the first ten years, after which the second mortgage would have been repaid.

It is interesting to note that when mortgages are written for low interest rates, the repayment period can be quite short. It is only the high interest rates that require lengthy repayment periods in order for mortgage terms to be reasonable.

The success of such a scheme depends on the propensity of people to save. Germans happen to be among the highest savers in the world. Thus it is not surprising that such contractual savings plans now account for more than 60 percent of housing transactions. (See table 8-4 for participation levels of various German housing-finance institutions.)

Housing Consumption

Housing Prices

The average level of rents in the FRG is kept low because of the widespread use of subsidies (see table 8-5). Fully 60 percent of the population is eligible for some kind of housing subsidy. Such subsidies can also be used by home

Table 8-4
Participation of Housing-Finance Institutions, Federal Republic of Germany, 1977

	Amount (Million DM)	Percentage
Savings banks	10,175	14.5
Mortgage banks	8,416	12.0
Insurance companies	1,959	2.8
Building societies (Bausparkassen)	22,691	32.5
Total private institutions	43,241	61.8
Government subsidies	3,039	4.3
Government savings bonuses	1,853	2.6
Total government	4,892	6.9
Total institutional finance	48,241	68.7
Household equity	21,699	31.3
Total housing investment	69,940	100.0

Source: Bundesbaublatt, *Der Wohnungsbau* (1977).

Table 8-5
Average Percentage of Disposable Income Spent on Rent

Household Type	1964	1973
Two-person households consisting of pensioners or welfare recipients with low incomes	13.9	18.5
Four-person households in the blue-collar, middle-income group	9.9	12.9
Four-person households in the white-collar/ civil-servant, higher-income groups	10.6	11.2

owners who otherwise meet the criteria of eligibility based on monthly housing cost and income.

Housing in West Germany tends to be quite expensive, especially single-family housing.

> Any visitor to West Germany is struck by the fact that, for all the many virtues of the German housing situation, to own a home of one's own is a luxury to which most people in this rich country usually aspire only late in life, if at all. [4]

In 1978 the average cost of a single-family house was DM 196,550 (DM 170,050 for building costs and DM 26,500 for land).

The Market for Existing Houses

A market for existing (used) housing is developing. However, the bulk of houses are purchased in the new sector, unlike the situation in the United States and the United Kingdom. There are significant differences that tend to account for this. There is no large and constant turnover of houses in the FRG comparable to that in the United States; German house purchasers tend to be much older when they do buy and are more likely to stay put. In the United States and the United Kingdom, young households are much more apt to purchase, providing more opportunities for changes in residence as family structure and life cycles change.

Home Ownership

In Germany the rate of home ownership is quite low; only 38 percent of households were owner occupants in 1976. The government would like the rate of home ownership to increase in order to make the filtering process work more efficiently through the chains of moves. People moving out of rentals to home ownership will free up some of the existing stock for those of lower income, thus relieving some of the state's burden in providing housing.

Owner occupation in Germany is largely in the rural areas and small towns. In the cities the rate of owner occupation is extremely low. Most of the construction after World War II in the cities has been of large apartment complexes and of smaller multifamily units owned by individuals. A significant number of owner-occupied houses was not built in the FRG until after 1960. Prior to that time, most of the effort had gone into increasing the housing stock by building a large number of rental units.

In order to expand home ownership in light of the low home-owner rate and high cost, the government has enacted a series of tax incentives. The most significant tax advantage to home owners is the ability to deduct from income an amount equal to 5 percent of the value of a house for a period of eight years. For owner-occupied housing, mortgage interest is not deductible. However, this special 5-percent deduction serves the same purpose as does interest deductibility in the United States. This deduction is available for both new and used houses, with a cost limit of DM 150,000 for a one-family house or condominium and DM 200,000 for a two-family house.

There is a tax on the net imputed rental income from housing. First the housing value is established as it is for property taxation. In practice this tends to be considerably below current market value, since the reference mark is the value in 1961, with a 40 percent update. One percent of the computed value is arbitrarily taken as the imputed rental income. Against this the owner occupier may deduct all maintenance expenses, but no mortgage interest. Depreciation is allowed, so that the computation of the net rental income is apt to be negative.

For new houses there is a further subsidy in the form of an exemption from real-estate taxes for ten years. There is also a waiver of the 7-percent land-transfer tax on the purchase of a new house or condominium. There is no capital-gains tax on the sale of real estate if the holding period is at least two years.

Rental Housing

In West Germany the government began decontrolling rents in 1960. Rents were gradually decontrolled in all areas of the country where the vacancy rate was more than 3 percent, which included most of the country by 1967.

Although rent control has been lifted in Germany, there are still constraints on the private rental sector. Tenants have had considerable security of tenure since the passage of the Tenancy Protection Act in 1974. Essentially, this law makes it impossible to evict a tenant unless he fails to pay rent or the owner needs the unit for his own family. In addition, rent increases that are contested are settled by court arbitrators. If rent is contested, the arbitration of the issue is based on the concept of comparable rents, less any shortage premium. As in the United Kingdom, there is an attempt to set rents based on some standard that would remove any premium due to the landlord because of shortages.

Housing Subsidies

In Germany there has been a shift away from objective subsidies (*Objektforderung*) to buildings, toward subjective subsidies (*Subjekforderung*), which are oriented toward people. Both renters and owners are eligible for rent or mortgage rebates. When either the rent or mortgage payments are too high, the government can provide supplements in the form of allowances, which in 1974 went up to 10 percent for tenants and 1 percent for owners.

In Germany housing allowances were first introduced in 1965. The allowance is based on a combination of income and family size. More than 1.6 million households received housing allowances in 1976. Both the state and federal governments share the expenses for funding housing-allowance subsidies. The public assistance given to individuals for housing is extremely generous. Fully 60 percent of all households in Germany are eligible for some type of housing assistance.

The housing-allowance system is based on a "tolerable rent" for a family, based on family size and income and usually estimated at between 5 and 20 percent of income. The difference between the actual cost and the tolerable rent is the subsidy or allowance, which is provided to the family if the rent is within bounds. Government standards require that the rent must not be unreasonable.

After World War II, subsidies were made available to the private sector to build rental housing. Grants to cover a portion of the capital costs were available to those who agreed to set rents on a cost-covering basis and to limit their profit to a reasonable amount, approximately 4 percent (see table 8-6). These incentives, along with favorable tax treatment for investors, were enough to insure that a large amount of rental housing would be provided through the private sector. Since the end of the war, one-half of all the rental units have been provided by private, profit-motivated investors, with the balance coming from the cooperatives and nonprofits. It is interesting to note that much of the rental housing has been in small units, owned by small investors and owner occupiers, as opposed to the large blocks of flats built by the nonprofits.

Table 8-6
Germany: Example of Housing-Subsidy Scheme Compared with Unsubsidized Development

	Nonsubsidized Prototype	Interest-Rate Subsidy	Comments
Development costs	$3,000,000	$3,000,000	Assuming comparable costs of construction
Mortgage	$2,400,000	$2,400,000	
Investor equity	$600,000	$600,000	
Debt service	$255,000	Years: 1-4 $122,000 5-8 163,000 9-12 205,000 13 + 255,000	Assumming below-market interest subsidy (3 percent) decreasing over a twelve-year period
Operating costs	$180,000	$80,000	
Return on equity	$40,000	$36,000	Assuming a 6-percent return
Rent required to break even	$395		
Actual rent to tenant	$395	Years: 1-4 $281 5-8 319 9-12 357 13 + 395	Rents will increase to market rate after twelve years
Subsidized rent as percentage of economic rent		70-100	Subsidy decreases over time

Germany provides a good example of the kind of problems encountered in subsidizing rents during a period of inflation. Because of inflation and greatly increased capital costs, the cost approach to rent setting meant that rents in newer dwellings would always be higher than rents in older dwellings. Thus those individuals that obtained the lowest rents were not necessarily those that had the greatest need, but merely those that got into the earlier units. Therefore, the system of subsidy was augmented in 1967 with a second program that instituted a degressive subsidy, which was calculated to be self-eliminating in time. An interest-rate subsidy would attach to the unit but would be available only for a limited number of years. This philosophy takes into account both inflation and the propensity of income to rise over time.

The full subsidy would be in effect for the first four years. Then it would be reduced one-third in years five through eight, reduced another third in years nine through twelve, and eliminated after twelve years. By that time, rising incomes should theoretically have been enough to compensate for the decrease in subsidies and the rise in rents.

References

1. Bunderministerium für Raumordnung, Baumeser and Stadtebau, "Die Finanziering in Wohnungswesen in der Bundersrepublik Deutchland" (May 1974).
2. Der Bundesminister für Raumordnung, Bauwesen und Städtebau, *Der Wohnungsbau* (1977).
3. Federal Minister for Regional Planning Building and Urban Development, Federal Republic of Germany, *National Report for the United Nations Conference on Human Settlement.*
4. Graham Hallett, *Housing and Land Policies in West Germany and Britain: A Record of Success and Failure* (London: Macmillan, and New York: Holmes and Meier, 1977).
5. Peter Marcuse, "Descriptive Summary: Governmental Housing Programs Federal Republic of Germany' (1978, mimeographed).

9 Housing in France

Housing Policy

Public Assistance and Private Effort

At the midpoint of the twentieth century, after two world wars, France faced the task of reconstructing a devastated housing stock. In 1945 it was essential to repair the war devastation and rapidly increase the housing stock so that there would be parity between the number of households and the number of housing units. The first priority was on reclamation of the habitable stock that remained; next in importance was the construction of large numbers of new units. France was successful on both counts, and the construction of a large number of units over a sustained period eventually eliminated the numerical housing shortage. Once this milestone was reached, it became evident that a new direction in housing policy was called for, one that would stress the quality of the housing stock and would also widen the choice of housing tenure for all families.

France has a long history of active public-sector assistance in the private development of housing, going back to turn-of-the-century measures to provide adequate housing for workers through the Habitation à Loyer Modéré (HLM) associations. As in other Western European countries, the French government's role in housing has been to encourage, and occasionally to direct, resources into housing. It has not relied on direct government construction or ownership of housing, but has worked through nonprofit-sector public corporations (HLMs), private individuals and builders, and the state-directed financial institutions.

The government's principal tool for implementing housing policy is its enormous leverage over the financial sector, tightly controlled through the Ministry of Finance, The Bank of France, and Crédit Foncier de France (the French Land Bank). The flow of money into the housing sector and its price are determined with the sanction of the government and the controlling financial institutions. By setting strict terms and conditions on eligibility for financing, the government can effectively determine the kind, quantity, quality, and location of most of the housing built, even though virtually all of it is built by private entities.

The French government has traditionally been an active participant in the mortgage market. For example, since World War II these subsidies and bonuses have been made available to builders, developers, and private individuals to construct houses for rent or ownership. Such assistance covers a wide spectrum of the French housing market. Special subsidies are given for first-time home purchasers under the "access-to-ownership" plan. There is a generous bonus saving scheme to encourage thrift for home purchase. Both public and private developers are eligible for low-interest subsidized mortgages for the construction of moderate-rent housing. These are all examples of the degree to which the government is involved. However, it should be remembered that most of the money for housing finance does come through the private banks from household savings.

In 1977 the housing-finance system in France was overhauled, with some very important changes that signaled a clear shift in housing policy. Since the wartime housing shortage had ended, there was no longer a need to gear policy toward sheer production. Once numerical parity had been reached and the worst of the devastation repaired, emphasis could be placed on improving the quality of housing and widening the choices available to families.

The housing reforms of 1977 had three principal features. First was the creation of programs aimed at giving assistance to families in need through individual assistance, tailored to the requirements of the particular household. This policy departed from previous public-sector subsidy programs aimed at building as much low-rent housing as possible without regard to the needs of individual families. The second step was to tailor specific programs to foster an increase in home ownership. Government policy explicitly recognized the need to increase the rate of home ownership by government-subsidy programs and encouragement through tax relief and savings bonuses. The third prong was to continue private-sector involvement in the provision of rental housing. France has a long history of the private sector providing low-rent housing, primarily through nonprofit associations.

Government and Local Development Policy

Housing policy has been aimed not only at improving the housing stock and increasing home ownership, but also at addressing regional imbalances caused by the depopulation of rural areas, among other things. What has happened in France is common to other advanced societies; rural areas are being depopulated and urban areas are growing. But even in the urban areas themselves imbalances exist. Although metropolitan areas continue to grow, the central cities, especially the inner areas of central cities, are experiencing decline. In Paris, Lyons, Lille, Bordeaux, and Nantes the situation is the same: decline at the center of the city and expansion out on the periphery and in the suburbs.

Land use is controlled primarily at the local level, using traditional permit and zoning procedures. However, the government has instituted a comprehensive program of land preemption to control urban development, through the creation of zones known as designated-development areas (*zones d'aménagement différe*, or ZAD). The system of land preemption is used in certain areas that are designated by public bodies for development or redevelopment. The program is especially appropriate to areas in the growing parts of suburbs and in some redevelopment districts in the inner cities. The aims of the system are to make sure that land is available for carrying out the public-development plan, and to ensure that the land price is not inflated because of the prospect of such future development. Giving the public the right of preemption of the land at existing values, and providing a system of arbitration for land prices, serves to dampen land speculation. At least, it keeps down land prices within the designated areas. However, land on the other side of the designated area is free to fluctuate with the market. Often such land outside the areas of demarcation may even inflate in price more rapidly as a result of the government action. Nevertheless, the program represents a significant departure from the traditional methods of planning and controlling urban land development.

Housing Production

Housing Investment

The rate of dwelling construction in France has been relatively high by European standards (see table 9-1). During the 1970s the rate of new building per 1,000 population exceeded 9, which was higher than that in

Table 9-1
France: Selected Housing-Production Statistics, 1953-1976

Housing Activities	1953	1960	1965	1970	1976
Dwellings completed (thousands)	115.3	316.6	351.0	471.5	448.9
Dwellings per 1,000 population	2.7	6.9	8.4	9.3	9.7
Housing construction as a percentage of gross domestic product	3.5	4.7	6.7	6.9	7.2
Percentage of total by type of investor					
State (reconstruction)	30.5	4.0	1.2	0.7	1.3
Public bodies (HLM)	20.9	30.3	30.2	32.2	21.6
Private	48.6	65.7	68.6	66.1	77.1

Source: United Nations, *Annual Bulletin of Housing and Building Statistics for Europe*.

most countries on the European continent. When the rate is analyzed in terms of the percentage of gross domestic product invested in housing, France again utilizes a very significant portion of its resources for the housing sector. In 1976 more than 7 percent of GDP was invested in new houses. To put this figure in perspective, it is approximately twice as much as the comparable percentage of GDP in either the United States of the United Kingdom. But it must be remembered that France was starting from a base of substantially greater housing need at the end of World War II than was either the United States or Britain and that it therefore required a higher level of investment to end the wartime shortage.

Housing Producers

In the years immediately after the war, state reconstruction agencies undertook a considerable amount of dwelling construction, accounting for 30 percent of such output as late as 1953. But these direct government activities eventually subsided, and the effort was assumed by private entities.

France has a variety of public and private housing developers. Until 1976 the bulk of the housing built had been collective housing, built by local semipublic housing entities (HLMs). However, in 1976 the amount of housing built by individuals exceeded collective housing for the first time, as a result of the activities of both individual merchant builders and individuals building houses for their own use.

Private construction has been increasing in France as public development has tended to decrease. Private developers can build both rental housing and condominiums. There are also merchant builders on the U.S. model, who build for owner occupation. The activities of these private development companies began after 1953.

Public construction is essentially done by the local housing associations known as HLMs, entities that construct publicly subsidized housing either for rent or for owner occupation. In 1976 there were 1,150 HLMs in France. An HLM operates within a specific geographic territory for its operation. During the 1950s and 1960s HLMs accounted for 40 percent of housing construction in France. The extent of their operation can be demonstrated by the fact that in 1976 HLMs owned 2.5 million rental units.

The private non-HLM sector, mostly for owner occupation, has continued to account for an increasing share of French housing. In 1976 more than three-quarters of all housing was accounted for by private construction, largely for owner occupation. The government incentives for owner occupation no doubt figure prominently in this shift.

Housing Finance

Prior to 1977 the housing-finance sector in France essentially comprised three separate parts. The first, concerned with HLM organizations, had developed since the turn of the century and was geared to building rental housing for moderate-income families. In order to finance such housing, special arrangements evolved between the savings-bank system and the HLM organizations, which had been institutionalized over the years. The second part of the housing-finance system centered on Crédit Foncier de France and its programs to support the market for financing moderate-income housing for owner occupation. The third part consisted of the commercial banks that provided housing finance largely without government support of any kind.

The housing-finance structure was geared overwhelmingly toward the financing of new housing. After all, for many years after the war, the primary need in France was for the provision of as many new housing units as possible because of the acute housing shortage.

The reform of 1977 steered the housing-finance sector onto a somewhat different course. The most important deviation was the introduction of a new program of personal housing assistance, *"l'aide personnalisée au logement"* (APL), which provides housing assistance to families based on their need and family circumstances.

New financing programs were offered as part of the 1977 reform; more importantly, the programs were extended to cover existing housing and also the purchase of older housing for the purpose of rehabilitation. An additional feature was the expansion of the program, which was aimed at encouraging home ownership among first-time home purchasers.

The French mortgage market is another quite mixed system between public and private utilization of capital (see figure 9-1). Private savings, the bulk of the funds that are utilized for mortgages, come primarily from savings banks and commercial banks. Although there are other institutions at work, such as insurance companies and credit unions, these tend to play a somewhat minor role in housing finance.

Mobilization of Savings

A variety of thrift institutions exist to accommodate the high propensity of the French to save. The savings rate in France is among the continent's highest, hovering between 17 and 18 percent of disposable income during the 1970s. All the principal thrift institutions channel some of their funds into housing.

1. The postal savings-bank system (Caisse National d'Epargne) is a traditional institution, which has been especially popular in small towns.
2. Community-based savings banks are chartered under the sponsorship of the community or department (state).
3. Building-and-loan associations (*epargne logement*) tend to specialize in savings for housing and the issuance of housing loans.
4. Commercial banks offer passbook and time deposits for household savers.

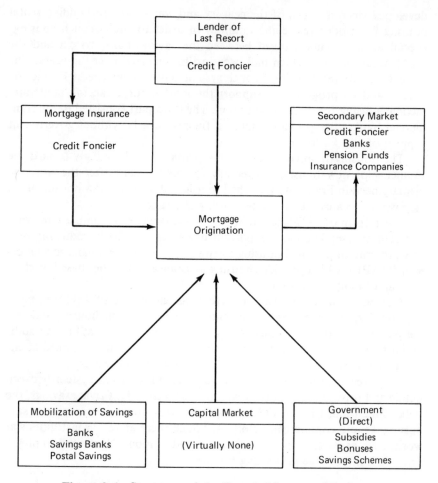

Figure 9-1. Structure of the French Mortgage Market

Financing of the HLM Associations

HLMs are community-based nonprofit enterprises that finance and build moderate-priced housing for workers. HLMs have a long history in France, going back more than a century. They began with the movement to improve the housing of workers and were originally sponsored by trade unions and private philanthropists. Over the years they have been assisted by a variety of pieces of legislation, which have molded the HLMs into the institutions they are today.

Traditionally, HLMs have relied on low-interest loans to keep down the cost of housing and the rents they charged. Initially they borrowed directly from the state, and later from private banks with government interest subsidies. Low rates of interest and capital subsidies have enabled HLMs to keep their rents relatively low. They have also built condominiums, which they sell to moderate-income families.

There is a central institution, the Bank for Loans to HLM Bodies (la Caisse des Prets Aux Organismes) that was created in 1966. This HLM Bank obtains most of its funds directly from the Deposit and Consignment Bank (La Caisse de Depots et Consignation), which is the government's central bank and repository of funds from the postal savings banks and a host of other thrift, pension, and insurance enterprises. The savings banks, postal savings banks, and some others are required to deposit their receipts in the Deposit and Consignment Bank. The HLM Bank has a direct line to the Deposit and Consignment Bank and therefore a sure source of funding (see figure 9-2).

The Deposit and Consignment Bank lends money to the HLM Bank at a low rate of interest—for example, 5.25 percent in 1977. The difference between the lending rate and market rate is made up by subsidies from the central government.

The HLM Bank in turn lends to local HLM societies at even more favorable terms of 4.5 percent per annum for a period of thirty years or more. In addition to borrowing from the Deposit and Consignment Bank, HLMs receive state subsidies and bonuses to defray their interest expenses. There is also the constant amortization of loans from the local HLM societies, which provide cash reflows. The local HLM societies, of which there are more than 1,200, make loans to builders and individuals both for rental housing and for condominium ownership.

Contractual Savings Schemes

The French have developed two interesting contractual savings schemes oriented to home purchase (see table 9-2).

1. The first contractual scheme was introduced in 1965 and is a special savings *account*. The account can be opened in an approved savings institution, which may be a building-and-loan association, a community savings bank, a commercial bank, or a post office.

The saver agrees to make a series of regular deposits to the account for a certain period, and the bank agrees to make a loan 1.5 times the contractual amount at the end of the period if the contract amount has been saved. The saver is paid interest at a rate of 2.5 percent, and an eventual loan is at 4.0 percent, or approximately 1.5 percent above the savings rate.

As an incentive the government provides a bonus equal to the amount of interest earned, thereby doubling the effective rate. The effective rate is made even higher since the total interest (including bonus) is tax free.

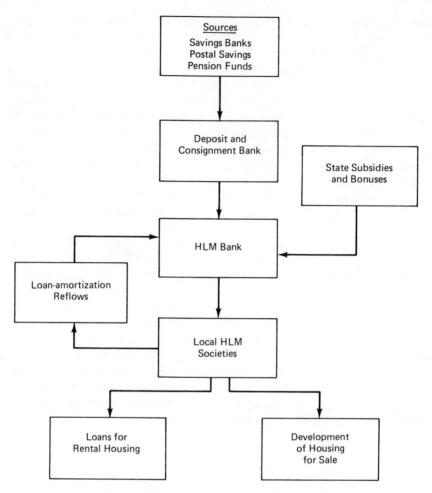

Figure 9-2. Financing the HLM Sector

2. In 1969 another scheme was introduced, known as the *house-savings plan.* A contract is required between the saver and lender in which the saver agrees to save for at least four years and to accumulate a certain sum. The institution is obliged to provide a loan 2.5 times the amount of savings. Savers receive a bonus equal to the accrued interest (tax free) if the account is not disturbed by withdrawal during the period. As in the case of the account, both the saving and borrowing rate are below comparable market rates.

In both the savings account and the savings plan, there is quid pro quo among savers and lenders. Savers accept a low rate on their savings for important reasons: (1) the government bonuses and tax exemption increase the

Table 9-2
Savings Accounts and Savings Plans in Selected Years

	1971	1977
Savings accounts (*comptes d'epargne logement*)		
Number of passbooks (thousands)	532	1,457
Amount on deposit (million francs)	6,595	24,579
Average passbook amount (thousand francs)	12.5	16.4
Number of loans (thousands)	22.3	45.5[a]
Amount of loans (million francs)	1,142	18,232[a]
Savings plans		
Number of plans (thousands)	797	3,682
Amount of deposit (million francs)	10,633	76,038
Average amount of plan (thousand francs)	11.3	20.4
Number of loans (thousands)	—	52.0[a]
Amount of loans (million francs)	—	14,508[a]

Source: Caisse des Depots et Consignations. (unpublished)
[a]Total to date.

effective yield and (2) a housing loan is guaranteed at a low rate. Lenders, on the other hand, have the advantage of receiving a steady stream of low-cost money, which can be loaned at the going rate, offering a considerable profit opportunity. This is tempered by the realization that eventually a below-market loan will have to be granted. But on balance it is a profitable situation for the lending institution.

The contractual savings schemes have been very popular as amounts under contract and in the accounts have grown dramatically. Their use in house financing has been equally extensive, figuring in about two-thirds of all individual housing transactions in 1977.

The amounts of the contractual savings plus the loan may not in themselves be enough for the entire purchase, so a second mortgage is often necessary. But the savings schemes are significant incentives to save for house purchase.

Capital-Market Resources

Capital-market resources do not play a prominent role in the primary mortgage market. Mortgage banking as it is practiced in Germany and some other countries is unknown in France. Mortgage money comes from the traditional savings and thrift institutions and from the government.

Government Social-Security Funds

In France there is a program requiring mandatory contributions from employers into a special housing fund. Each employer with more than ten employees must allocate 0.9 percent of total wages toward an investment in housing. The employer has several options for how the participation funds will be invested. Such funds can be put to either direct of indirect investment in the housing sector: new-house construction, housing loans for down payments, or home-improvement loans for workers.

Direct investment can take the following forms:

1. The firm itself may build housing.
2. The firm may have housing built on a cooperative basis in a consortium with others, such as local nonprofit HLMs.
3. Existing property may be acquired.
4. Loans may be made to employees to build their own housing.

Indirect allowable forms of the contribution are payments:

1. To nonprofit organizations specifically set up to collect such funds.
2. To professional associations that will build housing.
3. To a special government agency, the Interprofessional Housing Committee.
4. To local Chambers of Commerce.
5. To building societies.
6. To family-allowance funds.
7. To HLM organizations.

These employer contributions are significant. For example, in 1977 they accounted for 7 percent of the funds provided for building and lending on housing.

Government Bonuses

The French system of housing finance allows the finance minister to grant bonuses or premiums (*primes*) for certain kinds of socially desirable construction. Bonuses are paid to the lending institutions, and they result in a decrease in the interest rate charged. Such a decrease must be passed on in lowering the rents to tenants or the market prices of condominiums. The system of offering bonuses is rather complicated, with actual amounts paid based on the square footage of the housing built. Builders apply for these special premiums; if successful, they can then go to a variety of lending sources to obtain the loan. The conditions and terms of the loans are set by the finance minister.

Crédit Foncier de France

Crédit Foncier, established in 1852, is the overseer of the entire mortgage market and sets the policies for mortgage lending. Although it began as a private company, it has since been nationalized. It obtains its own funds by issuing bonds to the public as well as by accepting savings deposits from individuals. These funds are available to be reloaned to savings institutions or, under some conditions, directly to builders. Crédit Foncier has the guardianship of the mortgage market and serves a function somewhat analogous to that of both the Federal Home Loan Bank Board (FHLBB) and the Federal National Mortgage Association (FNMA) in the United States.

Although it is government controlled, Crédit Foncier is a commercial company that pays a corporate income tax and is required to make a return on its capital; its function and form are analogous to those of the Federal National Mortgage Association. As with the FNMA, its stock is held by private shareholders. It is a private, profit-making company, federally chartered but controlled by the state. The management of Crédit Foncier is in the hands of a governor appointed by the French cabinet who is always a high official in the French finance ministry.

Almost 30 percent of the funds provided in the mortgage market are from public-sector institutions, primarily for the HLM housing programs. Approximately half of the mortgage money is provided by the private banking sector. Crédit Foncier directly provides about 10 percent of housing finance.

Mortgage Loans

There are essentially four kinds of mortgage loans issued on noncommercial property: (1) assisted loans for moderate-income families aspiring to ownership, (2) unassisted loans approved by Crédit Foncier, (3) private loans not eligible for rediscounting by Crédit Foncier, and (4) low-interest loans under contractual savings accounts and/or plans.

Access to Ownership. The access-to-ownership program is designed for persons whose income and family situation meet certain conditions and who are buying a principal residence, usually for the first time. Lenders for the program are the government-controlled agencies, Crédit Foncier, Crédit Agricole, and Crédit Immobilier. Terms offered for such loans are quite favorable, and the interest is below market. The mortgage amount depends on the section of the country, the income of the family, and the family circumstances. For a house that qualifies, the loan can be for a maximum of twenty years at an interest rate of 8.10 percent for the first nine years, rising to 10.9 percent for the last ten years. Both the beginning and ending rates are less than the market mortgage rate, which, for example, was in the neighborhood of 12 percent in 1979. Mortgage loans can be for either new housing, existing housing, or older existing housing purchased for rehabilitation. The income limit for participation in the program in the Paris region for a family of six is approximately $25,000 per year. The maximum amount of the mortgage obtainable under such a program is in the neighborhood of $85,000 in the Paris region.

Eligible Conventional Loans. What are known as conventional loans (*prets conventionnes*, or PC) are those that meet conditions laid down by Crédit-Foncier. Eligible lenders of conventional loans are all banks, savings banks, and others that are approved by Crédit Foncier. Conventional loans (PCs) can be discounted in the secondary mortgage market by Crédit Foncier. This is the principal advantage to the private financial institutions participating in this particular program. Interest rates of PCs are set by Crédit-Foncier, based on reference rates of interest, which reflect the conditions in the market at the time. As of January 1978, for example, the rate for conventional loans was established as 12.60 percent.

Conventional loans have no ceiling on either the price of the house or the income of the purchaser. This program is designed for those households that do not meet the conditions of the access-for-ownership programs. Eligible properties can be either new housing, existing housing, or housing purchased for rehabilitation.

Ineligible Loans. Private banks make some loans that do not meet the eligibility conditions laid down by Crédit Foncier. Ineligibility might be the result of the loan-to-value ratio being too high, or the interest rate charged may exceed Crédit Foncier ceilings.

Contractual Savings Schemes. The rate of interest on contractual savings schemes is fixed below the market rate as part of the deal. Since the total amount of the contracted loan may be insufficient in itself for the entire price, an additional loan may be required.

Secondary Mortgage Market

The secondary mortgage market (*marché hypothecaire*) was established in 1966 under the direction of Crédit Foncier, which determines eligibility of those institutions admitted into the market (see table 9-3). Commercial banks, various savings banks, and other institutions such as insurance companies and pension funds may be members of this market. Standards for loans, in terms of appraisals, loan-to-value ratios, and other characteristics are established by Crédit Foncier. In the French secondary-market system, the mortgages themselves do not change hands. Rather, Crédit Foncier allows the lending institutions to issue *bills of mobilization*, which they sell in the capital market, backed by eligible mortgages. These sales enable lending institutions to obtain additional mortgage money from the capital

Table 9-3
Secondary-Mortgage-Market Activity, 1967-1978
(millions of francs)

Year	Total Activity	Annual Volume	As Percentage of Total Originations
1967	1,766	1,766	6.8
1968	6,128	4,362	14.2
1969	11,788	5,660	15.9
1970	15,329	3,541	10.1
1971	20,875	5,546	12.1
1972	30,624	9,749	16.0
1973	44,174	13,550	21.1
1974	53,891	9,717	15.2
1975	63,373	9,482	12.4
1976	80,192	16,819	17.0
1977	93,616	13,424	13.7
1978	114,833	21,217	18.7

Source: *Banque* (May 1979).

market. Crédit Foncier can, at its discretion, enter directly into this market and purchase such bills itself, using its own funds. However, the primary markets for such mortgage-backed securities are pension funds and banks. Secondary-market activity in France represents from 15 to 20 percent of total new-mortgage originations.

Lender of Last Resort

The lender of last resort is the Crédit Foncier de France. This venerable institution, established in 1850 as a private bank but since nationalized, is both regulator and lender in the housing market. It establishes conditions for mortgage lending and eligibility for participation in the secondary mortgage market, makes directs loans under some conditions, and accepts deposits. Its function is analogous to that of the FHLBB, the FNMA, and the Canada Mortgage and Housing Corporation all rolled into one.

Financing an Individual House

The most interesting point concerns the housing-savings plan that has some similarities with and some differences from the German contractual system. The example used previously can be utilized to demonstrate how it works in practice (see table 9-4). It will be assumed that it is possible to purchase a house with only one mortgage once the required savings have been ac-

Table 9-4
France: An Illustrative Example of Financing the Purchase of an
Individual House

1. Value of house: U.S. $50,000 (F 210,000)
2. Mortgage terms:
   a. 71% of value (U.S. $35,715, F 150,000)
   b. 5% per annum for 15 years
   c. Payment of U.S. $282.43 (F 1, 186) per month
3. Equity of 29% = U.S. $14,285 (F 60,000)

Notes:
1. The savings plan in the illustration requires deposits of U.S. $2,970 (F 12,474) per year for 4 years (or proportionately less for a longer savings period) in order to accumulate U.S. $14,285 (F 60,000) at the end of the term at a savings interest rate of 3.5%, in addition to a bonus of 3.5% from the state.
2. The loan is predicated on a maximum of 2.5 times the amount saved, which for a house with a value of U.S. $50,000 (F 210,000) requires a loan of U.S. $35,715 (F 150,000).

cumulated, and, once again, that the house has a value of $50,000. According to the terms of the housing-savings plan, a mortgage would be available to an individual for a maximum of 2.5 times the amount saved, which for a $50,000 house requires a loan of $35,715, which in turn requires savings of $14,285.

The French savings plan requires that savers have a plan in operation for at least four years at an approved savings institution. Savers are paid at the rate of 3.5 percent interest; if such savings meet the minimum time requirement and are used for house purchase, an additional 3.5 percent bonus is given. Thus the effective interest rate, if the funds are used for house purchase, is 7 percent—actually more, since it is tax free.

If the individual were to make deposits of $2,970 per year for four years at the contract rate of interest, plus the bonus, these funds would accumulate at the end of the four-year period to $14,285. This is a relatively high rate of savings, which could be approximately halved if the term were increased from four years to eight years. But there is flexibility on this point.

Once the savings have been accumulated, the individual can apply for a first-mortgage loan, which in this case would amount to 71 percent of value or $35,715, would have a maturity of fifteen years, and would bear an interest rate of 5 percent per annum. The interest rate of 5 percent represents the 3.5-percent savings rate plus a 1.5-percent fee for administrative charges. The owner's equity in this case amounts to 29 percent, or $14,285, which was the result of savings plus bonuses from the state. The result of this arrangement is a monthly mortgage payment of only $282.43 per month, which is considerably lower than what one would obtain on similar housing in the United States or the United Kingdom, or even under the German housing-savings plan.

Here again is another example of the benefit of a low rate of interest for house purchase. With the low 5-percent, it is possible to have a very short term to maturity of only fifteen years and yet to have a low monthly payment. This housing-savings plan produces a low payment and appears to provide the appropriate incentive to save. Here again, the success of the program depends on the ability to save a considerable amount, almost 30 percent of the value. But given the ability to save, which is characteristic of the French, this particular scheme produces considerable benefits for the home purchaser.

Housing Consumption

The Market for Existing Housing

In France approximately 75 percent of the mortgage funds are for new housing. This is considerably different from the picture in the United States and United Kingdom, where the reverse is true, with the majority of mortgage funds going for existing housing. This situation will undoubtedly begin to shift as owner occupation increases and as the new housing programs that specifically include housing finance for existing units become more operational. Prior to the housing reforms of 1977, mortgage money was not easy to come by for an existing house.

On the market an existing unit typically sells at a discount of about 20 percent compared with a comparable new unit. There is a market for older houses of pre-1930 vintage in the inner cities. With the availability of financing of rehabilitation under the 1977 housing programs, such housing is increasingly attractive since it often offers advantageous central location and prized architectural features that are lacking in new housing (see tables 9-5 and 9-6).

Home Ownership

The federal government is now supporting a policy of increasing owner occupation. "The guiding principle is to make home ownership a real possibility for every Frenchman." [3] In 1976, for the first time, construction of individual houses exceeded all collective housing. In 1977 the trend continued, there being 225,000 individual houses built as against 220,000 collective units. The various government incentives to finance home ownership, such as the access-to-ownership mortgages, bonus contractual saving

Table 9-5
France: Household Budget by Category of Expenditure for Selected Years

	1959	1974	1980
Food	37.3	25.9	22.4
Clothing	11.5	8.7	7.8
Housing	17.5	22.2	22.5
Loding	5.8	10.3	10.7
Utilities and other	11.7	11.9	11.2
Health related	8.3	13.8	17.3
Transportation and telecommunication	8.4	10.6	11.7
Culture and leisure	7.8	8.6	9.4
Hotels, cafes, and so forth	9.2	10.2	8.9
Total	100.0	100.0	100.0

plans, and favorable taxation, point to future dominance of owner occupation over renting.

Tax Policies Toward Housing

French tax policy toward housing is quite favorable. For an owner, interest on a mortgage is deductible during the first ten years after purchase. The limit on the amount of interest that can be deducted is 7,000 francs plus 1,000 francs for each person in the household. For a principal residence, no

Table 9-6
Loan Amounts by Purpose
(millions of francs)

Year	New House	Old House	Rehabilitation	Total
1967	20,351	3,666	1,795	25,812
1968	22,878	5,469	2,259	30,605
1969	26,786	6,199	2,576	35,562
1970	27,799	4,219	2,716	34,736
1971	34,427	7,440	3,754	45,621
1972	43,009	12,131	5,820	60,961
1973	46,365	11,953	5,571	63,882
1974	50,512	9,629	3,979	64,120
1975	58,307	12,554	5,338	76,199
1976	70,070	21,540	721	98,820
1977	71,800	18,700	7,700	98,200
1978	80,000	23,600	9,900	113,500

capital-gains tax is levied on the profit on sale. There are also substantial tax incentives for rental housing. Interest on loans is a deductible expense with no limit on the amount of the deduction. All real-estate taxes are also eligible for deduction. Depreciation is also allowed for rental properties. In addition, the French tax code permits a deduction of 25 percent of income for management insurance and other expenses. For owner-occupied housing, there is an exemption of local property taxes for fifteen years after purchase.

Rental Housing

Rent control began in 1914, during World War I, and was gradually extended to cover all of the housing stock. However, since 1950 there has been movement to eliminate the controls gradually. Today only 50 percent of the French housing stock is under control. Since the wartime shortage has ended, the reasons for enduring controls are no longer compelling. The extensive use of government subsidies to lower rent in the privately built sector, plus the existence of housing allowances, has kept rents at a reasonable level, thus dampening political pressure to extend controls (see table 9-7).

For personal housing aid a formula is used to determine the amount for which each household is eligible. The formula takes into consideration the family size, income, section of the country, and the amount paid in rent or

Table 9-7
Characteristics of Loans for Rental Housing

	HLM Organizations	Collectors of the 1% Housing Tax	Others
Amount	95% of estimated costs	65% of estimated costs	55% of estimated costs
Terms	34 years, during which no amortization of principal the first 2 years, and no interest payment until 2 years and 3 months	34 years, during which no amortization of principal the first 2 years	
Repayment Terms			
	First and second year: nothing	First and second year: 5.50% of the amount outstanding	
	Third year: 4.21% of the amount outstanding	Third year: 5.58% of the amount of loan	
	Fourth year: 5.7% of the amount outstanding	Fourth year and all following: interest increasing at a rate of 3.25% per annum	

in mortgage payments. Aid is not restricted to renters; owner occupants are also eligible if they meet the other criteria.

Assistance for rental housing, Prets Aidés Locatifs (PAL), is available to the HLM organizations and also to private, limited-profit corporations. Lenders are the HLM Bank for local HLM associations and Crédit Foncier for other developers that qualify for the program.

In order to qualify for loans under the rental-assistance program, developers must agree to fix rents at a low break-even level, based on below-market financing for the duration of the loan. The amount of the loan is 95 percent of value for the HLM and only 55 percent of value for the private developers. The repayment period is thirty-four years for both. The rate of interest is an average of 6.18 percent for HLMs and 6.88 percent for private developers. Terms of the loan are graduated from 5.5 percent during the first six years to 9.85 percent during the last 17 years. For the HLMs there is a two-year grace period for interest payments.

Illustrative Example of the Rental-Subsidy System (Les Aides a la Pierre—PLA)

In the example shown in table 9-8, the housing development would be eligible for a capital-cost subsidy from the government of up to 20 percent, which would lower the development cost and the mortgage and debt-service requirements accordingly. There would also be some exemption of property taxes. Since the HLMs are nonprofit, there would be no requirement for a return on invested capital.

Interest rates gradually increase, by 3.5 percent per year, up to the approximate market rate. Thus the break-even rent is lower in the earlier years than in the later years because of the degressive nature of this part of the subsidy. Nonetheless, for the first six years of operation, rent charged by the HLM would be 64 percent of the unsubsidized economic-rent level.

If the same housing were developed by a private developer, it would be subject to some of the same subsidies, but not as extensively. Under private development there would still be a cost bonus. However, the loan would be for only 55 percent of value, requiring a considerable equity investment on the part of the private developers.

It is interesting to note that the rents charged under both the HLM and the private-developer methods are not significantly different. This is because the HLM, having little equity in the development, has a relatively large debt service. On the other hand, the private developer with a considerable equity in the project has low debt service, but a return on the large equity investment. Thus both are able to offer to qualified tenants rents that are substantially below market levels.

Table 9-8
Example of Housing-Subsidy Scheme in France

	Nonsubsidized Prototype	Subsidized		Comments
		HLM Society	Private Developers	
Development cost (less state bonus)	$3,000,000 —	$3,000,000 (600,000) 2,400,000	$3,000,000 (600,000) 2,400,000	Special bonuses of up to 20% of development costs are available from the state
Mortgage Investor equity	2,400,000 600,000	2,280,00 120,000	1,320,000 1,080,000	95% loan for HLMs and 55% loan for private developer
Debt service	255,000	153,000	88,000	Local taxes not paid
Operating costs	180,000	150,000	150,000	Private developers can take a 6% return on investment
Return on equity	40,000	—	65,000	
Break-even rent	395	252	252	Approximate rent needed, first year of operation
Actual rent to tenant	395	Years: 1-3: $252, increasing each year thereafter	Years: 1-2: $252, increasing each year thereafter	Rents will rise each year because of the degressive nature of the subsidy
Subsidized rent as percentage of economic rent		63% in year 1, increasing to 87% after 30 years	63% in year 1, increasing to 87% after 30 years	Subsidy decreases over time as rents are allowed to rise

References

1. John S. Banta, "France: Public Ownership from ZUP to ZAD," in *The Government Land Developers*, Neal Alison Roberts, editor (Lexington, Mass.: Lexington Books, 1977).
2. Pierre Le Besnerais, "La Réforme du Financement du Logement," *Banque*, no. 371 (March 1978).
3. Crédit Foncier de France, "Réforme du Financement du Logement" (Paris, 1978).
4. "Current Trends and Policies in the Field of Housing, Building and Planning," National Monograph of France prepared for the United Nations, Economic Commission for Europe (April 1978).
5. Serge Montagnon "Le Marché Hypothécaire in 1978," *Banque*, no. 384 (May 1979).
6. Morris L. Sweet and S. George Walters, *Mandatory Housing Programs: A Comparative International Analysis*, (New York: Praeger Publishers, 1976).
7. Union de Crédit pour le Batiment, *Exercise 1978* (Paris 1979).

10 Housing in Switzerland

Housing Policy

The Swiss government had not been an active participant in the housing sector prior to 1942. Although not a combatant in World War II, Switzerland nevertheless suffered some effects of the war. The country experienced internal migration from rural areas to urban centers that greatly increased the demand for housing; but as in other European countries, housing was lower in priority than industrial production. As a result the housing situation worsened and the government was forced to intervene.

Actions that were considered temporary at the time included imposition of rent controls and capital grants to private builders to stimulate apartment construction. After the war these measures were difficult to reverse, since the housing shortage remained acute. Thus the government reluctantly continued controls on rents and incentives to apartment developers.

By 1970 formal rent controls were lifted. The housing shortage had been eliminated; in fact, in 1975 large numbers of vacant apartments became evident. But the government had become committed to formal support of the housing sector. There was strong political pressure for this support to continue. In 1972 this commitment was codified in the Confederation Constitution:

> The Confederation shall take measures aimed at encouraging the construction of housing, especially through a lowering of costs, and providing the opportunity to owning a dwelling or house. Federal legislation shall determine the conditions for giving assistance grants.
>
> The Confederation shall have the following particular powers:
>
> a) to facilitate the purchasing and development of sites for housing construction;
> b) to support efforts aimed at improving housing and environmental conditions for families, persons with limited capacity, the elderly, the disabled, and persons in need of care;
> c) to research into the housing market and into building methods as well as to encourage rationalization in building; and
> d) to ensure that capital is obtained for housing construction. [1]

Although it is constitutionally committed to housing, the Swiss government has only slight involvement in housing by European standards.

Since 1942 only 5 percent of the housing built has received some form of government assistance. And the assistance programs themselves tend to be modest interest-rate subsidies, with some capital grants. This no doubt reflects both the limited role of government in the Swiss social system and the high level of income and employment of its citizens.

In spite of a strong and stable economy and high income levels, the Swiss exhibit the lowest rate of home ownership in Europe. Scarcely 10 percent of the urban population are owners. In addition, the cost of owning a house is also the highest in Europe. The government has accepted the policy of increasing the rate of ownership; and in 1975 it adopted the Law on Assistance to Housing and Owner Occupiers of Dwelling, which gives assistance to those wishing to purchase housing in the form of government guarantees to lenders.

Housing construction is overwhelmingly private, with government accounting for a small fraction of building. Unlike the situation in other nations on the continent, cooperatives account for only a small share of dwelling construction. Most of the housing built is in the form of apartments for rental occupancy, although the number of condominiums for owner occupancy is increasing. See table 10-1 for housing-production statistics for Switzerland.

The Structure of the Housing-Finance Sector

Switzerland is a nation that does not have the array of specialized housing-finance institutions characteristic of most other advanced industrial nations. Although housing naturally requires a large share of national

Table 10-1
Switzerland: Selected Housing-Production Statistics, 1953-1977

Housing Activities	1953	1960	1965	1970	1977
Dwellings completed (thousands)	23.8	39.0	59.9	65.6	34.8
Dwellings per 1,000 population	6.0	9.4	10.1	10.5	5.5
Housing construction as a percentage of gross domestic product	5.0	7.1	7.3	6.7	—
Percentage of total by type of investor					
Public bodies	0.6	2.6	2.7	2.5	3.5
Cooperatives	15.9	12.6	11.9	13.7	8.3
Private	83.5	84.8	85.4	83.8	28.2
Individuals	45.0	47.1	45.0	44.1	52.4
Others	38.5	37.7	40.4	39.7	35.8

Source: United Nations, *Annual Bulletin of Housing and Building Statistics for Europe.*

financial resources, the needs of this sector are handled by commercial and savings banks, insurance companies, and finance-company subsidiaries of banks (see figure 10-1).

Savings Institutions

The Swiss banking system is unique because of its ability to attract money from all over the world. This attractiveness to worldwide investors has produced a banking system that is much larger than is required for the country's internal needs.

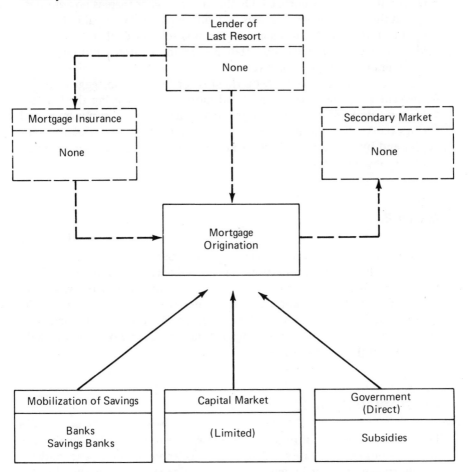

Figure 10-1. Structure of the Mortgage Market in Switzerland

The Swiss are thrifty, saving an average of 13 to 14 percent of personal disposable income. Thus the savings banks have been able to tap a large steady fund of money, which they utilize for mortgages and construction financing.

Mortgage Financing

In Switzerland mortgage practices tend to vary with the nationality of the cantons. In the German-speaking areas, it is customary to have interest-only mortgages (on the first mortgage). If a second mortgage is required, however, it is usually amortized. On the first mortgage there is no amortization and the mortgage never comes due, although it may be paid off at any time. For interest-only mortgages, the loan is redeemed when the house is sold. However, in French- and Italian-speaking cantons, mortgages are usually amortized over twenty years.

The common practice in Switzerland is for the first mortgage to be for 65 percent of value. Second and third mortgages may bring the loan-to-value ratio up to 85 percent. First mortgages are made by commercial and savings banks. Second mortgages are usually made through finance companies and by individuals. There is an active market in these junior mortgages among individuals.

Interest Rates

Swiss interest rates tend to be very low in comparison with those of other countries. This no doubt reflects of the very stable conditions in Switzerland since World War II and the country's low rate of inflation. The Swiss franc (Sfr) is the world's most stable currency. Interest rates on mortgages would typically be in the neighborhood of 6 percent in Switzerland when they might be close to double that in England and France and one and one-half times that in the United States.

Lender of Last Resort

There is no lender of last resort in the Swiss system, there being an absence of such a dominating entity. There is also no secondary mortgage market, and mortgages are not bought and traded. The system is marked by the absence of specialized circuits for housing finance.

Financing an Individual House

By transferring the previously used example to Switzerland, we can observe this unique mortgage system (see table 10-2). It is common in the German-speaking portion of Switzerland to have first-mortgage loans that are nonamortized and have no fixed maturity. Let us examine how this would operate, using the example of the $50,000 house. (A house in Switzerland would no doubt be much more expensive, but in order to maintain comparability the same example is used.)

The home purchaser in the German-speaking canton would more than likely obtain a first mortgage of 65 percent of value on a nonamortized basis with no maturity, at a rate of 6 percent per annum. Thus for the first mortgage the repayment required would be $162.50 per month. The first mortgage would be paid off only when there was a transaction involving the sale of the house.

Let us assume in this case that a second mortgage is needed and that one could be obtained for 20 percent of the value for a term of ten years, at a 7-percent annual rate. Second mortgages, unlike first mortgages, are usually on an amortized basis.

The owner's equity in this situation amounts to 15 percent of the value, and the total montly payments considering both mortgages are $278.60 per month. This is quite low, even with two mortgages.

Housing Consumption

Home Ownership

Home ownership in Switzerland is much less common than in other European countries. Three factors are usually cited for the low rate of ownership in Switzerland.

1. There is an adequate supply of rental housing. Real estate is a favored investment and investors seem satisfied with a low return from rents since capital appreciation is great.
2. Housing costs are quite high. In a small mountainous nation, urban land is relatively scarce and very expensive, tending to drive up housing costs. Also housing is constructed to very high-quality standards, because the Swiss believe that buildings should last forever, which also drives up the price.
3. Tax policies keep the prices high. Property taxes are low, so the cost of holding property is slight. However, when property is sold, a variety of taxes and levies are imposed, serving as a disincentive. As a result, little real estate is traded.

Table 10-2
Switzerland: An Illustrative Example of Financing the Purchase of an Individual House

1. Value of house: U.S. $50,000 (SFr 82,500)
2. Mortgage terms:
   a. First mortgage
      1. Nonamortized loan, no fixed maturity
      2. 6% per annum
      3. Monthly payment = U.S. $162.50 (SFr 268)
   b. Second mortgage
      1. 20% of value, U.S. $20,000 (SFr 33,000)
      2. 7% per annum for 10 years
      3. Monthly payments = U.S. $115.10 (SFr 192)
   c. Owner's equity = U.S. $15,000 (SFr 24,750)
3. Total monthly payment for both mortgages = $278.60 (SFr 460)

The government had adopted policies to increase home ownership. Legislation allowing condominium sales was enacted in 1970 to encourage sale of apartments to their occupants. In 1975 the government began a program to guarantee 90 percent of the purchase price to facilitate sales. Yet despite their efforts, actual housing purchases are slow because no one wishes to sell.

Rental Housing

From World War II to 1970, formal rent controls existed in Switzerland. Any rent changes were subject to official approval. The controls were completely removed in 1970 but were partially reintroduced in 1972 because of political pressure. The present situation in Switzerland is that a tenant may submit what he or she considers an unreasonable rent to a special court for arbitration; this is much like the system in West Germany. Tenants have very secure tenure, and it is difficult to obtain an eviction since notice to evict can be set aside for up to three years should the court decide that the eviction places the tenant in a difficult personal situation.

Housing Subsidies

Housing-subsidy policy in Switzerland has evolved through three phases. From 1942 to 1949 the government made available grants for a portion of building cost to private investors. From 1958 to 1966 the Swiss government made grants to cover a portion of the interest expense. The third phase of subsidies, beginning in 1966, again concentrated on subsidies to lower the interest rates paid on rental housing plus small capital grants for housing of special groups.

The method of calculating the subsidy is indeed quite interesting. For a qualified housing development, a break-even rent is calculated. Then the initial rents in the first year are set 23 percent below the rent required to break even. The rents are allowed to increase by 3 percent per year over a twenty-five-year period. The shortfall in the rents over the first ten years is met by a special loan for the deficit. At the end of ten years the rents will have risen to the break-even level. After that, as the rents continue to increase by 3 percent per year, the additional funds are utilized to pay back the earlier deficit loan. There are also supplementary subsidies for low-income families, which reduce the rent paid another 7 percent. For the elderly and other special groups, the supplement can be as high as 19 percent. These subsidies are granted in areas of the country where there is a demonstrated shortage.

The basic rent-reduction scheme in Switzerland allows eligible tenants to pay a below-market rent (see figure 10-2). The landlord is initially subsidized to cover the shortfall. The system requires rents to rise each year until the rents are equivalent to the original break-even rent when the subsidy is terminated. An example is shown in table 10-3. The rent is initially established at $310.00 per month rather than the required break-even rate of $395.00. However, the low rent will then rise by a rate of 3 percent per year. Over the first ten years, the increases would make the rent rise to the market rate.

The way the system works is that the landlord is issued a loan to cover the shortfall between the economic rent and the below-market rent that is being charged. At the end of ten years rents are up to the market rate, but the rent increases continue even beyond that. From years ten to twenty-five, the 3-percent increases are used to pay off the loans that were necessary during the first ten years to cover the shortfall. This is a complicated method of financing what is in effect a graduated-payment mortgage. The extent of the subsidy can be deepened, up to 30 percent for low-income families, and up to 49 percent of the economic rent for the elderly and the handicapped.

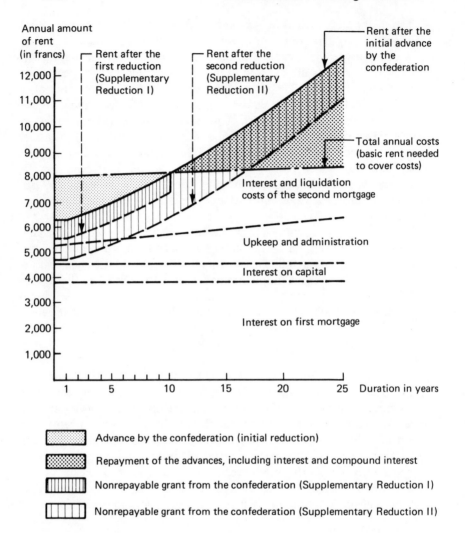

Figure 10-2. Diagram Illustrating the System of Rent Reduction in Switzerland

Table 10-3
Switzerland: Example of a Typical Housing-Subsidy Scheme Compared with Unsubsidized Development

	Nonsubsidized Prototype	Interest-Rate Subsidy	Comments
Development costs	$3,000,000	$3,000,000	Assuming comparable costs of construction
Mortgage	2,400,000	2,700,000	
Investor equity	610,000	300,000	
Debt service	255,000	286,000	
Operating costs	180,000	180,000	
Return on equity	40,000	18,000	
Break-even rent	395/month	403	
Actual rent to tenant	395/month	Years: 1 310 5 359 10 417 25 649	Rents are set 23% below break-even rent for first year, and rise 3.5% per annum thereafter until loan is amortized
Subsidized rent as percentage of economic rent	—		76% first year, increasing to 100% in 7 years

Reference

1. Federal Department of Economic Affairs, "Current Trends and Policies in the Field of Housing, Building and Planning in Switzerland" (Berne, 1978).

11 Housing in Sweden

Housing Policy

In the twentieth century the rate of urbanization among nations has certainly been uneven. Sweden, for example, is a country that urbanized late. Its status as an industrial nation was established only well after that of the other countries of Western Europe. In 1930 more than half of Sweden's population was still rural; yet today Sweden has been transformed into a nation that is 80 percent urban.

Such rapid urbanization did not come about without problems. Rapid urbanization created a severe housing shortage as the ability of the cities to provide housing was outstripped by the tremendous migration from the countryside. The problems in the 1930s became more acute in the next decade because of the housing shortage induced by World War II. Although Sweden was not a combatant, it, like other nations, had to curtail housing production during the war years because of economic disruptions. As a consequence of the severe housing shortage, which had been two decades in the making, the nation began an ambitious program of housing production following the war. Sweden's dedication is demonstrated by the fact that it had the highest rate of home building of any nation in the world during the 1960s. The fruit of this effort became evident by 1970, when the housing shortage was finally over after two decades of steady achievement.

The Role of Government in the Housing Sector

Swedish housing policy, as stated by the Riksdag, is as follows:

> The whole population should be provided with sound, spacious, well planned and appropriately equipped dwellings of good quality at a reasonable cost. [1]

To meet these ambitious goals, the government has assumed a very active role in the housing sector. Housing as an activity has substantial levels of both public and private participation, which have been institutionalized since the end of World War II. In fact, the distinction between public and private roles is blurred.

Implementation of housing policy is organized around certain principles.

Well-Organized Municipal Planning. Sweden has a tradition of strong planning at the local (municipal or commune) level. Private housing production must be coordinated with local plans in order to occur and in order to obtain special government assistance.

Active Municipal Land Policy. Through an extensive land-banking system, most land that is developed into housing and related urban uses must be purchased from or through the local municipalities. A private market for land, such as exists in most countries in North America and Europe, is nonexistent in Sweden.

Rational Housing Production. Each year the government sets housing targets and manipulates the provision of credit into the housing sector to meet the stated production goals, using both direct and indirect methods of allocation.

State Aid. This takes the form of loans and grants for construction and modernization of dwellings. Almost every housing transaction involves some meaningful participation by the state in the form of preferential low-interest loans or other lenient government loan policy.

Grants. Special housing allowances and grants are available to groups with limited economic resources or special housing needs, such as low-income persons, the elderly, and the handicapped.

Rent Legislation. Although rent controls as such have been phased out in Sweden, the government is still active in arbitrating and legislating issues that are mutual concerns of owners and tenants.

Tax Policies. Consideration of housing-policy goals is a factor in formulating taxation measures. The government believes that tax policies should be relatively neutral as incentives between choice of tenure.

Housing-Policy Administration

Housing policy is administered at the national level by the Ministry of Housing and Physical Planning, which has five divisions that carry out the regional allocation of funds provided by the government for housing construction, administration of regulations concerning loans and grants, establishing standards, and conducting technical studies (see figure 11-1).

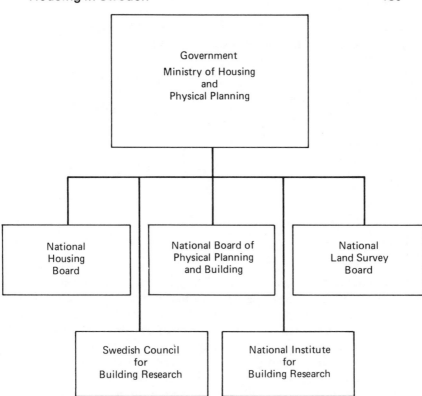

Figure 11-1. Organization of the Ministry of Housing and Physical Planning

The state and the municipalities have joint responsibility for implementing housing policy. The central government's function is mainly to provide the economic resources, usually in the form of loans and grants to housing producers and even to households. Grants to the municipalities, enable them to implement their land-banking programs. Municipalities, on the other hand, are responsible for ensuring the quality of the housing that is produced, for the housing environment, and for the provision of local public services.

Housing Production

Construction during the postwar period has been very high, with Sweden, a small country, producing more than 1 million units each decade (see table 11-1). Between 1945 and 1964, 1.2 million units were produced. From 1965 to 1974 another 1 million units were completed. Thus for a considerable

Table 11-1
Sweden: Selected Construction Statistics, 1953-1977

Housing Activities	1953	1960	1965	1970	1977
Dwellings completed (thousands)	51.9	68.3	96.8	109.8	54.9
Dwellings per 1,000 population	7.3	9.1	12.5	13.6	6.7
Housing construction as a percentage of gross domestic investment	5.0	5.0	6.2	4.9	3.9
Percentage of total by type of investor					
State, local authorities	38.7	31.1	41.1	4.3	1.6
Semipublic bodies	—	—	—	38.3	16.9
Cooperatives	20.6	29.5	22.2	15.6	9.7
Private	40.7	39.4	36.7	41.8	71.8
Percentage given state aid	—	—	91.9	88.3	87.5

Source: United Nations, *Annual Bulletin of Housing and Building Statistics for Europe.*

time Sweden had the highest home-building rate in all of Europe. In the early 1960s the rate of dwelling construction averaged over 12 units per 1,000 inhabitants. Since then it has gone down considerably, as the basic housing shortage is now over. In 1977 the rate of dwelling construction was down to 6.6 new units per 1,000 inhabitants (see table 11-2).

Sweden has one of the highest standards of housing in the world by almost any measure. One such measure that is often used is the ration of dwellings to population. In 1975 Sweden had a total of 430 housing units per 1,000 inhabitants, one of the world's highest ratios. Ratios approaching 400 are considered excellent.

Table 11-2
Housing Construction over the Period 1951-1977

Year	Average Number per Annum	Completed Dwellings Number per 1,000 Population per Annum	Percentage of Single-Family Houses
1951-1955	50,300	7.0	23
1956-1960	64,200	8.6	27
1961-1965	82,800	10.8	29
1966-1970	102,900	12.9	29
1971-1975	93,800	11.5	44
1972	104,000	12.8	36
1973	97,500	12.0	45
1974	85,300	10.4	55
1975	74,500	9.1	63
1976	55,800	6.8	72
1977	54,900	6.7	75

Source: Ministry of Housing and Physical Planning (unpublished).

Although there is substantial government support, publicly owned residences account for less than 4 percent of Sweden's housing stock. The amount of housing owned by the large nonprofit housing enterprises and by cooperatives is quite substantial, accounting for 20.2 percent and 14.3 percent, respectively. Such housing has been constructed with considerable government assistance, due both to the nature of Swedish housing finance, and to the government's commitment to the private nonprofit sector.

The percentage of single-family houses has grown dramatically since the mid-1970s. Immediately after World War II, most of the houses were built in large blocks of flats, primarily to be rented. However, in 1976 more than 70 percent of new houses were single-family units. There has been a decided shift away from the apartment unit toward owner occupation.

The Land-Development Process

In Sweden unimproved land may be purchased ahead of development by the municipality. Further, what development occurs must usually be on land that has already been purchased by local government and that has at one time been under government ownership. In this way land passes first from private hands—usually in agricultural use—into public hands, where it remains until it is resold or leased to private builders or to private individuals for their own homes. During this process the speculative element of profit will have been wrung out of the transactions.

Sweden's expropriation law allows a public body to take land and, in case of dispute, to have the matter of compensation settled by the courts. However, the courts will put a very exacting test on the land owner to prove that the current land price is higher than what the government is prepared to offer. The government will set the price at what it was ten years before, with some allowance made for inflation. The object is to take away that component of the land value attributable to speculation about a potential urban use. In this way Sweden has been successful in keeping the price of land low. It has therefore been able to keep new housing prices low, since the land component is not grossly out of line. However, a problem exists in the case of resale. Once a house has been sold initially at the low price, which has been dictated by the government, it can be resold at a price frequently one-third to 50 percent higher, which is more reflective of the going market price. This is more of a theoretical than a practical problem, since the person who realized the gain would be ineligible for a repeat of all the special subsidies and would have a long wait for a new house.

In Sweden there is an additional lever, since government financing is not available to those developments that do not conform to local land-use regulations. This means, in effect, that housing built on land that has not gone through the wringer of public ownership is not eligible for government subsidies, which puts such housing at a considerable disadvantage in Sweden.

Money is made available through the central government through loans to municipalities so that they can acquire land for future use. The local government has to repay these loans, and therefore must charge enough for land to be able to recoup the public investment. But the municipalities are under severe constraints as to what they can charge for land they own, since the government will not allow a municipality to charge a developer more than what it considers a reasonable price. The central government maintains an extensive system of prototype costs developed for various kinds of buildings in different parts of the country. If the prices that are charged for housing, including the land component, exceed these prototype costs, then government financing will not be made available. Thus municipalities may even be forced to lower the price they wish to charge for land in order to make it conform to the central-government prototypes.

Structure of the Housing-Finance Sector

In Sweden the typical dichotomy between private and public finance tends to vanish, since almost 90 percent of all construction is financed in some way by state housing loans. Thus the usual distinctions between private and public tend to be less meaningful in discussing specifics of housing finance in Sweden (see figure 11-2).

Mobilization of Savings

The rate of savings for Sweden has fluctuated widely during the postwar period. During the late 1960s it hovered at a low 3 percent of disposable income. However, that rate rose significantly in the 1970s. Still, the nation's historic rate of savings is perhaps the lowest in Europe. This low savings rate may be partially explained by the "cradle-to-grave" social-welfare system, which dampens one of the prime motivations to save—providing for personal emergencies, for example, or for unemployment—burdens assumed by the state in Sweden. Nevertheless, Sweden has a system of savings banks and an efficient postal savings network.

Capital-Market Resources

A considerable amount of housing finance comes through mortgage banks: specialized credit institutions affiliated with commercial banks that raise funds by issuing long-term mortgage bonds. There is a very active market for

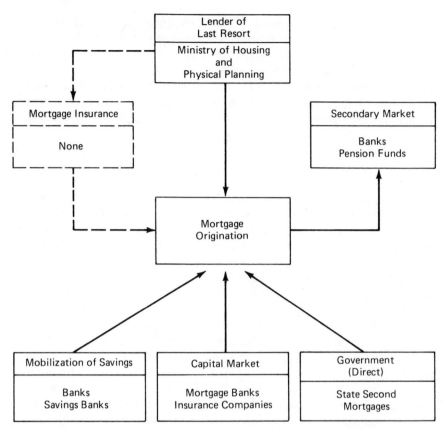

Figure 11-2. Structure of the Mortgage Market in Sweden

such securities in Sweden, with mortgage bonds accounting for more than 50 percent of all bond-market offerings. Such bonds are sold primarily to the National Pension Fund, other pension funds, banks, and insurance companies. The government urges private institutions to participate in purchasing these mortgage bonds, thus ensuring the supply of mortgage money.

The issuance of bonds is controlled by the central bank, Sveriges Riksbank, which regulates the flow of bonds onto the market. Preference has traditionally been given to housing bond issues. Bond financing accounted for more than half of mortgage lending in 1977.

Direct Government Lending

There is extensive direct government lending in Sweden. Almost every housing transaction involves two loans, one from a private source and a second mortgage from the government. The government loans will typically amount to 20 to 30 percent of the value and the private loan for 70 percent.

Direct state loans are available if the housing meets certain conditions. The housing must be new construction or rehabilitation and not merely a resale of an existing unit. The cost of the house must be within certain limits established by the government as reasonable. And the land on which the housing is constructed must meet all local and land-planning regulations.

Mortgage Finance

To finance housing, a first mortgage is usually obtained from a savings bank or mortgage bank for 70 percent of the value. This loan is typically a sixty-year, long-term rollover loan renegotiated and refinanced at ten-year intervals. A second loan is provided by the government and can be for a term of up to sixty years, provided the property meets certain specifications. The essence of the system is that the government second loan is issued at a below-market interest rate, but with the subsidy decreasing each year.

The details of the government second-mortgage programs have tended to shift over time. The government loan was formerly known as a "parity" loan because its objective was to have the amortization period and terms vary with construction-market conditions in such a way as to make new construction competitive with less-expensive older construction. Today the notion of parity as such has been dropped, and the government second mortgage has the more limited objective of merely reducing the cost of new housing—not necessarily of keying it to movements within the construction sector.

The actual operation of the state financing is somewhat complicated, but it can be illustrated as follows. The state issues the below-market interest-rate loan with an interest rate that varies over time, usually increasing at the rate of 0.2 percent per year until it reaches the market rate. The rate of increase has tended to change with conditions. For example, in 1980 the annual rate of increase of the government loans was 0.25 percent per year for rentals and 0.355 percent for owner-occupied houses.

As an example, the market rates of interest for the first mortgage will probably be in the neighborhood of 9 to 10 percent per year, whereas the guaranteed rate by the government on the second mortgage will start at 3.4 percent for rental properties and at 5.0 percent for owner-occupied houses. But it must be remembered that these are the initial rates and that these rates will be increasing each year by approximately 0.2 to 0.335 percent per year. Thus in about eight to twelve years the second mortgage will be at the market rate, and the subsidy will disappear. The degressive nature of the subsidy is a recognition that inflation will increase nominal incomes.

The government has established various interest-rate schedules and loan-to-value ratios depending on the kind of development. Public developers obtain a 30-percent loan from the state, which comes on top of a 70-percent first mortgage from private sources, leaving no equity requirement. For cooperative-housing developers, the state loan is 29 percent on top of a 70-percent first mortgage, leaving an equity balance of only 1 percent. Private persons can obtain loans for their own houses for 25 percent of value from the state and 70 percent from private sources, leaving an equity balance on only 5 percent. All other borrowers get only 22 percent from the state, leaving an equity requirement fo 8 percent. By all standards, these are very generous terms for mortgage lending.

However, to be eligible for the state-assisted loans, all property must conform to certain strict government guidelines. First, there is the development requirement that the housing meet community land-planning requirements that are very stringent. Requirements are placed on how much the land cost represents as a percentage of the total development cost. Total costs cannot exceed the costs that are developed by the government for certain housing prototypes. These requirements are very strict and must be met if the government loan is to be made available. Not surprisingly, they are met in 90 percent of the cases.

The terms of repayments on loans are quite long in Sweden, with repayment of the first and second mortgages amortized over sixty years. There are rollover provisions every ten years when rates are renegotiated.

Lender of Last Resort

The lender of last resort in Sweden is the government itself, operating through the Ministry of Housing and Physical Planning. It tends to participate in almost all housing loans, to set loan conditions, and generally to make available whatever money is necessary for the construction of houses. There is no semigovernment entity involved in performing this function as there is in the United States. Through formal and informal means, the state allocates the amount of housing credit, making money available as needed to meet housing goals.

Financing an Individual House

Sweden has one of the most complicated systems for financing home purchase, at least in a technical sense (see table 11-3). The government is involved in almost every transaction in terms of issuing a second mortgage. The function of the second mortgage, which typically amounts to from 20 to 30 percent of value, is to lower the housing burden.

Table 11-3
Sweden: An Illustrative Example of Financing the Purchase of an
Individual House

1. Value of house: U.S. $50,000 (SK 225,000)
2. Mortgage terms:
   a. First mortage:
      1. 70% of value
      2. 10.2% per annum for 60 years with provision for renewal (rollover) every 10 years.
      3. Monthly payment = U.S. $298 (SK 1,266)
   b. Second mortgage:
      1. 25% of value
      2. 5.5% per annum the first year, then increasing for the next 12 years at a rate of 3.5% until rate reaches 9.95%, and then constant for remainder of term.
      3. Monthly payment of U.S. $59 (SK 250) in first year and U.S. $102 (SK 434) in twelfth year and afterward.
   c. Owner's equity is 5%, U.S. $2,500 (SK 10,625).
3. The total of the two loans produces payments of U.S. $357 (SK 1,517) per month the first year and U.S $400 (SK 1,700) per month in the twelfth and subsequent years.

In order to understand the operations of this more complicated system, let us take the same example of a house with a value of $50,000. A first mortgage can likely be obtained from a commercial bank, mortgage bank, or insurance company at an interest rate of 10.2 percent (the prevailing interest rate in 1978) for 70 percent of the value amortized over a period of sixty years. This loan can be rolled over every ten years, and thus there may be some modification in the interest rate. Essentially, however, it is a long-term, fixed-rate mortgage.

There is a second mortgage, in this case for an owner-occupied house, of 25 percent of value for a similar long term of sixty years. Thus the home owner would have to come up with 5-percent equity. The second mortgage is written on a sliding interest rate that starts at a low 5.5 percent and then increases by 0.35 percent per year until it becomes constant at 9.95 percent per year. Thus after approximately twelve years, the mortgage rate becomes constant at 9.95 percent and remains so for the remainder of the sixty-year term.

The amortization of such a loan, including first and second mortgages, is shown in table 11-4. It is interesting to note that the amortization of the long-term second mortgage with the increasing rate of interest proceeds extremely slowly, and that principal repayment is almost nil. However, it does have the effect of producing a very low initial payment on the second mortgage of only $59 per month in the first year, increasing in the twelfth year to $102 per month and stabilizing thereafter.

The total of the long-term first and second mortgages produces an overall payment in the first year of $357 per month, rising to $400 per month for each year after the twelfth.

Table 11-4
**Loan-Repayment Schedule Assuming Fixed-Payment First Mortgage and
Graduated-Payment State-Provided Second Mortgage**

Year	First Mortgage Annual Payment	Second Mortgage			
		Annual Payment	Principal	Interest	Outstanding Balance End of Year
1	3,580	716	29	688	12,472
2	3,580	756	26	730	12,442
3	3,580	796	25	771	12,417
4	3,580	836	23	813	12,394
5	3,580	876	21	855	12,373
6	3,580	917	20	877	12,253
7	3,580	987	18	939	12,335
8	3,580	998	17	981	12,318
9	3,580	1,039	17	1,022	
10	3,580	1,080	16	1,064	12,285
11	3,580	1,121	15	1,106	12,270
12	3,580	1,162	15	1,147	12,255
13	3,580	1,203	14	1,189	12,241

Housing Consumption

Home Ownership

The rate of housing production in Sweden has been very high by world standards, but the majority of housing produced consisted of large blocks of flats
for rent. However, after the housing shortage had been met, consumers tended
to reject these large blocks of rented housing. The national decrease in housing production in the early 1970s came at the expense of rental units, while
single-family housing remained strong. In 1977, 75 percent of the housing
built in Sweden was for owner occupancy, dramatically illustrating the shift.

Although the Swedish housing shortage is over, there are still long
waiting lists for new housing for owner occupation. A new-house buyer
must wait until he receives the state loan with which to buy a new house.
This opportunity is given only once. The established price for a new house
does not necessarily reflect the market value, but rather reflects the prototype cost, which is based on estimated construction cost plus a low land
value. It is interesting to note that once the house is obtained, it can be
resold on the existing house market, for a significant profit, to persons who
do not want to stay on the waiting list for a period of five to ten years. In
this way, a person willing to pay the premium can avoid the waiting period.
However, it may not be in the best interest of an individual to sell a house in

the open market, since the subsidy is a one-time occurrence. This inhibits transactions of this kind.

Taxes and Housing

The Swedish tax system has two essential parts. First there is a steeply progressive national income tax, and then a proportional local tax with a flat rate, which is used to finance municipal government. The property tax per se is only a small levy. Despite the high rate of Swedish taxes, housing for owner occupation does not receive special tax breaks. Interest and property taxes are deductible, but only as offsets to the imputed value of the rental income.

In Scandinavia imputed rent on a house is required to be reported as income. In Sweden, imputed rent is calculated as 2 percent of value up to $30,000. 4 percent from $30,000 to $45,000, and 8 percent over $45,000. However, offsetting this would be the expenses of interest on the mortgage, operating expenses, and an allowance for depreciation. Therefore, the net income for tax purposes would be the amount of the imputed rent less all of the allowed deductions.

Rental Housing

Although there is no longer rent control, there are rules that govern the relationship between tenants and owners. Rents are set at utilization rent value, determined on the basis of the quality of the unit and the location of the dwelling. The intent of the regulations is to eliminate rent premiums due to scarcity. Tenants possess considerable security of tenure. A tenant is entitled to have the rent agreement renewed when a lease expires. The only way to evict a tenant is for the personal use of the flat by the landlord or gross behavior on the part of the tenant. Disputes are arbitrated by a special rent tribunal.

Housing Subsidies

Sweden's national policy is not to have rents exceed 20 percent of income. For those whose incomes are relatively low, rent allowances are given up to a maximum of 80 percent of the allowable housing costs. In 1977 subsidies were paid on more than 1.2 million housing units.

The housing-allowance system is used in lieu of subsidies for the production of low-income housing. Such subsidy programs directed at lowering costs of builders and developers no longer exist in Sweden. Almost all housing is subsidized to a slight degree because of the ubiquitous state second mortgage at below-market rates. But deep subsidies to housing producers are not a part of housing policy. Rather, money is made available to needy families through housing allowances so that they can obtain their own housing in the market, as long as the housing meets price guidelines.

References

1. Ministry of Housing and Physical Planning, "Housing, Building, and Planning in Sweden," Monograph to the United Nations (1978).
2. Michael Sumichrast, John Hart, and Robert Arquilla, "Central European Housing Study" (Paper prepared for the National Association of Homebuilders, Washington, D.C., 1974).

12 Housing in Eastern Europe

Housing Policy

In the centrally planned economies of Eastern Europe, there is no real counterpart to the housing-market concept familiar in the West. Housing is not a commodity that is freely bought and sold in organized markets, nor is it the subject of trade and exchange to the extent that it is in the West. But to say that there is no market activity in housing in Eastern Europe would be misleading; even there, some housing-market functions are performed, albeit quite differently.

Perhaps one of the most important differences between the approach to housing in the Eastern socialist countries, as opposed to that in the West, is that in the West housing represents a significant personal investment, whereas in the Eastern countries it is seen primarily as an important consumption item. The policies that emanate from these differences in perceptions differ in significant ways. If housing is seen as an investment, people will want to own their own personal houses and will save toward that end. A house becomes a very valuable possession, one that can be transmitted to one's heirs, and often the bulk of the estate that a family will accumulate during a lifetime. On the other hand, if housing is not viewed as a personal investment, then the essence of housing allocation is the provision of shelter, disassociated from any investment aspects. There would be no incentive to save for a house if it could not be possessed and could not be passed on to one's heirs.

In most societies, housing is a little of both: consumption and investment. Although a house is not strictly an investment item in the West, one of the prime motivations for house ownership is obviously the investment aspect. This factor is not entirely absent in Eastern socialist countries, some of which do allow forms of ownership and even the ability to bequeath property to one's children. But this depends on the individual country, since policies and practices tend to vary.

The most doctrinaire of the socialist countries in Europe is the Soviet Union. Its principal housing policy is that it is the duty of the state to provide housing for its citizens. Thus government tends to build, own, and maintain the housing stock. The least doctrinaire is Yugoslavia, a country with a centrally planned economy, but one is which the responsibility for providing housing is left primarily to the household, and in which housing is

201

built, owned, and maintained by individuals. The other socialist countries
are arrayed between these extremes in terms of the relative degree of state
provision and ownership of the housing stock.

One important difference between housing in the Eastern socialist countries and in the West is that in the East housing is not a freely traded commodity. Even though most socialist countries admit some form of home
ownership, few allow houses to be traded at the sole initiative of the occupant. Housing tends to be allocated by the state, rather than by a market
where people bid for units. None of the Eastern countries allows profit on a
real-estate transaction in which housing is sold or otherwise transferred.
Local governing councils at the communal level decide on housing allocation. Needless to say, no private real-estate industry exists in these countries.

The Eastern European socialist countries permit private land ownership, especially in the agricultural sector and for individual residential units.
For example, in Yugoslavia 71 percent of all dwellings are in private ownership. In other countries, such as Poland and Bulgaria, there is also private
ownership of residential land. Collective ownership of land, although extensive in the agricultural sector, usually affects only plots over a certain
minimum size. Small farms are still in the hands of private owners, even in
the USSR.

However, it is important to note that in the socialist countries land is
not a marketable commodity. Land cannot be bought and sold by individuals. Hence there is no such thing as private land speculation; a land
market, as such, does not exist.

In Eastern Europe rents are kept low for ideological reasons, since rent
is considered one of life's necessities that should be greatly assisted by the
state. Housing costs, therefore, tend to be met not from personal income
but from deep subsidies from the state. In Czechoslovakia the average rent
for a state-owned apartment with 38 square meters of living space is 5 percent of gross wages. In the USSR a three-room flat (not including kitchen)
or a two-bedroom apartment costs approximately 8,000 to 9,000 rubles to
build, but would rent for only 18 to 20 rubles per month, or what would
amount to 5 to 6 percent of family income. In the USSR rent tends to be 4
percent of family income, on average. Rent has been kept at the same level,
on a per-square-meter floor-space basis, in the Soviet Union since 1928; the
boast is that rents have not risen in seventy-five years, since the time of
Lenin.

Behind the facade of state ownership, one finds in Eastern Europe an
increasing emphasis on mobilizing the desire of individuals to contribute to
their own housing. This has been accomplished in a variety of ways, but
mostly through the use of cooperatives.

Cooperative housing is very important in Poland, Czechoslovakia, and even the USSR. There is more cooperative housing in Eastern Europe than in Scandinavia, which is most often identified with the cooperative-housing movement. Coops receive extensive state aid.

> Cooperative building and individual building benefit equally from very extensive aid: in the German Democratic Republic, repaying of credits is spread over fifty-two years, in Poland over thirty to sixty years. In both countries, interest on credits for people who build their own houses comes to two percent and cooperatives receive interest-free loans (in Poland, this applies to tenant cooperatives: home ownership cooperatives pay 1%). In Hungary on the sale of state dwellings, the loan is granted at 1% for twenty-five years. [4]

In Czechoslovakia cooperatives can obtain long-term loans from the state for thirty years at an interest rate of 1 percent. Also, state savings banks offer loans to individual citizens to purchase their own houses at a rate of 2.7 percent for a repayment period of ten years.

The cooperative movement in Eastern Europe has as its basis the realization by the state that individuals have both the means and the desire to provide for their own housing. Their personal wishes exceed what the state is usually willing to provide. The privately owned cooperative apartments are substantially larger and with more amenities than typical state-owned apartments. On the other hand, the monthly payments on a coop are much higher than the subsidized rent on a state-owned apartment. Increasingly, however, individuals are expressing their preferences for owning their own units even at higher cost.

Prior to World War II the Eastern countries, with the exception of the Soviet Union, had long traditions of private-property ownership. Home ownership was widespread, especially in the rural areas. When these countries became socialist after the war, most of their wealth was nationalized, with the exception of the housing sector. Today, home ownership coexists with state ownership of the means of production. In fact, rates of home ownership in Eastern Europe exceed those in the West.

The Union of Soviet Socialist Republics

In the USSR housing is considered an extremely important item of household consumption. In fact, the revised Soviet constitution specifically mentions housing as one of the basic rights of the Soviet people. It is the responsibility of government to provide adequate housing for all citizens.

The housing situation in the USSR differs in many ways from that in the other socialist countries. The housing stock of the Soviet Union had for many years been allowed to deteriorate. From the Bolshevik revolution until the end of World War II, very little housing had been built in the entire nation. During the infancy of the new socialist state under Lenin, emphasis was on building the industrial structure of the country and making significant improvement in agriculture. Housing was not a priority item, and little housing was built for the entire first half of the twentieth century.

Not until after World War II did the Soviet Union embark on a massive home-building program. During the war a large amount of the Soviet housing stock had been devastated, the USSR having been the scene of some of the most vicious fighting during the war. Thus after the war the USSR faced a tremendous need for rebuilding, caused not only by the war damage but also by the accumulated neglect of the housing sector for the first half of the century.

In the 1950s the Soviet Union began building at a prodigious rate (see table 12-1). The rate of new-housing construction was approximately 8 units per 1,000 population during the 1950s and 1960s. The guiding principle was to build as much housing as possible, often without regard to quality, in order to put a satisfactory roof over each family. As an example, housing construction accounted for almost 15 percent of the total investment in the national economy, an amount four times as high as the comparable figure for the United States.

In the USSR the planning for housing is carried out by the state planning-committee of the Council of Ministries (GOSPLAN of the USSR), the state building entities of the republics, and the planning commissions of the various Soviets' Working Peoples Delegates. Their five-year plans are developed, including the construction of housing. The resources allocated by the state and by the industrial enterprises are made part of the economic plan.

Of all the socialist states, the Soviet Union has been the most doctrinaire in insisting on government construction, ownership, and financing of hous-

Table 12-1
USSR: Selected Housing-Production Statistics, 1955-1977

Housing Activities	1955	1964	1965	1970	1977
Dwellings completed (thousands)	1,512	2,912	2,227	2,266	2,190
Dwellings per 1,000 population	7.7	13.6	13.6	9.7	8.5
Housing construction as a percentage of gross domestic product	15.5	18.0	—	16.0	14.0
Percentage of total by type of investor					
State and cooperative	41.3	48.5	67.8	76.0	81.7
Employees on their own account			15.1	10.9	8.9
Collective farms and rural	58.7	51.5	17.1	13.1	9.4

Source: United Nations, *Annual Bulletin of Housing and Building Statistics for Europe.*

ing units. The state takes this responsibility as its almost exclusive province. Yet in the small towns and rural areas there is still considerable widespread home ownership. In addition, the practice of owning a private second house or *dacha* in the countryside is still an entrenched way of life for many of the well-to-do technocrats.

Still, there has been increasing private home ownership in the cities through the vehicle of cooperative housing. The Soviet people are increasingly turning toward cooperative housing as the primary means of upgrading their own housing situation. Admittedly, much of the housing built in the immediate postwar years was of low quality because the emphasis was on quantity of production. Over the years, the standards used in constructing flats have gradually been increased.

Nevertheless, many households seeking even higher standards have sought to join cooperatives that would build housing with more amenities than are found in those built by the state. Today, cooperative apartment buildings account for almost 10 percent of housing construction. Land for the cooperatives is provided free of charge by the state. Loans are granted to the housing-cooperative associations on very favorable terms, typically at a rate of 0.5 percent a year for a period of ten to fifteen years. Individuals are required to put up 40-percent equity, and the government loan will finance 60 percent. More and more households are willing to save for the required equity in order to own their own cooperative housing unit.

Rent is deliberately kept low in the Soviet Union. The USSR boasts that the original levels of rent set by Lenin are still in operation. Since the income of workers has increased significantly, rent has become a smaller and smaller percentage of a family's household budget.

A rising standard of living within a nation usually leads to an increased demand for better housing. Certainly this is indicated by the progress made in the Soviet Union. In the last five years, consumer-goods production has increased by 37 percent, with a corresponding expansion in the volume of services. Sales of high-quality furniture, refrigerators, television sets, washing machines, and other sophisticated consumer durables have increased rapidly. At the present time, seven out of ten households have television sets and two out of three have refrigerators. There were nearly 1 million cars sold to the population in 1975, seven times the amount in 1970. During the same period the average per capita space standard increased. The standards for sanitary and other equipment in the house have been upgraded considerably. Conveniences such as central heating, hot running water, and bathrooms are now common in state-owned housing. The stated goal of Soviet housing policy is that "the ultimate aim of long-term governmental programs of housing development is to secure every family with a self-contained flat insuring most favorable living and sanitary-hygienic conditions [1]. The policy to be implemented by the economic plan for the fifteen-year period 1976-1990 calls for

> . . . one family in one flat, the demolition of houses of little value, and the provision of every urban household and most rural households with a well-appointed flat. The creation of comfortable living conditions for households of different sizes, providing each adult member of the family with a separate room and eliminating sleeping space in the living room. [2]

In the USSR one-third of all housing is owner occupied. However, most of this owned housing tends to be in rural areas and small towns. In the urban areas the level of owner occupation is quite small, but growing. There is a spreading cooperative movement within the Soviet Union, and increasingly families are opting to take care of their own housing requirements through cooperatives that receive low-interest loans through the state. However, in the urban areas about 80 percent of the housing stock is owned by the state.

Even in the USSR there is diversity in housing finance; over 65 percent of the housing is financed through state appropriations, with 35 percent being financed by other means. Ten percent is from state enterprises that at their own expense invest some of their money in housing for their workers. Another 10 percent comes from cooperatives, which raise some of their money privately. There is some state assistance for cooperatives with 0.5-percent interest loans. But as much as 15 percent of the housing built in the Soviet Union is privately built by individuals with the assistance of state loans, mostly in the rural areas. In the cities most of the housing is done by public corporations or cooperatives.

Yugoslavia

Yugoslavia is a nonaligned socialist country with strong ties to the West. Its economy is centrally planned, although implementation is not as rigid as that found in the other Eastern nations. In spite of central planning, market incentives play more of a role in the Yugoslav's economy than is true in other socialist states. The state-controlled enterprises operate with management and incentive systems common to market economies. This also holds true for the housing sector, in which there is a very strong tradition of individual initiative and home ownership, which countinues under the socialist regime. Fully 71 percent of all households in Yugoslavia own their dwellings, the highest rate in Europe.

All the national economic institutions set aside a percentage of their funds for housing purposes. In 1977 the amount set aside was approximately 6.7 percent of the gross personal income of all employed workers. The individual enterprises retain approximately two-thirds of these housing funds for construction of units for their employees. The other one-third goes to the local commune (which is the local political organization) and is used for general housing purposes, that is, for workers whose own enterprises do not put aside sufficient funds, for subsidizing families with low incomes, and for administrative purposes related to housing at the commune level. The amount set aside in each enterprise can be higher than the state-prescribed minimum. It has been reported that some enterprises set aside, by common agreement, from 8 to 10 percent of gross wages for housing.

Enterprises may use their funds to build or purchase dwellings, which are then given to the workers with a protected tenure. Or the funds can be used to grant favorable credit to those workers who wish to buy or build their own apartments. At each enterprise there is a worker council in charge of determining the exact procedure to be used in allocating funds for housing. They establish the terms of loans, including interest rates and repayment periods for those who wish to borrow funds to purchase their own apartments.

The use of private funds for housing finance has been quite significant in Yugoslavia. Banks exist in which citizens accumulate their savings. A considerable down payment is usually required to finance an individual unit, usually an equity of 40 to 50 percent of value. Loans are granted for fifteen to twenty years at interest rates of from 2 to 4 percent. For housing construction, the total amount of private funds is approximately equal to the amount of social funds committed in that sector.

Although there is private ownership of real estate in Yugoslavia, it is somewhat modified from the traditional Western patterns. Land has been nationalized, but people can still own individual buildings. In fact, citizens may own as many as three flats for their own use or for investment purposes. There is consequently a private rental market, but rents are controlled. In Yugoslavia two-thirds of all housing construction is private.

The price of housing in Yugoslavia tends to be somewhat high in relationship to family income. A two-room apartment requires approximately nine years of work for the average paid worker, which is considerably higher than is true in most of Western Europe or in North America.

The rate of housing construction in Yugoslavia has increased significantly since the end of World War II (see table 12-2). At the end of the war, there was a tremendous housing shortage caused both by war damage and by the industrialization and urbanization that had occurred. In order to alleviate the housing shortage, investment in housing had to be greatly increased.

One result of the postwar building rate is that the housing stock is quite young by Western standards. More than 65 percent of Yugoslavia's present housing stock was constructed or reconstructed in the period from 1945 to 1977. Fortunately, the increase in housing production went hand in hand with an increase in the general economic prosperity of the country. As the economy improved over the years, the obligatory contribution to the housing sector increased, permitting ever larger amounts to be devoted to the

Table 12-2
Yugoslavia: Selected Housing-Production Statistics, 1953-1976

Housing Activities	1953	1960	1965	1970	1976
Dwellings completed (thousands)	38.2	75.7	122.0	128.8	149.9
Dwellings per 1,000 population	2.2	4.1	6.3	6.3	7.0
Housing construction as a percentage of gross domestic product	—	—	—	—	—
Percentage of total by type of investor					
State	23.8	42.1	36.5	34.5	40.6
Private	76.2	52.9	63.5	65.5	59.4

Source: United Nations, *Annual Bulletin of Housing and Building Statistics for Europe.*

housing sector. Also, the increase in wages meant that more savings could be devoted by individuals who wished to use their private funds to build their own housing.

Czechoslovak Socialist Republic

Czechoslovakia provides an interesting example of a position between the extremes represented by the USSR and Yugoslavia. Czechoslovakia is a centrally planned economy in which the state controls the housing sector. However, it differs from the USSR in that the state depends on private initiative to provide housing, with some state aid. The housing sector is not as flexible as in Yugoslavia, nor as rigid as in the USSR (see table 12-3).

In Czechoslovakia the utilization of private initiative and resources for housing is clearly stated as public policy.

> The principle aim of housing policy in the Czechoslovak Socialist Republic (CSSR) is the satisfaction of the housing needs of all social groups of the population while endeavoring that the housing needs of every citizen be satisfied with an adequate standard, corresponding with the possibility of the national economy. On the other hand, endeavor is being made to enable an improvement of the housing standard to those citizens who are willing to expend their work and money to improve their housing conditions. The prerequisites for an increased participation of the population and the financing of housing construction are being continuously improved: the real income of the population is continuously growing, the saturation of the population with basic products is increasing, the rate of saving is increasing and the security of old age is improving. [3]

Table 12-3
Czechoslovakia: Selected Housing-Production Statistics, 1955-1977

Housing Activities	1953	1960	1965	1970	1977
Dwellings completed (thousands)	50.6	76.3	87.7	122.6	143.9
Dwellings per 1,000 population	3.9	5.6	5.8	8.6	9.5
Housing construction as a percentage of gross domestic product	22.5	14.5	14.0	17.3	13.8
Percentage of total by type of investor					
State	70.4	58.6	29.9	19.3	24.5
Enterprises	—	6.3	0.3	17.0	22.1
Cooperatives	—	11.5	46.5	38.2	24.3
Private	29.6	23.6	23.3	25.5	29.1
aided	—	6.5	12.4	15.6	21.6
unaided	—	17.0	10.9	9.9	7.5

Source: United Nations, *Annual Bulletin of Housing and Building Statistics for Europe.*

In Czechoslovakia there are four principal kinds of housing investors.

1. The state builds housing through organs of local government called national committees. Such housing is financed from the budgets of the local governments, which in turn are part of the official state budget. Such housing built by the national committees is usually allocated to citizens who have some special housing needs due to family size, age, or physical condition.
2. State-run industrial enterprises are significant builders of housing. The enterprises engage in housing construction, usually in large blocks of flats, with their own funds earned in their operations and also with occasional credit from the state bank. Special tax credits are allowed to those enterprises that utilize their free assets to build housing. These enterprises usually build housing for their employees; such housing is owned by the enterprises, which are also responsible for their maintenance.
3. Cooperatives are established by employees of enterprises or other institutions. The housing that is built is owned by the cooperative membership. Sometimes the cooperative is a self-help housing cooperative in which equity comes from the members own labor.
4. Individuals may build or purchase their own houses with their own funds.

State-provided housing is fully financed by the state. Cooperative housing is financed partly by special state loans and partly by individual savings. The state looks favorably on the construction of cooperative housing and under some conditions will defray 30 percent of the construction costs with a state grant. The state bank of Czechoslovakia will extend long-term credit for housing cooperatives at rates of 1 percent for thirty years. The state savings bank will also offer private citizens low-interest loans for cooperative apartment ownership.

The Czechoslovak government anticipates that cooperative housing construction will be the principal vehicle for meeting its housing needs. Accordingly, it is seen as being in the best interest of the state to encourage this particular form of tenure and to encourage the industrial enterprises to cooperate in supporting cooperative housing for their workers.

Loans can be obtained for purchasing individual cooperative apartments for two-thirds of the cost at an interest rate of 6 percent for twenty-five years. The system of savings banks will make loans in an amount of twice the savings on deposit. The industrial enterprises will also make loans with their housing funds.

The government is especially interested in having young families acquire their own dwellings. There is a special savings plan for young people between the ages of 15 and 27 who wish to accumulate money for the procurement of a flat and furnishings. Savings accounts are paid a rate of interest of 2 percent per year. After five years savers are awarded a premium of 200 to 2,500 koruna, in accordance with the amount of the accumulated deposit. With the premium, the actual rate of interest is 5.3 percent, which is the highest rate of interest paid in Czechoslovakia. Deposits can be made by parents on behalf of their children. In this way 400,000 young people are enrolled in this saving scheme in Czechoslovakia.

In Czechoslovakia, although land has been nationalized, there is extensive private ownership of housing. In 1970 half of all the housing was privately owned. In rural areas and in small towns there is a considerable amount of individual ownership.

The Czech government has encouraged private ownership in order for the state to escape the high cost of providing housing. Mobilizing individual savings and individual desires for home ownership has greatly reduced the burden on the central government for providing housing.

References

1. Research Institute for Building and Architecture (Prague), "Housing, Building and Planning in Czechoslovakia 1979," United Nations monograph.
2. Standing Conference of Towns of Yugoslavia, "Current Trends and Policies in the Field of Housing, Building and Planning in Yugoslavia, 1978," Country monograph for the United Nations, Economic Commission for Europe.

3. Czechoslovak Socialist Republic, "Current Trends and Policies in the Field of Housing, Building and Planning," Country monograph for the United Nations, Economic Commission for Europe (June 1976).

4. United Nations, *Human Settlements in Europe: Postwar Trends and Policies* (ECE/HBP/18).

5. Committee for the People's Councils' Affairs, Socialist Republic of Romania, "Current Trends and Policies in the Field of Housing, Building and Planning," National monograph for the United Nations, Economic Commission for Europe (1976).

6. State Committee for Civil Construction and Architecture (USSR), "Current Trends and National Policy in the Field of Housing, Building and Town Planning in the U.S.S.R." (Prepared for United Nations, Economic Commission for Europe, 1976).

13 Housing in Japan

Housing Policy

The Postwar Situation

Japan's housing deficit at the end of World War II was estimated at 4.2 million units, enough to house 20 percent of the population. Japan experienced tremendous damage in its cities because of its participation in the war, but its housing problems predated the war. The major cities were built up largely with narrow wooden structures constructed at high densities and constituting fire and health hazards. Thus at the end of the war Japan faced two difficult problems in terms of its housing stock. First, it had to construct enough new dwellings to provide shelter for each family. The second task was to replace the substandard housing with dwellings constructed to higher standards and having more space per capita and more amenities.

The task of eliminating the quantitative housing shortage was accomplished within two decades after the war. The census of 1968 reported that the number of housing units equalled the number of households. The quantitative housing problem was not a static one after the war, as the target kept enlarging with the increased urbanization. Japan's spectacular economic recovery required a greater labor force, and the consequent migration to the urban centers put strains on the available housing.

Assault on the qualitative housing problem continues. A rising standard of living has brought higher expectations for what constitutes acceptable housing. Workers are no longer satisfied with small, narrow apartments, but aspire to large apartments, condominiums, and individual houses of their own. A 1978 survey revealed that 40 percent of all households were dissatisfied with their present housing, primarily because of the small size of units and their age [1].

The traditional housing structure in Japan has been the wooden house, because of the availability of forests and lumber. However, postwar Japanese policy has been away from the traditional wood-frame house and toward fireproof construction relying primarily on concrete. Japanese cities are quite dense, and land is at a premium. Therefore, the older wooden houses packed densely into neighborhoods are serious fire hazards. Today most housing is likely to be in large apartment complexes constructed of brick and concrete.

213

Government and the Private Sector

The Japanese economy relies on private initiative and free markets. Yet the government and the private sector are characterized by close cooperaton and a supportive rather than an adversarial and regulatory relationship, an arrangement unique in a capitalist system. In the industrial sphere this system has proved its practicality with Japan's gigantic success in world trade.

Japan's housing sector also is based on close working relationships between government agencies and private housing-development entities. Government involvement in housing is quite complex, running through several different ministeries. The most prominent is the Ministry of Construction, which oversees both the Housing Loan Corporation and the Japan Housing Corporation. In addition, some housing is also developed through the Ministry of Welfare, utilizing the Welfare Pension Corporation, which lends money to employers for building housing for workers. Also, the Ministry of Labor sponsors housing in conjunction with new factories or new mining enterprises being developed through the Employment Promotion Projects Corporation.

Land Development

In Japan the public sector is increasingly involved in the land-development process. Land is scarce, especially available land that is usable for urban requirements. As a result the price of land is extremely high, and land assembly by private persons is very difficult. Public organizations financed by the government now dominate the development process and attempt to buy developable land in an area and put in the infrastructure. After assembly and improvement they sell the finished lots to public or private developers. It is anticipated that such local development companies will provide 30 percent of the buildable sites. However, most urban sites—usually about 50 percent of the total—are still provided by private real-estate developers. The rest of the sites are those furnished by individuals as well as sites from the new towns that are being built by the Japan Housing Corporation.

Housing Production

Housing and the Economy

Japan's rate of housing production during the 1970s has been the highest in the world (see table 13-1). Its sustained rate of housing construction during this period has never been approached by any other nation. A rate of 10 dwellings per 1,000 population is quite high and is reached by few nations in any given year. But the Japanese rate of 14 to 15 dwellings per 1,000 inhabitants for almot a decade is without precedent.

Table 13-1
Japan: Selected Housing-Production Statistics, 1950-1975

Housing Activities	1950	1960ᵃ	1966	1970	1975
Dwellings completed (thousands)	25.8	79.9	109.2	162.1	1,541
Dwellings per 1,000 population	—	—	10.5	15.6	14.8
Housing construction as a percentage of gross domestic product	—	4.2	6.1	7.1	—
Percentage of total by type of investor					
Public housing	38.2	30.5	37.1	37.1	40.8
Private	61.8	63.5	62.9	62.4	59.2

Source: Japan Ministry of Construction, *Housing in Japan.*
ᵃAverage annual production during period.

During the immediate postwar years and the 1950s Japan's rate of dwelling construction was moderate, with about 4 percent of its gross domestic product devoted to housing. The nation's first priority was industrial production, so resources went primarily toward export industries. The rate of housing construction increased during the 1960s, rising to more than 6 percent of GDP at a rate of over 10 units per 1,000 inhabitants. During the 1970s housing production greatly increased, accounting for more than 7 percent of GDP (see table 13-2).

The extremely high rate of housing construction during the 1970s did not come about by accident. In 1966 the government instituted the first of its five-year plans for housing construction. Goals were set for construciton for both publicly and privately financed housing. Since then there have been two additional five-year plans, for 1971-1975 and 1976-1980. In order to meet the goals of the five-year plans, the government makes money available directly to public developers and indirectly and directly to private developers and individuals through the state-run Japan Housing Loan Corporation (JHLC). Also, building activities of the state-run Japan Housing Corporation can be adjusted as circumstances require. As a result, the ambitious goals of the first and second five-year plans were substantially met. The third five-year plan for 1976-1980 was even more ambitious (see table 13-3, 13-4, and 13-5).

Japan Housing Corporation

The Japan Housing Corporation (JHC) was established by the government in 1955 for the purpose of constructing dwellings for workers, principally in the urban areas. Its specific charges are to: (1) build and manage rental housing, (2) develop housing for sale, (3) redevelop blighted areas of

Table 13-2
Percentage of the Housing Investment in the Gross National Product

	1960	1965	1966	1967	1968	1969	1970	1971	1972	1973
Housing Investment/ GNP	4.2	6.2	6.1	6.6	6.7	7.2	7.1	7.0	7.9	9.0
Gross fixed capital/ GNP	32.2	30.2	31.2	32.8	33.6	35.2	35.2	36.0	35.1	37.0
Housing investment/ Gross fixed capital	13.1	20.4	19.5	20.1	20.0	20.2	20.3	19.5	22.6	24.3

Table 13-3
Number of Houses Constructed after World War II in Japan

Fiscal Year	Classification						Private Houses with Private Funds	Total
	Public	Redevelopment	Housing Loan Corporation	Japan Housing Corporation	Other Publicly Funded	Total Publicly Funded		
1945-1950	274	—	62	—	297	633	2,136	2,769
1951-1955	223	—	256	20	118	618	944	1,562
1956-1960	247	2	459	148	130	986	1,594	2,580
1961-1965	288	22	640	188	321	1,459	2,537	3,996
1966	73	45	168	53	107	405.5	686	1,092
1967	82	5	199	61	118	465	764	1,229
1968	88	5.5	223	65	122	503.5	795	1,298
1969	100	8	246	79	149	582	918	1,500
1970	103	10.5	252	77	168	610.5	1,011	1,621
1971	112	12	282	84	154	644	973	1,617
1972	100	10	303	48	132	593	1,294	1,887
1973	96	8	309	50	126	589	1,285	1,874
1974	77	6	369	50	121	623	811	1,434
1975	85	6	329	60	148	628	913	1,541

Source: Ministry of Construction, *Housing in Japan*.

Table 13-4
Numbers of Dwellings Constructed by Japan Housing Corporation, 1955-1975

Classifications	1955-1959	1960-1964	Fiscal Year 1965-1969	1970/1974	1975	Total
Danchi dwellings	80,589	94,307	160,992	138,485	14,000	488,373
Dwellings for rent						
Apartment dwellings in ordinary urban areas	4,917	15,050	18,525	20,181	2,000	60,170
Apartment dwellings in block develop- ment urban areas	0	0	16,850	36,903	8,000	61,753
Subtotal	85,503	109,357	196,367	195,569	24,000	610,296
Dwellings for sale						
Dwellings for sale for individuals	6,732	2,804	48,977	61,657	29,000	149,170
Dwellings for specified sale for firms and other corporations	47,277	55,490.5	65,313	46,091.5	7,000	221,172
Subtotal	54,009	58,294.5	114,290	107,748.5	36,000	370,342
Grand total	139,512	167,651.5	310,657	303,317.5	60,000	981,138

Source: Ministry of Construction, Japan Housing Corporation. (unpublished)

Table 13-5
The First, Second, and Third Five-Year Housing-Construction Programs for Japan
(thousands of units)

| Classification | First Five-Year Plan, Fiscal-Year 1966-1970 | | Second Five-Year Plan, Fiscal-Year 1971-1975 | | Third Five-Year Plan, Fiscal-Year 1976-1980 |
	Planned	*Actual*	*Planned*	*Actual*	*Planned*
Public houses	440	446	597.2	470	500
Redevelopment houses	80	33	80.8	42	60
Housing Loan Corporation houses	1,080	1,087	1,370	1,592	2,200
Japan Housing Corporation	350	335	460	292	380
Other public-funded houses	480	664	945	681	700
Number of units adjusted	270	—	385	—	—
Total number of public-funded houses	2,700	2,563	3,838	3,077	3,840
Number of private houses with private funds	4,000	4,174	5,738	5,276	4,760
Grand total	6,700	6,739	9,576	8,353	8,600

Source: Ministry of Construction, Japan Housing Corporation (unpublished).

cities, (4) assemble and develop land, and (5) build public and community facilities.

The only subsidies that the Japan Housing Corporation obtains are low-interest loans from the government. The Japanese government funnels low-interest loans to the JHC, then utilizes these funds to construct moderate-or middle-income housing for workers. Housing for the poor is a function of Japan's public-housing program, not of the JHC.

The JHC has specialized in building large-scale apartment developments in the suburbs. These have become quite commonplace in Japan and are frequently known as *danschi* housing, synonomous with "JHC housing." Since its inception, the JHC has built more than 1 million units. Annually, it has accounted for approximately 4.5 percent of all housing produced.

Other Developers

In 1965 a system of local housing-supply corporations was encouraged by the government to build housing for workers, both rental units and condominiums. These local housing-supply corporations are nonprofit entities, much like their counterparts in Germany and France. They obtain their money by borrowing from the Japan Housing Loan Corporation. There are fifty-six such local corporations in operation.

Sixty percent of Japan's housing is constructed without any government assistance. Rental housing accounts for one-quarter of private housing, whereas individuals building their own house account for one-half. The remainder is housing built by developers for sale and housing built by companies for employees.

Structure of the Housing-Finance Sector

Mobilizing Household Savings

The Japanese have the world's highest savings rate, greatly outdistancing those of the other industrialized countries. Since the 1960s, the savings rate has been above 20 percent, more than three times the rate in the United States and twice as high as that of the Germans. The average Japanese household in 1979 had savings of U.S. $22,000.

The Japanese save for many reasons, including: (1) guarding against long or catastrophic illness, (2) educating one's children, (3) accumulating for vacation, and (4) accumulating for house purchase. Given the very high cost of housing in Japan, the typical household needs a considerable amount to purchase a house. A major incentive to household savings is the fact that interest on savings accounts is tax exempt up to U.S. $45,000 per family member.

Japan is now beginning the process of developing an extensive and specialized circuit for housing finance. For many years the Japanese conscientiously put most of their savings to work in expanding their industry. From the end of World War II through the 1960s, almost all of the investment capital generated by savings in Japan was funneled into industrialization and manpower-training projects. Savings were not devoted to housing, but rather to the industrial sector. As late as 1967 residential debt in Japan held by private financial institutions was less than 1 percent of all private debt. A comparable figure for the United States would be in the neighborhood of 30 percent.

But now that a greater emphasis is being placed on providing a higher level of housing satisfaction for the population, considerable effort is being put forward to develop the kinds of specialized mortgage-lending entities that will be necessary to finance the housing (see figure 13-1).

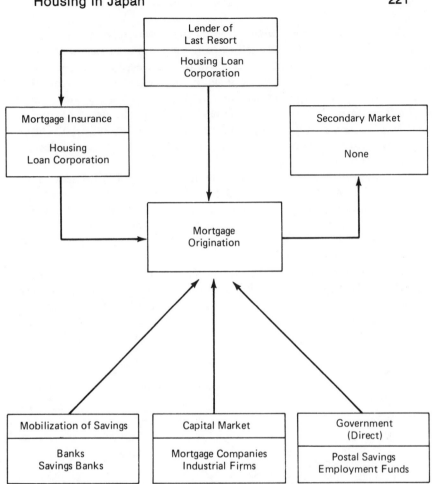

Figure 13-1. Structure of the Mortgage Market in Japan

Housing Loan Corporation

The Housing Loan Corporation (HLC) was established in 1950 to finance housing for moderate-income families. It has its own network of twelve branches throughout Japan, but it also utilizes the private banks throughout the nation as collection and servicing agents. HLC provides loans for personal housing for individual units, housing for developers building housing for sale, housing for rental, and loans to the JHC.

The Housing Loan Corporation puts size and cost limits on its loans, and the kinds of houses on which it will lend are restricted. HLC- eligible houses tend to be smaller and cheaper than those that are privately financed.

HLC was established on the base of the postal savings system. The postal savings system in Japan is one of the country's largest financial institutions; it is utilized by the government to finance several important activities, including the Japan Development Bank, the Export-Import Bank of Japan, and the HLC. In 1978 accounts in the postal savings system totaled $217 billion. Over the years the HLC has augmented its source of funds, so that in 1978 the postal savings system accounted for only half of its resources. The remainder consists of private funds from bond sales, investments, and reflows of principal payments (see figure 13-2).

Mortgage lending was dominated by the HLC for almost twenty years after the end of World War II. It was the only place an individual could obtain an institutional mortgage. Over the past decade the dominance of the HLC has tended to subside as other private institutions—notably commercial banks, specialized mortgage-finance companies, and savings banks—have begun to make mortgage loans.

The rate of interest charged by the HLC is below the market rate. HLC begins in the favorable position of being able to borrow from the postal savings system and also directly from the government. Thus it can offer rates considerably below the market clearing rate. It is a feature of the Japanese

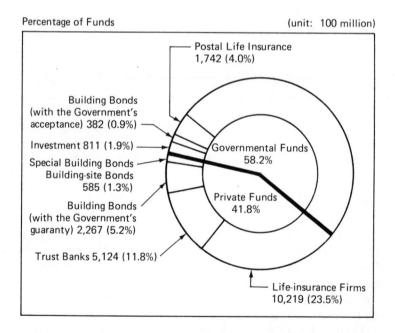

Figure 13-2. Sources of Funds, Japan Housing Loan Corporation

financial system that key interest rates are established by the government under leadership of the Bank of Japan. Exact rates are determined by both discussion and negotiation among other monetary authorities, with representation of the affected financial institutions. Both deposit-rate ceilings and key interest rates are determined collegially. Once the key rates are set, all other rates find their levels in the market.

The lending rate of the HLC is a socially favored rate and is kept below market. On the one hand, this is an incentive for housing production; on the other, it is a lever that can be employed to stimulate housing to the degree thought necessary for countercyclical purposes.

Because HLC rates are below market, there are at any given time more applicants than available funds. Funds are rationed by restricting HLC loans to moderately priced and moderate-sized housing units and to developers who specialize in worker housing (see figure 13-3).

Private Sources of Housing Finance

Private financing of housing in Japan is increasing rapidly and is becoming the major source of financing, supplanting both the Housing Loan Corporation and direct government support. Now the commercial banks, savings banks, and other specialized housing-loan companies are making mortgage loans on housing. The terms are not as generous as those offered by the HLC; interest rates are higher and maturities shorter. These private

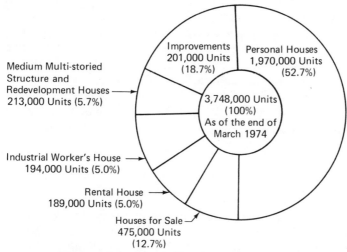

Figure 13-3. Japan Housing Loan Corporation

institutions must pay their savers and investors a competitive rate of return; thus their rates are market rates. Still, private-sector finance of housing continues to increase. During the period immediately after World War II, when investment funds were in extremely short supply, the government was the logical place to turn for housing finance. The HLC was virtually the only game in town. With the extraordinary economic success of the Japanese, and their increased standard of living and per capita income, it is only natural that government assistance would begin to wane. The private market is being relied on increasingly to provide the bulk of money for housing.

In Japan all the traditional financial institutions tend to make some mortgage loans. However, commercial banks and life-insurance companies in Japan, as everywhere else, have a low percentage of their assets in mortgages. There are specialized housing-loan corporations and special government-assisted entities that are responsible for the bulk of private mortgage financing. The rates they charge are twice the rate offered by the HLC (see table 13-6).

Employer-Provided Housing

Employer-provided housing has been an important part of the housing sector in Japan. Such employer involvement goes back to the turn of the century, but especially to the 1930s. Women were then entering the labor force, and there was considerable popularity for employer-provided boarding houses for single female workers.

Although employer housing accounts for only 6 percent of all housing, 73 percent of manufacturing firms in Japan have some form of company housing. This is most pronounced in manufacturing, where 77 percent of the firms have such housing. Production of employer housing has been steady, accounting for approximately 7 percent of the housing built annually since the end of World War II. It tends to be more prevalent in remote areas than in the cities.

Mortgage Insurance

There is a system of mortgage insurance administered by the JHLC and based on the same principles as that of the FHA in the United States. Insured mortgages amounted to a small proportion of all outstanding mortgages in 1976. But with the increased utilization of private sources of funds, the use of mortgage insurance is likely to increase.

Table 13-6
Housing Loans Originated and Outstanding, 1978

	New Loans			Total Outstanding		
	Number (thousands)	Value (million yen)	Percentage	Number (thousands)	Value (million yen)	Percentage
City banks	203.9	1,357,871	14.0	981.2	4,715,170	15.9
Local banks	243.9	1,270,131	13.1	1,109.3	4,295,826	14.6
Trust banks, trust accounts, and long-term credit banks	132.2	670,321	6.9	621.5	2,418,241	8.1
Total banks	580.2	3,298,323	34.0	2,712.0	11,429,237	38.6
Mutual-loan and savings banks	114.7	662,071	6.8	500.3	2,142,418	7.2
Credit associations and cooperatives	331.1	2,606,286	27.0	1,337.9	6,400,060	21.7
Insurance companies	59.4	473,814	4.9	242.7	1,375,448	4.7
Specialized housing-loan companies	93.0	783,256	8.1	292.1	1,861,268	6.3
Total private nonbank	598.2	4,525,427	46.8	2,373.0	11,779,194	40.0
Japan Housing Loan Corporation	462.3	1,839,819	19.2	3,128.1	6,287,009	21.4
Grand total	1,640.7	9,663,569	100.0	8,213.1	29,495,440	100.0

Source: Bank of Japan (unpublished).

Secondary Mortgage Market

There is no secondary market as such in Japan at this time. All the preconditions that seem to be necessary for the creation of a secondary market exist, however. There is mortgage insurance, a variety of all kinds of lenders, and an active capital market. In time, as mortgages as a percentage of all debt increase, secondary-market activity may become more desirable as the private institutions compete for funding in the capital market. But there is no secondary-market activity along the lines of either the United States or France.

Lender of Last Resort

The lender of last resort in Japan is the Housing Loan Corporation, which provides a variety of functions including direct lending, as well as setting the standards used in the mortgage market. It is able to utilize government funds to influence the direction that the mortgage market takes at any time, and to provide some insulation of the market against the cycles of the economy.

Financing an Individual House

The same $50,000 house can be financed in Japan in four ways (see table 13-7). In order to gain a better understanding of the Japanese system, consider the possible ways that such a house would be financed.

    1. The JHC would issue a loan, if the house were new, for 80 percent of a value for a period of twenty-five years. The interest rate would be a low

Table 13-7
Japan: An Illustrative Example of Financing the Purchase of an Individual House

1. Value of house: $50,000 (105 million yen)
2. Mortgage terms:
   A. Japan Housing Loan Corporation loan (new), terms: 80% of value, $40,000 (84 million yen) for 25 years at an interest rate of 5.5% per annum. The mortgage payment is $245.63 per month and the owner's equity is $10,000 (21 million yen).
   B. Japan Housing Loan Corporation loan (existing), terms: 55% of value for 20 years at 6.75% per annum. The mortgage payment is $209.00 (43,890 yen) per month and the owner's equity is $22,500 (47 million yen).
   C. Commercial bank, terms: 80% of value for 20 years at a rate of 9.5%. The payment is $372.85 (78,300 yen) per month.
   D. Housing Finance Company, terms: 88% of value for 25 years at a rate of 11.5%. The payment is $406.58 (85,380 yen) per month.

5.5 percent per year. If one were able to obtain a loan from the JHLC at this rate of interest, it would produce a mortgage payment of $245.63 per month, requiring an owner's equity of $10,000.

2. If the house were an existing one rather than new, the HLC would offer a loan for only 55 percent of value, for only twenty years, and at 6.75-percent interest. Under these arrangements the mortgage payment would be $209.10 per month, and an equity of $22,500 would be required.

3. A loan could also be obtained from commercial banks, which are increasingly becoming involved in real-estate finance in Japan. A loan from a commercial bank would likely be for 80 percent of the value for twenty years, at an interest rate of 9.5 percent. The required payments would be $372.85 per month, and the equity would be $10,000.

4. Specialized housing-finance companies, which are often subsidiaries of commercial banks and insurance companies, are becoming much more active in housing finance. However, the terms would be the most stringent of all, with an interest rate of 11.5 percent on 80 percent of value for twenty-five years. Under these conditions, the mortgage payment would be $406.58 per month, and the owner's equity would be $10,000.

Thus in Japan, depending on the institution, the amount required in repayment of a loan can vary enormously. For those fortunate enough to be able to receive financing from the HLC, there are substantial benefits. However, as might be imagined from the preceding example, the HLC has a long waiting list for its loans. It is now tending to be much more selective in the kinds of loans it gives and is rationing loans to those who are most in need. Now that the private market is providing mortgage loans, the HLC is retrenching in some of its activity, at least that portion that can be met in the private market. But at this point there is a large discrepancy between the rates charged in the private market and those offered from the Housing Loan Corporation.

Housing Consumption

Housing Costs

Housing in Japan is expensive by any measure. Considering absolute cost in 1975, a house of 100 square meters on a 200-square-meter lot in a suburb an hour away from the city center would cost U.S. $83,500 (25 million yen). This is approximately ten times the average worker's income. In terms of income, a house in Japan is more expensive than a comparable house in Europe and more than twice as expensive as in the United States.

One factor consistently pointed to as a factor in Japan's high housing prices is the enormous cost of land. In Japan the pressures of urbanization and the concentration within a few metropolitan areas has caused land prices to be very high. To begin with, Japan does not have enormous amounts of land as do the United States and Canada or most of the European countries. Land is precious throughout Japan. Land prices, which have always been very high in Japan, have within the past several years increased rapidly. During the decade from 1964 to 1974, construction prices in Japan rose by a factor of almost three. However, during the same period land prices increased by a factor of almost five. This is especially true in Tokyo, where land prices inflated even more rapidly than in the rest of the country.

The increase in land prices in Japan did not result primarily from inflation, as in some other countries. The rate of inflation in Japan has been modest by world standards. Nevertheless, land prices have increased as rapidly as anyplace in the world. Pressures were derived not so much from inflation as from the increased demand for land.

Home Ownership

Home-ownership rates in Japan have declined during the postwar years. Whereas in 1951 more than 65 percent of households were owners, that figure had fallen to 59 percent in 1973. The most obvious reason for the decline in the rate of owner occupation is the high cost of a house in relation to income. Even with the exceptionally high rate of personal saving, a house is out of reach for a large sector of the population.

Rental Housing

Because of the high cost of housing, many families have no alternative but to rent. For those fortunate enough to occupy a company-owned unit, rent is only a fraction of the market rate; the rate for an issued house is only 20 percent of the going rate for a private rental unit.

Housing Satisfaction

Japan has a high level of dissatisfaction with its housing (see figure 13-4). The most frequently voiced complaint concerns the small size of the units, a complaint registered by both renters and owners.

In Japan the *tatami* is the basic unit of floor area measurement. A tatami is a straw mat that is 90 by 180 centimeters. Floor area is measured as the number of tatami that can be accommodated on it. In Japan the average

What Makes Them Think
Their Housing is Poor?

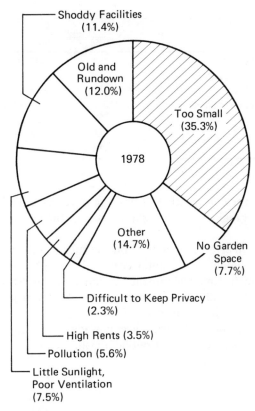

Source: *Japan Economic Journal*, May 22, 1979.

Figure 13-4. Housing Satisfaction in Japan

tatami per person in 1973 was 6.6 mats, or 10.9 square meters. Per capita space per unit has been steadily increasing, with a 20-percent increase in tatami space between 1968 and 1973 (see table 13-8).

Housing Subsidies

Japan has a low-rent public-housing program that was modeled closely after the public-housing program in the United States when it was introduced in 1951. Public housing utilizes the method of government capital

Table 13-8
Rental per Tatami (Approximately 90 cm × 180 cm)
(yen)

Classification	Nationwide		Metropolitan Tokyo	
	1968	1973	1968	1973
Public rental house	289	446	394	582
Private rental house (with exclusive facilities)	553	1,015	1,121	1,981
Private rental house (with common facilities	769	1,163	1,237	1,880
Issued house	111	210	178	306
Average	430	750	827	1,358

subsidies for the construction of housing developments. The rents are then calculated to break even, taking into account the extent of the capital subsidy.

There are in effect two public-housing subsidy schemes, one providing a subsidy for one-half the capital cost and the other for two-thirds. The deepest subsidy is for developments aiming at the lowest-income group. The two-thirds capital subsidy will produce a break-even rent 48 percent of what the rent would be in the absence of the subsidy.

Demand for public-housing accommodations is higher than available supply. Therefore, tenants for public housing tend to be chosen by lottery.

References

1. Japan Housing Loan Corporation, "General Information on the Housing Loan Corporation."
2. Japan Real Estate Institute, "Indexes of Urban Land Prices and Building Cost of Frame Houses in Japan" (Tokyo, September 1976).
3. Hidetoshi Kato, "Japanese: Wealthy Because Homeless," *PHP* 9, no. 9 (September 1978).
4. Ministry of Construction and City Planning Association of Japan, *City Planning in Japan* (Tokyo, 1978).
5. Ministry of Construction, *Housing in Japan 1975* (Tokyo, 1977).

14 Housing in Brazil

With a population of 120 million, Brazil is the seventh-largest country in the world. It is generally classified as a developing country, using World Bank standards, since its per capita income is approximately $1,275. However, it is one of the most advanced of the developing nations.

The housing sector of Brazil is of special importance for two reasons. First, since Brazil is a developing country, its institutions have not had time to develop to the same extent as have those in the United States and Europe. Nonetheless, Brazil must house its large population, an exceedingly difficult task because of the country's low average income. Yet Brazil has developed housing institutions that emulate features of the sophisticated financial systems of North America. Thus it is interesting to review what a developing country like Brazil has been able to accomplish in housing.

A second important reason to study Brazil is that since the 1960s Brazil had had to face a sustained inflation that at times has been a hyperinflation. It is of interest to learn how Brazil has managed to cope with one of the world's highest inflation rates and still to produce housing using institutions based on North American and European models.

Structure of the Housing-Finance Sector

Banco Nacional de Habitacão

Brazil's housing-finance sector was created in 1966 with the development of the National Housing Bank—the Banco Nacional de Habitacão (BNH). At that time inflation had become a deeply ingrained feature of the Brazilian economy. Throughout the early 1960s inflation had averaged more than 60 percent per year. Subsequently, the rate of inflation would even exceed 100 percent. Developing a housing-finance system in light of this tremendous inflation was an extremely difficult task, one that required considerable innovation. Inflation intensifies the basic problem of securing funds for long-term investment such as housing, because there is considerable uncertainty about the protection of capital.

High rates of inflation have the very practical effect of eroding the savings habit of a nation. In order for savers to put their money in any kind of financial intermediary, there must be some reasonable guarantee that their capital will not be depreciated through time. One way of guarding against the depreciation of capital is through the indexing of capital balances. This can be applied both to savings accounts in financial institutions and to financial assets such as mortgage loans. The durability of the housing-finance system in Brazil is testimony that at least under the Brazilian circumstances the indexation applied to both savings and lending has worked well enough to permit the development of a housing-finance system.

Housing finance in Brazil is dominated by the BNH, which provides money and also controls and directs the other institutions in the housing-finance system (see table 14-1). BNH also finances urban infrastructure, such as sewer and water projects. Altogether, 70 percent of BNH's activities are housing and 30 percent are for the provision of urban infrastructure. Low-income housing represents about 20 percent of the BNH commitment.

BNH is a government-owned institution, which is under the control of the Ministry of the Interior. However, it has considerable autonomy, with its own board of directors appointed by the government. It conducts its business in eleven regional offices. BNH combines almost all the functions we normally associate with HUD, FHLBB, FNMA, GNMA, and the other specialized housing agencies in the United States. It is indeed the wide umbrella organization for the entire housing sector.

The BNH was established as part of a comprehensive housing-finance system. Another important ingredient was the establishment of a system of savings-and-loan associations patterned after those found in the United States. In addition, savings banks and mortgage companies were created (see figure 14-1).

The Sistema Financiero de Habitacão (SFH) consists of 81 real-estate institutions: 36 savings-and-loan associations, 40 real-estate credit associations, 5 state savings banks, and 1 federal savings bank. The savings-and-loans in Brazil are similar to their U.S. counterparts. In fact, the U.S. savings-and-loan industry played a large part in setting up the savings-and-loan system in Brazil and in other Latin American countries.

In addition to the savings institutions, the other intermediaries that carry out Brazil's housing policy with respect to low-income housing are those known as popular housing companies, or COHABS, which are owned jointly by state and local municipalities. Currently there are 34 of these in the country, carrying out low-income housing programs.

Money to finance BNH came primarily from the government unemployment fund. Brazil has what is known as a Time of Service Guarantee Fund (TSGF), which is funded by deposits by employers of 8 percent of all payrolls (see table 14-2). The funds are deposited in the name of the employee in individual accounts in the fund. The fund balance is appropriated by the BNH and used to make housing loans. Interest is paid on the use of the guarantee funds at a rate of between 3 and 6 percent per

Table 14-1
National Housing Plan, Consolidated Balance Sheet

Items	Years									
	1968	1969	1970	1971	1972	1973	1974	1975	1976	1977
Assets										
Total	1,386	2,235	3,335	4,496	6,647	8,721	11,711	15,622	20,611	31,333
Loans:										
Housing	1,177	1,914	2,619	3,342	3,462	5,807	7,569	9,802	13,252	15,924
Sanitation	—	—	60	92	154	384	464	693	934	3,074
Building materials	—	—	153	268	354	424	644	772	951	564
Other assets	209	314	490	794	1,504	2,032	2,892	4,183	5,096	2,958
Pending classification	—	7	13	—	273	74	142	172	378	8,813
Liabilities										
Total	1,386	2,235	3,335	4,496	6,647	8,721	11,711	15,622	20,611	31,333
Capital and reserves	162	246	351	434	616	940	1,485	1,679	1,796	2,198
TSGF	773	1,246	1,747	2,306	2,953	3,710	4,446	5,379	6,509	8,125
Savings accounts	135	306	604	898	1,541	2,496	3,908	6,135	8,710	11,524
Housing bonds	219	358	526	677	930	1,084	1,112	988	814	646
Other liabilities	92	67	91	181	270	343	588	1,011	2,138	1,413
Pending classification	5	12	16	—	337	148	172	430	644	7,427
Number of loans granted	286	446	604	732	835	985	1,082	1,230	1,470	1,738
Number of savings accounts	—	583	1,349	2,239	3,234	4,837	6,808	9,956	13,486	17,730

Source: Banco Nacional de Habitacao (unpublished).
Note: All balances in millions of U.S. dollars and loans and accounts in thousands.

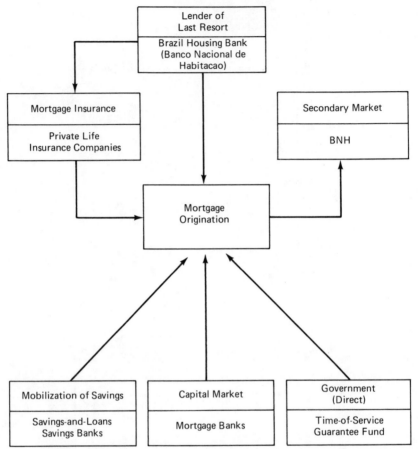

Figure 14-1. Structure of the Mortgage Market in Brazil

annum. The funds are also indexed to protect against inflation. Although BNH has the power to issue mortgage bonds, this is only a small part of its assets; the bulk coming from the TSGF.

Brazil has traditionally had a very strong system of job tenure through laws that give employees a right to job stability. An employee can be dismissed only through a severe fault of his own. When an employee is dismissed, a lump-sum benefit is paid. The fund was created to adapt this system of worker protection to the needs of a developing and expanding economy, which often requires job relocation. The TSGF as institutionalized permits employees to receive installments each month in the form of deposits from employers of a percentage of their earnings. These funds

Table 14-2
Time-of-Service Guarantee Fund, 1967-1977
(millions of U.S. dollars)

Years	Deposits	Withdrawals	Net
1967	39	1	38
1968	77	14	63
1969	114	36	78
1970	159	63	96
1971	223	97	126
1972	313	142	171
1973	431	186	245
1974	618	265	352
1975	949	441	499
1976	1,410	714	696
1977	2,211	1,143	1,067
Total	6,533	3,103	3,432
Interest credited			551
Monetary correction			4,142
Balance, 12/31/1977			8,125

Source: Banco Nacional da Habitacão (unpublished).

go into the employee's personal account and can be transferred should the individual change jobs for any reason. Such funds can be withdrawn by the employee should he be dismissed or lose his job through no fault of his own or should work be cancelled. Also, if the worker is disabled or retires the funds will be available to him or, in case of death, to his family.

Over time the fund accumulated a significant amount that was used for investment in housing. From 1966, when the fund was established, to 1978 it grew to over $8 billion. In the late 1960s these were virtually the only funds available for housing. Since then, the funds available through voluntary savings have grown large enough so that they now exceed the amount from the guarantee funds.

In 1977 the TFGS was 128 billion cruzeiros (about $8 billion). However, the amount in voluntary savings in the housing-finance system was 193 billion cruzeiros. There were 17.5 million passbooks, and in 1977 alone 3.5 million new savings accounts were opened. Thus at the end of 1977 the amount of money in voluntary savings greatly exceeded that in the involuntary sector. Although the social-security fund is still a vital part of the housing-finance system, the system is more and more dependent on private savings. More importantly, Brazil has proved that private savings can be mobilized even from low-income households. The growth of savings-and-loan assets, which were more than U.S. $20 billion in 1977, has indeed been impressive. The savings-and-loan system is now the fourth-largest system in the world.

Brazil's real-estate credit companies are private-stock companies whose funds come from the sale of mortgage-backed bills and from BNH advances. Savings banks in Brazil also tend to make real-estate loans, although only 30 percent of their assets are in mortgages.

The success of BNH and the housing-finance system (SFH) can be seen from the fact that, over the twenty-five years prior to its implementation in 1966, only 125,000 units had been financed with mortgages. Since then the rate of home building in Brazil has been approximately 150,000 units per year. This figure represents units that received financing but does not include the large number of units built in Brazil without formal financing, namely the slums and squatter settlements.

There is secondary-market activity in Brazil through the operations of BNH. As an incentive to the private companies not to overspecialize in the higher-valued mortgages, BNH has a sliding scale of rediscounting. For rediscounting mortgages the rate of the discount is inversely related to value: lower-valued units are discounted at a lower rate and higher-valued units at higher rates. Thus the net yield to the originators is highest for low-value mortgages. This unique method of discounting mortgages has as its objective to equalize the flow of mortgage funds across income lines (see table 14-3).

The Brazilian housing sector has four segments. The first of these is for families with good incomes, who are served by the private market. The savings-and-loans and mortgage banks provide mortgage money for families with incomes of more than U.S. $16,000.

Table 14-3
Mortgage Terms According to Size of Loan

Loan Amount (U.S. Dollars)	Maximum Interest Rate (%)	Maximum Payment-to-Income Ratio (%)	Maximum Loan-to-Value Ratio (%)	Maximum Maturity (Years)
0- 2,570	1.0	18	90	25
2,570- 3,855	2.6	20	90	25
3,855- 5,140	3.3	25	90	25
5,140- 6,425	6.0	25	90	25
6,425- 7,710	6.6	25	90	25
7,710- 8,995	7.3	25	90	25
8,995-10,280	7.9	25	90	25
10,280-11,565	8.6	25	90	25
11,565-12,850	9.3	25	90	15-25
12,850-44,975	10.0	25-40	70-90	15-25

Source: Richard Anderson and Donald R. Lessard, "Price Level Adjusted Mortgages in Brazil," *New Mortgage Designs for Stable Housing in an Inflationary Environment* (Boston: Federal Reserve Bank of Boston, 1975).
Note: These rates went into effect in 1975.

Middle-income families, those with between U.S. $5,000 and U.S. $16,000, tend to be served jointly by private enterprise and public coopera-tion. Most of their housing is provided by the cooperatives, which build a large amount of housing in Brazil, especially for the middle-income market. They obtain their financing from BNH and also from the commercial banks and savings banks.

The low-income population, considered to include those workers earn-ing up to U.S. $5,208, are served by the developers of popular housing, who are financed by the BNH. The programs are executed at the local level by the COHABS, which are government entities.

For the last segment, the very low-income families who are unemployed or only marginally employed, there is a sites-and-services policy. Low-interest loans at 0.0 or 1.0 percent are made available for the purchase of a lot and the supporting infrastructure and sometimes for the purchase of building materials.

Indexation of Mortgages and Savings

The unique feature of Brazil's housing-finance structure is its use of monetary correction through indexation. Since 1964 all bank assets and liabilities have been indexed. The indexation of financial assets exists in an overall structure in which all wages and prices are indexed to compensate for the high rate of inflation.

Brazil has had one of the highest rates of inflation in the world, which for a period was well over 100 percent. The rate of inflation has subsided dramatically; but by American and European standards the rate of inflation in Brazil is still very high, having leveled off at about 30 percent annually by the late 1970s.

The Ministry of Finance maintains an index that is related to wholesale prices measured in Standard Capital Units (UPC), which tend to be revalued each quarter, varying with the movement of the index. The index was revalued 24 percent in 1975, 34 percent in 1976, 35 percent in 1977, and 32 percent in 1978.

The principal value outstanding on mortgages is adjusted each quarter by applying a monetary correction factor, which is linked to the official price index. Mortgage payments are also adjusted by the monetary correc-tion factor, so that the adjusted payment will amortize the adjusted prin-cipal over the remaining mortgage term. This means that each period the mortgage payment has to be increased because the outstanding balance of the mortgage has been increased. Passbook savings accounts are also price-level indexed and adjusted for inflation. The nominal interest rate on all savings accounts is 6 percent.

When indexation was adopted in 1964, it was seen as a temporary measure to stimulate the economy. However, like many such controls it has been difficult to remove and has been essential since the rate of inflation in Brazil has remained very high.

In Brazil the system of indexing seems to work, at least to the extent that money is kept in the system and lenders are willing to extend long-term loans. In the absence of indexation the high rate of inflation would no doubt drive out all private capital and limit the time of transactions to month to month or week to week. For those workers whose wages are indexed the system works well because they are able to keep their standard of living intact as prices increase.

Nominal interest rates are low in Brazil because of the indexing. Nominal rates can be low because they do not have to take into consideration the premium for inflation, which is built into mortgage interest rates. Rather than place the burden of preserving capital on a high interest rate, the principal is revalued to compensate for currency depreciation, allowing the nominal interest rate to remain low.

Illustration of Financing an Individual House Under an Indexed System

A mortgage loan could be made available from a savings-and-loan association or savings bank in Brazil for 90 percent of value for twenty-five years at an interest rate of 10 percent. The interest rate would remain constant for the term. What would tend to vary, however, would be the outstanding principal of the loan and the required payments.

Table 14-4 shows the method by which the outstanding principal would be adjusted, assuming an annual inflation rate of 30 percent. This rate is not out of line for Brazil; in fact, it is slightly low by historical standards. Using the system of revaluing the outstanding debt quarterly, it can be shown how such adjustments would affect the mortgage loan.

Consider the first year, in which the outstanding principal at the beginning of the year is $45,000. The first quarter payment of $1,229 consists of both principal and interest. At the end of the first quarter the outstanding balance is $44,896. But during that quarter a 30-percent rate of inflation requires application of a correction factor of 7.5 percent on a quarterly basis. Thus inflation has required that the outstanding nominal balance at the end of the first quarter of $44,896 be adjusted upward by an amount of $3,367. At the beginning of the second quarter the adjusted principal is therefore $48,263. To amortize $48,263 over the remaining ninety-nine quarters of the term of mortgage requires payments during the second quarter of $1,321. Here again, the payment consists of principal and interest.

Table 14-4
Financing an Individual House in Brazil

1. Value of house: U.S. $50,000 (1,485,000 cruzeiros)
2. Mortgage terms:
   a. 90% of value
   b. 10% per annum
   c. Monthly payment = U.S. $410 (12,095 cruzeiros) price level adjusted every quarter by indexation.
3. Repayment schedule of the price-level-adjusted mortgage, assuming a 30% annual rate of inflation and quarterly adjustments, is as follows:

Quarter	Adjusted Principal	Quarterly Payment	Principal	Interest	Balance	Adjustment
1	45,000	1,229	104	1,125	44,896	3,367
2	48,263	1,321	114	1,207	48,149	3,611
3	51,760	1,420	126	1,294	51,634	3,873
4	55,507	1,527	139	1,388	55,367	4,153
5	59,520	1,641	153	1,488	59,367	4,453
6	63,820	1,764	169	1,596	63,652	4,773
7	68,425	1,897	186	1,711	68,239	5,118
8	73,357	2,039	205	1,834	73,152	5,486

At the end of the second quarter the balance is $48,149. The same process is encountered again when the outstanding balance is readjusted by a factor of 7.5 percent (an amount of $3,611) to account for the annual 30-percent rate of inflation. This process is repeated every quarter.

The example in table 14.4 shows how such a repayment schedule would look over a two-year period, based on a quarterly revaluation of the principal. In spite of the increasing nominal balances from the adjusted principal, it is theoreticaly possible to amortize such a loan, paying the principal down to zero over the original twenty-five year term. As in all amortization schemes, the bulk of the principal reduction occurs within the last few years anyway, and this is no exception. As long as the payments are increased in a manner to amortize the loan, it will eventually be reduced to zero, although it certainly does not look like it in the first few years.

The Brazilian example is indeed quite interesting from the point of view of observing how measures must be taken to cope with double-digit inflation, when increases in the rate of interest are not enough to make up for the erosion of capital. When there is indexing of the principal it becomes unnecessary to try to capture the inflation rate in the nominal rate of interest. Therefore, the nominal rate of interest is kept low at 10 percent, and the adjustments for inflation occur with the changes in the principal. The situation seems to work in Brazil since it keeps funds in the housing sector. Not only are mortgages revalued quarterly; so are savings accounts and, most important of all, wages. The system seems to work as long as wages keep up with prices, although it does appear that everything is on a treadmill.

Chile and Argentina also have indexing systems for wages, financial assets, and mortgages much like that in Brazil. However, the Brazilian experience may be working best. Although inflation in Brazil has been extremely high by U.S. and European standards, it still is moderate in terms of its neighbors, Argentina and Chile.

Other Aspects of the Brazilian System

Income-Tax Deductions

Mortgage interest is deductible as an expense against income without declaration of imputed rental value. Such a deduction is of value to upper-income taxpayers. However, Brazil has attempted to grapple with the fact that income-tax deductibility of interest is a nonprogressive item and that low-income persons obtain no real benefit from income-tax deductibility of interest. Therefore, in Brazil low-income mortgage holders receive a cash benefit equal to 12 percent of their annual loan repayments, from a minimum of $50 up to a maximum of $333. This is available to all mortgage holders but is of specific benefit to low-income families.

Financing Existing Housing

Brazil's mortgage-finance system places sole emphasis on creating new housing. Because there is such a housing shortage in the country, the financing of existing housing is discouraged and eligibility for loans is restricted to new construction. It is thought at this time that the money is better utilized by having the funds stimulate new construction. Also, there is not much turnover in the housing stock, as families tend to stay put once they have obtained their house.

Interest Rates

Because of indexation, the nominal interest rates charged for mortgages are low in spite of double-digit inflation. The rates themselves are established by BNH and are set to give preference to the lower end of the spectrum. Brazil maintains a cross-subsidization system with a graduated system of mortgage interest rates; there are low interest rates for low-income housing and high interest rates for upper-income housing. Also, the more prosperous regions of the country are charged higher rates in general than are the depressed areas. For low-income housing the interest rates average from 0 to 3 percent, and the higher-income housing rates range from 3 to 10 percent.

Housing for the Poor

The low-income sector is served by BNH through the national low-income housing program Plano Nacional de Habitacão Popular, known as PLANHAP. These programs are implemented through the states. In conjunction with the COHABs, they build low-cost housing with BNH loans. The interest rate charged for these low-income housing developments is between 1 and 6 percent a year, depending on the ultimate sale price and the region of the country.

In Brazil there is still a problem in financing housing for the very low-income families, those that are not reached through the PLANHAP program. For families of very low income, Brazil relies on a system of sites and services, wherein the state agency will provide land and essential sewerage and water connections, and will assist the individual family in building its own housing unit. It may also provide low-cost building materials.

Brazil has no direct housing-subsidy programs such as are found in Europe and North America. Rather, the housing subsidies that exist are those aimed at providing home ownership rather than the usual kinds of housing allowances or subsidies for construction of rental housing. As a developing country, Brazil seeks to avoid the kind of subsidy programs that require a continued financial commitment from the government. Housing allowances and subsidies for tenants are expensive and interminable. But low-cost housing that is owner occupied may require only a one-time subsidy, after which the person is on his own.

In Brazil housing subsidies take several indirect forms. There is (1) the indirect subsidy using the workers' trust fund, (2) interst-rate differentials according to house value and location, and (3) the financing of site- and-service development and of building materials at low cost.

References

1. Richard Anderson and Donald R. Lessard, "Price-Level-Adjusted Mortgages in Brazil," *New Mortgage Designs for Stable Housing in an Inflationary Environment*, Federal Reserve Bank of Boston, Conference Series no. 14, 1975.

2. Jose Carlos Melo Ourivio, "Compulsory Savings as a Basis for the Setting Up of a Savings and Loan System for Home Financing, The Brazilian Experience," *Fifth Annual Conference on Housing in Africa* (Washington, D.C.: U.S. Agency for International Development, 1978).

Index

About the Author

Chester C. McGuire is an economist and urban planner. He is currently visiting professor of economics at Howard University, and president of Capitol Economics Incorporated, an economic consulting firm. He previously served in the U.S. Department of Housing and Urban Development as assistant secretary for fair housing and equal opportunity. Other affiliations have included: faculty member in the Department of City and Regional Planning, University of California, Berkeley; vice president of Berkeley Planning Associates; economist for Real Estate Research Corporation. He received the A.B. from Dartmouth College, and the M.B.A. and Ph.D. from the University of Chicago Graduate School of Business.